CHINESE PHILOSOPHY IN AN ERA OF GLOBILIZATION

SUNY series in Chinese Philosophy and Culture

Roger T. Ames, editor

CHINESE PHILOSOPHY IN AN ERA OF GLOBILIZATION

Edited by

ROBIN R. WANG

State University of New York Press

Published by
STATE UNIVERSITY OF NEW YORK PRESS
ALBANY

For information, address
State University of New York Press
90 State Street, Suite 700, Albany, NY 12207

Production, Kelli Williams
Marketing Michael Campochiaro

Library of Congress Cataloging-in-Publication Data

Chinese philosophy in an era of globalization / Robin R. Wang, editor.
    p. cm.
Includes bibliographical references and index.
ISBN 0-7914-6005-3 — ISBN 0-7914-6006-1 (pbk.)
    1. Philosophy, Chinese. 2. Philosophy, Modern—20th century. I. Wang, Robin R.

B5231.C5134 2004
181'.11—dc22   2004043379

10 9 8 7 6 5 4 3 2 1

CONTENTS

ACKNOWLEDGMENTS

"The stones from another mountain may provide the best whetstones for polishing one's own gems."

—*The Book of Poetry*

This project has been a long and complex journey. It was inspired by the changes that I witnessed in the field of Chinese philosophy during my annual travels to China since 1992. The initial thought was rooted in a few Sino-American philosophical conferences held in Peking University. However, bringing that idea to fruition required a very kind collaboration among many friends and colleagues.

I particularly wish to thank Stephen Davis, Philip J. Ivanhoe, and Bryan Van Norden, who helped me refine my primary inspiration and offered me many valuable suggestions on the book's basic dialogical structure and format. The faculty and graduate students at Peking University were also great resources to me; they especially identified representative essays. I am grateful to the Chinese scholars, Zhao Dunhua, Wan Junren, Zhang Xianglong, and Chen Lai, for their enthusiastic participations. Many thanks are also due to Roger Ames for his invaluable support and Paul R. Goldin for his assistance in inviting good translators for the project. Anita Fisher and Nick Pinto have my gratitude for a careful reading of the manuscript. I was also supported by Loyola Marymount University 2000 summer research grant. Special thanks to Dennis McCann for his editorial effort. Finally, I am deeply indebted to all the contributors of this project. Their intellectual sagacity and generous support will always have a special place in my mind and heart.

R.R.W

FOREWORD

Whenever we attempt to understand another, we engage in interpretation. When the others we are attempting to understand are expressing complex and subtle philosophical ideas, the process of interpretation can be difficult and daunting; when they are speaking or writing in another language and out of a different and only dimly understood tradition, the challenges grow, but so too can the rewards.

The epigram for this volume recalls another line from the *Book of Poetry*, which was quoted by one of Kongzi's disciples to describe his ongoing struggle to understand and embody the teachings of his own tradition, "Like cutting, like filing; Like grinding, like polishing." (*Analects*, 1.15) In both passages, the idea is that something beautiful and enduring—the gems that result from the process of dressing jade or other precious stones—requires hard and steady work by well-trained hands. These stones don't yield their beauty easily; preparing them is a demanding art. The same is true in the case of cross-cultural philosophy. It is a task that requires the hard and steady work of those skilled in the art of philosophical interpretation. It presents imposing challenges but can also yield remarkable and distinctive gems of its own.

The present volume is an exercise in "cutting, filing, grinding, and polishing." These essays and responses, by prominent representatives of the Chinese and Western philosophical traditions, offer a wealth of insight into important aspects of their respective traditions and into the different styles in which philosophy is pursued in each. These writings also show that there is much more "cutting, filing, grinding, and polishing" to be done before these two traditions can fully benefit from one another. We need much thicker and more nuanced understandings of one another before we can truly appreciate the full richness and subtlety of each other's views and engage cooperatively in the ongoing task of self-understanding. This volume makes an important contribution toward realizing these worthy goals and illustrates the unique benefits that such work can bring to both East and West.

Philip J. Ivanhoe

INTRODUCTION

In the more than twenty years since the start of economic reforms in 1978, the People's Republic of China has become a full partner in the era of globalization. Recently, for example, it has gained World Trade Organization (WTO) status and received permanent normal trade relations (PNTR) recognition from the United States. The dramatic economic and social changes that have ushered in the era of globalization, have also been accompanied by a virtual renaissance in the study of philosophy in China. Philosophers have once again taken up the challenge of thinking critically about society and its future development. Earlier in this century, Chinese reformers claimed that modernization required abandoning traditional beliefs and practices and embracing Western methods and values. But is this also to be China's philosophical response to the challenge of globalization? Philosophers are now asking themselves: Have traditional ways of thinking endured? Have they been replaced by Western approaches and priorities? Alternatively, has there been a synthesis of Eastern and Western perspectives? Is there any continuity between the more than two thousand year old Chinese philosophical tradition and current philosophical trends? If so, what is the nature of such continuities and what may they contribute to the development of a genuinely global conversation about philosophy?

This book is designed to contribute to this conversation by presenting essays by some of the leading philosophers of modern China, on both their own traditions and their impressions of influential contemporary Western philosophers, and by offering the reactions and comments of prominent Western philosophers, all of them committed to expanding the horizons of philosophical inquiry globally. Before giving readers a brief outline of their essays, it may be useful to provide you with a sketch of the historical context in which philosophy is done in today's China. Seen in this context, the rapid development of contemporary philosophy in China is almost as astonishing as China's extraordinary, but more familiar economic and social development.

AN OVERVIEW OF PHILOSOPHY IN CHINA SINCE
ECONOMIC REFORM (1978 TO PRESENT)

Philosophy in China suffered during the Cultural Revolution (1966–1976), where mindless conformity was king. The slogan "philosophy must serve politics" plunged philosophy into darkness for many years. Philosophers were caught in a storm of ideological struggles and often had to write a justification of whatever the party in power's policy happened to be. Furthermore, the philosophical field was completely isolated from more recent developments in other countries. Marxism was only one of several Western ideologies that had entered China earlier, but it had been given an authoritative position. In the Marxist method of analysis, philosophical traditions (either Chinese or Western) were classified simplistically as either materialist or idealist, with the former being good and the latter bad. The history of philosophy was viewed as an eternal struggle between these two trends. China's great intellectual tradition had indeed fallen on hard times. Then on May 11, 1978, the *Guangming Daily's* article "Practice Is the Only Criterion for Testing the Truth" sparked a national debate about the standard of truth. This was a landmark for the movement of intellectual freedom and a breakthrough for social change. A main goal of this controversial article was to discredit dogmatism and to promote the idea that practice is the only and ultimate authority. This pragmatic view (more Deweyan than Rortyean in spirit) was based on Deng Xiaoping's commitment to results rather than to ideological purity. His famous quotation: "White or black, if it catches mice, it is a good cat" became the official justification not just for policy, but also for China's intellectual life. Economically, of course, Deng's approach sparked the transition away from a planned economy and toward a free market. But it also had a profound effect on academic research, leading to increased freedom of expression. This has increasingly emancipated philosophy from political and ideological bondage. Philosophers no longer are required to employ Marxist methodology as a tool.

As the old ideology lost ground, Western culture invaded all areas of life. The focus of philosophical debate moved from the criterion of truth to the problem of alienation versus humanism. This debate was over the legacy of the Cultural Revolution in the past, how to understand Western culture in the present, and how to realize the value, rights, dignity, and freedom of human beings. There was intense philosophical turmoil around issues of "culture" *(wenhua),* focused on two concerns: *(a)* The relationship between tradition and modernity: Is tradition compatible with modernity? Does the process of modernity mean one has to resist tradition? What role, if any, does tradition play in assisting the transition to modernity? *(b)* The relationship between Chinese and Western cultures: What are the differences between them? How can one absorb the outstanding cultural achievements of all countries and at the same time resist the corrosive influence of some aspects of capitalism?

This "cultural fever" (*wenhua re*) replays the perennial Chinese battle over the old and the new, conservatism and change. For example, more than two thousand years ago, the Mohists had fought in favor of technological innovation and social reform against the Confucian reverence for tradition and honor. In the 1980–89 period, however, Chinese intellectuals now desperately tried to discover China's distinctive identity in the world, and to find a way to combat the alienating and dehumanizing aspects of modern societies. During this time intellectual life was flourishing together with a rise of cultural self-consciousness.

One important event was the "River Elegy," a controversial, interpretive, six-part television series on Chinese cultural roots and ethos, on tradition and modernity, straightforwardly attacking the historical, mythological, and social foundations of China—the legends of the Yellow River, the Great Wall and the Dragon. This documentary, watched by 70 million Chinese, regarded these venerable legends as an albatross. It blamed the river and a reverence for what it represented for China's failure to enter the modern world. While the Europeans were sailing the high seas and discovering the world and its riches, China had paddled along the silted Yellow River, hardly venturing out of sight of land. The high seas symbolized the open, dynamic, and exploratory spirit of the West, while the Yellow River symbolized the closed, stagnant, and insular mentality of China. Similarly, the Great Wall, a symbol of historical continuity, was seen as a manifestation of close-minded conservatism. The Dragon, a symbol of the all-powerful emperor who ruled China by virtue of the Mandate of Heaven, was condemned for legitimating an outmoded imperial authoritarianism. The message of the *River Elegy* evoked memories of the May Fourth movement of 1919 in its intertwining of nationalism (patriotism) and iconoclasm (antitraditionalism). But it also provoked even more difficult questioning: If Chinese intellectuals in China proper are so thoroughly disgusted with Chinese culture, does this mean that they have voluntarily forfeited their right to have any distinctive Chineseness? This was a hard conclusion for many Chinese to accept.

The economic reforms had enriched people and enlarged their views of the world. They started to adopt Western slogans, symbols, and styles. In sharp contrast to the Cultural Revolution, students were quoting Abraham Lincoln and Thomas Jefferson to back up their demand for democracy. Many Chinese intellectuals took a great interest in Western philosophical currents and attempted to introduce them into their research and writings. Many Western philosophical books and articles were translated into Chinese. Continental European philosophy had a particular appeal to reflective minds in China at this time. Jean-Paul Sartre, Friedrich Nietzsche, and Martin Heidegger became very popular on every university campus—a phenomena that came to be known as "Sartre fever," or "Nietzsche fever." Together they inspired the students' call for "self-liberation" and their hope that the promotion of Western beliefs would provide a way to construct a new vision of personal individuality. This cultural movement partially contributed to the June 4, 1989 student movement, some of whose leaders were philosophers and authors.

Despite the brief backlash after the June 4 incident, Chinese philosophers today are flourishing in the climate of diversity and prosperity that economic reform has created. Here are some numbers: before economic reform, all of China had only four philosophical journals; now there are over sixty academic journals in philosophy. There have also been at least one thousand Western philosophical books and over a thousand articles translated into Chinese since the economic reforms. While publications are still censored by the government, and discussing some social problems can lead to reprisals, many people from cabdrivers to college professors apparently feel quite free to speak their views. The inclusion of China in the global telecommunication network has contributed to the opening of Chinese society and has transformed Chinese academic research. Never before have Chinese academics been able to reach out so easily and become so well acquainted with Western philosophical perspectives. It is a revolution by e-mail, websites, fax machines, and direct-dial telephone calls.

There is no single current that can encompass the diversity characteristic of the current atmosphere. The superficial aspects of "the Western fever" have cooled down. The slogan "Back To Philosophy Itself" captures the latest trend. It seeks to focus on academic and rigorously philosophical activities. There are scholars studying and writing about Western philosophy, while many other philosophers in China are making a considerable effort to modernize, while also preserving, the millennia-old heritage of Chinese thought. The latter, hoping to restore and deepen what they see as a distinctive wisdom tradition, blend a Confucian ethos with a respect for the achievements of modern science and capitalist markets.

AN OVERVIEW OF OUR CONVERSATIONS

With that historical context in mind, here is a map of the terrain upon which our philosophical conversations will proceed. The six exchanges have been divided into two parts: Part One: "Reflecting on Chinese Philosophical Tradition," and Part Two: "Bringing Chinese Philosophy into the Global Discourse." Those in the first part feature contemporary Chinese philosophers reflecting primarily on China's intellectual tradition and its possible contributions to philosophical conversation in an era of globalization. Those in the second part allow the reader to eavesdrop on Chinese philosophers critically appropriating the work of major Western philosophers in order to understand their own tradition from different global perspectives. In both parts, each Chinese perspective is given a critical response, usually by a prominent Western philosopher whose work or field of inquiry is addressed in the lead essay. Thus, each set is an invitation to conversation, rather than a transcript of a conversation that has already been completed.

The first of these consists in an exchange between Zhang Dainian and Kwong-loi Shun on the presence or absence of "axiology" or value-theory in representative works of pre-modern Chinese philosophy. Zhang Dainian's magisterial survey not only discovers a robust discussion of axiology running throughout that history, but also seeks to develop a typology that will locate ancient Chinese philosophers within the range of contemporary axiological discourse and facilitate an evaluation of their relative strengths and weaknesses. Kwong-loi Shun, however, warns that such a project runs the risk of distorting a genuine understanding of these works. Given the absence in the ancient texts of any clear equivalent to the modern meaning of "value" *(jiazhi)*, Shun is skeptical of construing their richly evaluative discourses as a contribution to value-theory.

Besides the specific merits of their debate over the presence or absence of axiology in premodern Chinese philosophy, Zhang and Shun model many of the challenges that must be faced if the old East-West "dialogue" about Chinese philosophy is to be transformed into a genuinely open and collaborative conversation. Zhang has mastered modern Western value-theory, and seeks to apply it to Chinese classical philosophy. As Shun suggests, such an approach seems to assume that contemporary Western philosophy must set the terms of the dialogue, and that Chinese scholars can make their contribution by reconstructing their tradition within the Western paradigm. The risks of distorted interpretation that he emphasizes suggest that this approach has not yet reached the level of either cross-cultural dialogue or collaborative conversation. On the other hand, all conversations, however haltingly proceeding, must begin somewhere. Shun's attempt to deepen the reader's appreciation of the otherness of the ancient texts and traditions succeeds only by challenging the modern conventions of analytic discourse within which Zhang has laid out his lucid and perhaps all too familiar picture of Chinese "axiology."

The second philosophical conversation, between Zhao Dunhua and Stephen Davis, concerns analyses of the historical origins of not only Chinese religion but also theories of religion in general. As Davis points out, Zhao's paper indirectly testifies to the extent that philosophy of religion in China is now liberated from Marxist dogma, particularly the evolutionary view of the origins of religion, presupposed by Marx, among others, and later canonized in the writings of Frederick Engels. Contrary to this "Progressive Theory," Zhao argues that the worship of the "Lord on High *(Shangdi)*" and "Heaven *(Tian)*" (characteristic of the Shang and Zhou dynasties respectively) cannot be explained as evolving from "lower" forms of religiousness, such as, ancestor worship, animism, shamanism, or polytheism. Indeed, subsequent to the Shang and Zhou dynasties the pattern of development is just the opposite: "polytheism" apparently emerges from "monotheism" as the "Lord on High" and "Heaven" become increasingly vague, impersonal, and removed from the existential concerns of ordinary Chinese people.

While Zhao's argument is constructed painstakingly from the data of Chinese history, he does situate it in the context of philosophical theories developed to explain the origins of religion generally. At this point, his differences with Davis become apparent. Davis does not dispute Zhao's interpretation of

Chinese religion, but he does warn that such an interpretation does not warrant the hypothesis of an original, universal monotheism that Father Wilhelm Schmidt, for example, had memorably proposed in opposition to the reigning evolutionary theories of religion in the 1920s. Whatever their remaining differences, Zhao and Davis are agreed that the philosophy of religion can no longer be identified with speculative explanations of the origins of religion, especially those motivated by apologetics seeking either to subvert religious faith and practice or to justify them rationally. Such tacit agreements make a genuinely philosophical conversation about religion both possible and necessary.

The third set features a discussion of the theory of human nature found in the writings of the most famous Neo-Confucian philosopher, Zhu Xi. Chen Lai attempts a painstaking reconstruction of Zhu's reflections on the relationship between the heavenly principle (*li*) animating all things and the physical endowment (*qi*) specific to each individual. Chen asserts that Zhu's reflections are an advance beyond the teachings of his philosophical forebears, the Cheng brothers, and seeks to establish the basic coherence and adequacy of Zhu's position, particularly with reference to the question of how to explain the evil that human beings do, assuming that Mencius was correct in asserting the essential goodness of humanity. Chen's reconstruction is particularly helpful in articulating the cosmological presuppositions of Zhu's perspective on human nature, and how it might illuminate certain vexing problems in moral psychology, such as accounting for the unstable mixture of good and evil in human emotions.

Bryan Van Norden offers a very useful complement to Chen's reconstruction, for he helps readers not already conversant with the debates among Neo-Confucians to understand what is at stake in Zhu's reflections, and why they still matter. While Van Norden takes issue with Chen's estimate of Zhu's originality beyond the teachings of the Cheng brothers, his contribution lies in noting the differences between the entire school of Neo-Confucianism (*Dao xue*) and what is and isn't actually said in the classic texts. Van Norden challenges the reader to think through the Way of moral self-cultivation proposed by the tradition as a whole. The metaphysical disputes over the relationship of "*li*" and "*qi*," he persuasively argues, have profound ethical significance, not only for understanding what kinds of moral demands can reasonably be made of human beings, but also for highlighting precisely what must be cultivated in human nature, and with what resources, if one is seriously concerned to become a moral person. Van Norden thus illuminates the very different strategies that might emerge were Zhu's program of self-cultivation to be followed, as in the "School of Li," rather than that offered by Lu Xiangshan and later developed by Wang Yangming, as in the "School of Mind." The reader thus is invited to participate in a conversation on how the practice of self-cultivation might be enhanced by a philosophical understanding of human nature, both in general and as it is emergent in the strengths and weaknesses of each living person.

The fourth set, featuring Wan Junren and Alasdair MacIntyre, allows us to observe a conversation already well launched by two philosophers who have learned much from each other. The ostensible topic is further reflections on the divergences and convergences between Confucian and Aristotelian theories of virtue, with Wan tending more and more to emphasize divergence and MacIntyre convergence. Wan's interpretation of the otherness of Confucian tradition is couched to a great extent in the categories that MacIntyre developed in *After Virtue*. Only now his conversation partner MacIntyre, less a Marxist and more a Thomist in his interpretation of Aristotle, is committed to exploring the ways in which both perspectives on virtue make universal claims that are not only internally consistent, but also rationally compelling for all serious students of moral philosophy.

Thus, Wan contrasts Confucian virtue theory with the Aristotelian by asserting that the former's core is constituted by a normative pattern of cosmically ordered social relationships carrying deontological obligations, such that virtue can never be reducible to an individual's personal pursuit of any teleological end, however objective, or conceptualized apart from the social practices in which they are embedded as part of a specific community's moral tradition. MacIntyre, in turn, not only refuses to accept Wan's characterization of Aristotelian virtue theory, as if it were simply the point of departure for modern Western moral rationalism; but he also challenges Wan's interpretation of Confucian ethics, emphasizing the centrality of ritual propriety (*li*) in self-cultivation, although claiming that this social practice requires a rather different account of the relationship of individual autonomy and the achievement of exemplary moral character, than that provided by Wan. Understanding the differences between these two interlocutors requires as much thoughtful attention to what is not said, as to what they actually choose to address in each other's theories. Both are deeply committed to the comparative study of moral philosophies, and both help readers to appreciate the ways in which cultural differences, giving rise to different ontological presuppositions and epistemological commitments, will inevitably come to the foreground as the conversation gets more intense as well as more productive.

The fifth set offers us a chance to imagine how a conversation comparing epistemological commitments might proceed. Kelly James Clark and Liu Zongkun seek to compare Zhuangzi's and Alvin Plantinga's philosophies on how a natural knowledge of, on the one hand, Dao, and on the other hand, God, is possible. While conceding that such a comparison may at first seem strange, Clark and Liu argue that Zhuangzi and Plantinga share a common adversary in the classical foundationalism, identified with René Descartes and David Hume, and epitomized in the ethics of belief formulated by W. K. Clifford. In order to make this comparison work, Zhuangzi's criticisms of Confucian "rationalism" must be interpreted, not as warranting epistemological skepticism and moral relativism, but as tantamount to a form of "perspectivism" that allows what may be known naturally about the Dao to count as genuine "knowledge" capable of guiding a person's efforts at self-cultivation. Similarly, Plantinga's philosophical dissent against classical foundationalism is understood as a form of Christian apologetics, a philosophical defense of the beliefs of the reformed tradition in Protestantism, asserting that such beliefs, though unprovable on rationalist assumptions, are nevertheless rational and can be regarded as true knowledge by those who adhere to them.

While Clark and Liu are content merely to suggest the fruitfulness of such a comparison, Plantinga seems more concerned to defend his own position, by expressing some reservations about just how closely Zhuangzi can be made to agree with him. Plantinga, in short, sees more skepticism in Zhuangzi than Clark and Liu allow, and worries that Zhuangzi, in the end, may actually agree with classical foundationalism that the "unsettle-ability" of disputes about the nature of Ultimate Reality means that no one can claim to have any genuine knowledge of it. Nevertheless, in defending as genuine the knowledge of God that reformed Christians profess, Plantinga would seem required to accept similar claims from Daoists and other non-Christians, and for similar reasons. Thus, though comparative philosophy inevitably raises epistemological questions, substantively diverging claims about Ultimate Reality, for example, the nature of Dao and God, are not likely to be resolved by appeal to any one epistemology or another.

The final set, an exchange between Zhang Xianglong and Merold Westphal on how understanding what Laozi and Zhuangzi meant by Dao can be deepened through an appreciation of Heidegger's theory of language (*Sprache*), goes beyond conversation toward modeling a collaborative philosophical inquiry. Zhang and Westphal discover that they are in deep agreement on many things. Zhang's reconstruction of the meanings of Dao, and how they are used in Lao-Zhuang thought—contrary to standard interpretations—to convey the nonrepresentational, nonconceptual nature of "Dao-language," that is, the "great speech" of the Dao beyond the "petty speech" of ordinary work a day language, all this is accepted by Westphal. They also agree as to the relevance of Heidegger for understanding Dao-language, and the constructive role that his later works may play in rethinking philosophical Daoism. Both believe that a proper understanding of Dao-language is necessary to correct "skeptical and relativist" interpretations of Lao-Zhuang thought, which tend to legitimate "intuitionism" and "mysticism" as the only possible approaches to the Dao. They imply that leaving the field only to skeptical relativists and mystics is to force philosophical Daoism to commit intellectual suicide.

They disagree only on what Westphal concedes is a relatively unimportant question, namely, whether the later Heidegger's theory of language is already present in his earlier *Being and Time*. With that much consensus, what is left to talk about? At this point, Westphal introduces another perspective, that of Augustine of Hippo, claiming that Augustine (and orthodox Christianity generally), also held a nonrepresentational view of "God-language," similar to the view shared by the later Heidegger and Lao-Zhuang thought. The major difference, according to Westphal, is that Augustine's God is capable of "speech-acts," indeed that these are pictured in the Bible as the primordial pattern of God's dealing with the world that God created through his Word. The Dao, in Westphal's view, may call us beyond the reach of language, but the Dao may not be understood as someone calling. Thus, the reader is left to imagine a future conversation in which Zhang might either clarify the Dao's impersonal nature, especially in its superior moral wisdom, or might modify it in ways that make it more congruent with what Westphal (and Augustine) find so compelling about the personal nature of God.

Thus, the exchange between Zhang and Westphal, along with the preceding two sets, take us around full circle to certain basic questions animating the first part of this collection: What is it that humanity must value as constituting the core of a good life? How is our quest for wisdom about these things related to our religious inklings about Shangdi, Tian, Dao, and God? And, finally, what in our natures should be cultivated, and how, so that we might find in ourselves a greater integrity between our inner dispositions and what life itself requires of us. The passion for philosophical reflection that we see represented in these conversations has been one of the important ingredients in Chinese mentality throughout Chinese history. An average educated Chinese person has had an interest in (or at least has felt he ought to have an interest in) philosophy from classical Confucian times to the contemporary revolutionary period. Confucius' saying, "if one learns without thinking one will be bewildered," is still a widely held belief. This volume has brought together leading scholars to further the conversation between the Western and Chinese philosophical traditions. Consistent with China's traditional respect for philosophical reflection, contemporary Chinese philosophers display a remarkable openness, in which they rigorously study and make use of Western philosophy. By the same token, the history of Western philosophy yields impressive precedents of openness to learning and incorporating ideas from eastern traditions. Gottfried Leibniz, John Dewey, Bertrand Russell, Martin Heidegger, and many other Western philosophers were inspired by traditional Chinese thought. The underlying question animating the English language publication of this volume is: Can contemporary Western philosophers also benefit from contemporary Chinese philosophy? In exploring the possibilities for mutual intellectual enrichment, this book presents philosophical inquiry in a global context and creates a new style, which opens new possibilities for intriguing and meaningful philosophical exchange. The flourishing of philosophy in China deserves to attract the attention of modern speculative and critical minds more keenly than ever before.

PART ONE

REFLECTING ON CHINESE PHILOSOPHICAL TRADITION

Axiology in Pre-Modern Chinese Philosophy

Zhang Dainian

Translated by Eric L. Hutton

"Axiology" is a term that only came into existence in recent times, but thinking about value is something that was present from ancient times, both in China and the West. In China, it can be traced at least as far back as Confucius, and in the West, it can be traced back at least as far as Plato. In the pre-Qin period, there is an important divergence between Confucius' axiology, in which "the benevolent person rests at ease in benevolence," and Mozi's axiology, in which "the greatest benefit for the state and the people" is the highest standard. There is an even greater opposition between Mencius' axiology, in which "It is in the nature of things for them to be unequal," and Zhuangzi's axiology, in which "The myriad things are all one and equal." When we come to the Song, Yuan, Ming, and Qing periods, all the major philosophers each have their own views on the standards of value. We should recognize that axiology is an important aspect of pre-modern Chinese philosophy. Most works on the history of Chinese philosophy do not much discuss the question of axiology, and so in the present work I would like to try to describe its main points.

"Pre-modern Chinese philosophy" refers to philosophy from the pre-Qin period to the middle period of the nineteenth century, before 1840. "Pre-modern Western philosophy" also refers to philosophy from before the period of the 1840s in the nineteenth century. In terms of years, they resemble each other. However, pre-modern Western philosophy includes recent Western bourgeoisie philosophy, whereas pre-modern Chinese philosophy does not include recent Chinese bourgeoisie philosophy, and this is an important difference.

The most commonly discussed "value" is economic value or commercial value. However, beyond economic value and commercial value are more fundamental values. Fundamental values which people often discuss are truth, beauty, and goodness. Confucius says: "The *Shao* is completely beautiful, and moreover it is completely good"; "The *Wu* is completely beautiful, but it is not completely good" (*Analects*, 3.25). Laozi says: "All people under Heaven know the beautiful as beautiful, and thus there is the ugly. They all know the good as good, and thus there is the not-good" (*Daodejing*, chap. 2). This is sufficient to show that Confucius and Laozi both speak of beauty and goodness. "Truth" is a relatively later term. Among the surviving pre-Qin works, the earliest appearance of "truth" as an important term is in the *Zhuangzi*. Zhuangzi says: "Wherein does the Dao contain 'truth' and 'falsehood'?"(*Zhuangzi*, chap. 2) and takes truth and falsehood as opposites. In the *Laozi*, the term paired with "truth" is "trustworthiness." The *Laozi* states: "Trustworthy words are not beautiful. Beautiful words are not trustworthy" (*Daodejing*, chap. 81). The term "sincerity" also has the same meaning as "truth." The *Commentaries on the Yijing* says: "In refining one's words, establish their sincerity" (*Yijing*, *Wenyan*). Here "sincerity" means "truthfulness."

"Value" is a later term, but in pre-modern times the word *gui* (noble) was equivalent to what is nowadays called "value." The word *gui* originally referred to high status, but later it was extended to refer to things of superior quality. Mencius says: "A desire for nobility is what people's hearts all share in common. Everyone has that which is noble in themselves, but they simply do not reflect on it. What people regard as nobility is not the pure nobility. For, those whom Zhao Meng ennobles, he can also debase." (*Mencius*, 6A17). "Those whom Zhao Meng makes noble" refers to status. That "everyone has that which is noble in themselves" is a value that people originally have.

There are two main questions concerning axiology. One is the question concerning the types and levels of value. The other is the question concerning the significance and standards of value. There are not simply one or two values. Rather, value can be divided into different kinds. For example, truth is an epistemological value, goodness is a value of conduct, beauty is an artistic value, and so forth. If a thing is useful to people, then it can be said to possess utilitarian value. If what is useful to people has value, then people themselves should have a certain value. Although there are different types of value, they necessarily have some common substance, and this is where the significance of value lies. Value, moreover, has a fundamental standard; there must be a certain standard with which things accord before there can be said to be a value. In what does this standard consist? This is an even more fundamental question.

These questions about value are all very abstract questions. Discourse about value is highly abstract thought, but we should not deny its great significance simply because of its highly abstract quality. Thought about value indeed has great significance for conducting oneself in the world. In a story in chapter seventeen of the *Zhuangzi*, the question is posed: "Well, then what should I do?

And what should I not do? In refusing and accepting things, pursuing and abandoning things, how should I act in the end?" Although chapter seventeen rejects this question by saying that "They [i.e., things] will originally transform of themselves," this question in fact cannot be rejected. "Refusing and accepting things, pursuing and abandoning things" contains the question of value. Does human life have value? In what does the value of human life consist? What manner of living has value? These are questions that every person who seeks self-awareness cannot but answer. The question of the value of human life encompasses the questions about the values of truth, goodness, and beauty.

I will try to describe the axiologies of the important philosophers since the Spring and Autumn Era in order of their period.

THE "THREE IMPERISHABLES" VIEW OF THE SPRING AND AUTUMN ERA

The *Zuo Zhuan,* Duke Xiang reign-year twenty-four, relates the following story:

> Mu Shu went to Jin. Fan Xuanzi greeted him and questioned him, saying, "The ancients had a saying, 'to be dead but imperishable.' What does this mean?" . . . Mu Shu said . . . "I have heard it said that the greatest thing is to establish virtue. Next is to establish deeds. Next is to establish teachings. Even though a long time may pass, these things will not be forgotten, and so they are called 'imperishable.'"

Mu Shu is Shu Sunbao, a nobleman of the state of Lu. What he calls "the greatest thing" is what has most value. To take establishing virtue, establishing deeds, and establishing teachings as the three types of imperishability is to affirm that virtue, deeds, and teachings all have value. And to take establishing virtue as the greatest thing is to affirm that virtue is the highest value. This "three imperishable" view had a deep and long-lasting influence on later people.

CONFUCIUS' THEORY OF MORALITY AS SUPREME IN HIS VIEW THAT "RIGHTEOUSNESS IS HIGHEST" AND "THE BENEVOLENT PERSON RESTS AT EASE IN BENEVOLENCE"

Confucius advances the claims that "The gentleman takes righteousness as what is highest" (*Analects,* 17.21), and "For those who are fond of benevolence, there is nothing that tops it" (*Analects,* 4.6), and thus he believes that virtue is supreme. The words "high" (*shang*) and "top" (*shang*) are interchangeable, and both indicate value. What Confucius calls "righteousness" refers to the principle of morality. The content of righteousness is benevolence, and benevolence is the highest moral norm. In Confucius' theoretical system, righteousness is a "contentless term," and is not a concrete moral norm in itself. (In "Tracing the

Source of the Way," Han Yu distinguishes "contentless terms" from "fixed terms," and this has great theoretical significance.) Confucius does not link benevolence and righteousness as a pair (the linking of benevolence and righteousness as a pair begins with Mozi). Confucius also says: "The benevolent person rests at ease in benevolence, and the wise person takes benevolence as profit" (*Analects*, 4.2). To "rest at ease in benevolence" is to find comfort in benevolence and so practice it. To "take benevolence as profit" is to consider benevolence as profitable and so practice it. The benevolent person truly practices the virtue of benevolence, and does not do it because he regards it as profitable; he does not take benevolence as a means, but rather takes benevolence as his end. When "the wise person takes benevolence as profit," it is a case of acting with an ulterior motive. When "the benevolent person rests at ease in benevolence," it is a case of acting without an ulterior motive. Thus, when "the benevolent person rests at ease in benevolence," it is a case of recognizing that benevolence possesses a value internal to itself. This kind of viewpoint can be called a theory of intrinsic value.

Confucius views being moral as the highest value, and so he says: "Among men of proper purpose and benevolent men, there are none who will seek life to the point of harming benevolence, but there are those who will bring about their own destruction in order to accomplish benevolence" (*Analects*, 15.9). The benevolent person rests at ease in benevolence, and the wise person takes benevolence as profit, and in these circumstances of resting at ease in benevolence and taking it as profit, there is no contradiction between being benevolent and living out one's life. However, under certain circumstances, life and benevolence cannot both be preserved, and so one should sacrifice life in order to realize the virtue of benevolence. When one brings about one's own destruction for the sake of benevolence, then one has achieved the highest level of morality.

Confucius also distinguishes "the Way" and "righteousness" from wealth and noble status. He says: "Wealth and noble status are what people all desire, but if one has gotten them by not following the Way, then they will not stay. Poverty and lowly status are what people all hate, but if one has gotten them by not following the Way, then they will not depart" (*Analects*, 4.5). He says further: "If a well-bred man has his intentions on the Way but is ashamed of poor clothes and poor food, he is not worthy to discuss things with" (*Analects*, 4.9). He also says: "To have crude eats and only water to drink, to crook one's elbow and use it as one's pillow—there is also joy to be found amidst these things. Wealth and noble status obtained through being unrighteous are to me like clouds floating by" (*Analects*, 7.16). There are thus wealth and noble status "gotten by following the Way" and wealth and noble status "gotten by not following the Way." The formers do not conflict with the Way and righteousness, whereas the latter are "wealth and noble status obtained through being unrighteous." In Confucius' view, the value of wealth and noble status is relative, and only the Way and righteousness are the highest values (Confucius admits that there is wealth and

noble status "gotten by following the Way," and so he affirms hierarchical ranking is correct; this expresses his classist character).

The relation between the Way and righteousness, on the one hand, and
wealth and noble status, on the other, is the question of the relation between
moral principle and material profit. Confucius distinguishes between righteousness and profit, saying, "The gentleman understands righteousness. The petty
man understands profit" (*Analects*, 4.16). Confucius does not completely reject
profit, as when he says that one must "profit the people according to what they
consider profit" (*Analects*, 20.2), but he does believe that righteousness has a
higher value than profit.

In Confucius' belief that the value of morality is higher than that of material
profit, his true meaning is that he believes people's spiritual needs are more
important than their material needs. People's basic spiritual need is that they
must have an independent character, and so people must respect each other's
independent character. This is the basic principle of morality. Confucius affirms
that people have independent thoughts and purposes when he says, "The three
armies can have their leader taken away, but even a common man cannot have
his purpose taken away" (*Analects*, 9.26). To have independent thoughts and
purposes is to have independent character. Confucius asserts that Bo Yi and Shu
Qi "sought benevolence and obtained benevolence," and he says further that Bo
Yi and Shu Qi "did not lower their purpose, and did not disgrace their persons."
This is asserting that Bo Yi and Shu Qi had no regrets about sacrificing their
own lives in order to maintain their own independence of thought and purpose.

Confucius also distinguishes between strength and virtue. He says, "A fine
horse is not praised for its strength, but is rather praised for its virtue" (*Analects*,
14.33). This expresses a tendency to assign greater weight to virtue and less
weight to strength. Confucius also says, "That Duke Huan was able to call the
feudal lords to convene nine times without relying on armed force was due to
the strength of Guan Zhong. Such was his benevolence! Such was his benevolence!" (*Analects*, 14.16). This affirms the effects of strength, but his overall
attitude is to emphasize the value of virtue and relatively neglect the value of
strength. The question of the relationship between strength and virtue is an
important question concerning the value of human life.

In the period from the end of the Western Zhou to the Spring and Autumn
Era, there was discussion of "harmony" and "sameness." Shi Bo and Yanzi both
emphasize the importance of harmony. Confucius also says: "The gentleman
harmonizes with others but does not merely make himself the same as them"
(*Analects*, 13.23), and one of Confucius' disciples says, "Among the functions of
ritual, harmonizing people is most noble" (*Analects*, 1.12). What is meant by
harmony here is a kind of pluralistic unity. Shi Bo pronounces: "Harmony truly
gives birth to things, but if they were all the same, they could not be continued.
Using one thing to balance against a different thing is called 'harmonizing

them.' Thus, one can flourish and grow, and other things will come to one as well. But if one simply adds the same thing to the same thing, taken to the end it is untenable" (*Guoyu, Zhengyu*). This is to believe that "harmony" has value, and mere "sameness" has no value. This idea that "harmonizing people is most noble" can be said to be a claim about the standard of value, and has great theoretical significance. In the Warring States period, the term "harmony" was understood as following along with things uncontentiously, but, in fact, in the Spring and Autumn Era it referred to the combining of dissimilar things.

MOZI'S EXALTATION OF PUBLIC PROFIT AS A UTILITARIAN THEORY OF VALUE

Mozi is different from Confucius, for he takes "profit for the state and common people" as the highest value. Mozi advocates that "proposals must conform to three standards." What are the "three standards?" He says: "There is finding a precedent for it. There is having a source for it. And there is showing its effective use," and the most important of these is "showing its effective use." "How does one show its effective use? One employs it in setting punishments and issuing government decrees, and observes the profit it brings to the state and common people" (*Mozi*, chap. 35). "Profit for the state and common people" is thus the most important. Mozi emphasizes that one must "bring about profit for all people under Heaven." He says: "What the benevolent person takes as his work is surely to bring about profit for all people under Heaven, and eliminate what is harmful to all people under Heaven" (*Mozi*, chap. 15). Mozi takes profit as the highest norm for both discussions and actions. "In all talk and every action, if it is profitable to Heaven, ghosts, and the common people, do it. In all talk and every action, if it is harmful to Heaven, ghosts, and the common people, abandon it" (*Mozi*, chap. 47).

Mozi also discusses "righteousness" and believes that "of all the myriad affairs, none is more valuable than righteousness" (*Mozi*, chap. 47). The reason why righteousness is valuable is that it brings profit to the people. He says: "Now if one were to use righteousness to conduct the government of one's state, then one's subjects would surely become populous, one's punishments and government decrees would surely become well-ordered, and the state altars of grain and soil would surely be secure. The reason why one values precious treasure is that it brings profit to the people, and righteousness brings profit to people. Thus, I say: Righteousness is the most precious treasure in all the world" (*Mozi*, chap. 46). Moreover, the "Mohist Canons" use "profit" to define "righteousness," saying: "To be righteous is to bring profit" (*Mozi*, chap. 42). This "profit" refers to "public profit," so that what is righteous is public profit.

Mozi rejects music, and he once debates the issue of music with a Confucian:

Master Mozi asked a Confucian, "For what reason does one make music?"

He answered, "One makes music for the sake of entertainment."

Master Mozi said, "You haven't answered me yet. Now if I were to ask, 'For what reason does one make houses?' and you were to say 'In winter, one avoids the cold by means of them, and in summer, one avoids the heat by means of them, and the rooms make for an appropriate separation of men and women' then you would have told me the reason for making houses. Now I asked you, 'For what reason does one make music?' and you answered, 'One makes music for the sake of entertainment.' This is like saying, 'For what reason does one make houses? I say: One makes houses for the sake of houses.'"[1]

Mozi believes that everything must have a definite usefulness in order for its existence to have value. Otherwise, it has no value. Xunzi criticizes Mozi, saying that he "took accomplishment and usefulness as highest, gave great importance to restraint and frugality, and neglected differentiations and ranks" (*Xunzi*, chap. 6). Mozi's axiology may be termed a utilitarian theory of value.

As another point of difference with the Confucians, Mozi gives relatively higher regard to the value of "strength." Mozi believes that humans are unlike other animals in that they must rely upon "strength" in order to survive; "Now human beings are certainly different than the birds, beasts, and insects. . . . For those who rely on strength survive, and those who do not rely on strength do not survive" (*Mozi*, chap. 32). He means "strength" in a broad sense: the "judging cases and controlling government" of kings, dukes, and grand ministers, the "arts of plowing and planting" of farmers, and the "spinning, weaving, sewing, and embroidery" of women all count as using one's strength. He emphasizes the importance of strength, saying: "In the past, when Jie was creating chaos, Tang brought things under order. When Zhou was creating chaos, King Wu brought things under order. . . . That the whole world became well-ordered was due to the strength of Tang and Wu. . . . Now if a good and worthy person honors the worthy and is fond of the true Way and its arts . . . and subsequently gains a glorious reputation throughout the world, how could this be fate? Rather, it is because of his strength" (*Mozi*, chap. 36). Mozi sets up "strength" as opposite to "fate," and does not set up "strength" as opposite to "virtue." In Mozi's system of thought, strength and virtue are united.

MENCIUS' PRAISE OF "HEAVENLY HONORS" AND "PURE NOBILITY" AS A THEORY OF VALUE OF HUMAN LIFE

Mencius clearly proposes a view about the value of human beings. He believes that every person has an original value, which he terms "pure nobility" or "Heavenly honors." He says, "A desire for nobility is what people's hearts all share in common. Everyone has that which is noble in themselves, but they simply do not reflect on it. What people regard as nobility is not pure nobility. Those whom Zhao Meng ennobles, he can also debase. The *Book of Poetry* says: "Already drunk with wine, Already satiated with virtue." It means that when one is satiated with benevolence and righteousness, one has no wish to taste the flavor of others' Gaoliang liquor, and when one has a broad-ranging and glorious reputation on one's person, then one has no wish to wear others' embroidered clothes" (*Mencius*, 6A17). He also says: "There are Heavenly honors, and there are human honors. Benevolence, righteousness, loyalty, trustworthiness, delighting in goodness without tiring—these are the Heavenly honors. The position of Duke, Vizier, or Grand Minister—these are the human honors" (*Mencius*, 6A16). To say that everyone has that which is noble in themselves is to say that everyone has an original value, and this original value is bestowed by Heaven and cannot be taken away. The nobility of ordinary titles and honors is given by those in charge, and it can be taken away. These original "Heavenly honors" and "pure nobility" are precisely moral character.

Mencius believes that everyone has material needs of their "eyes, ears, and belly," but they also have spiritual needs of their heart, and the values of these respective needs are different. He says: "People's attitude toward their bodies is that they love all their parts. Since they love all their parts, they nourish all their parts. . . . But within the body there are noble parts and lowly parts, greater parts and lesser parts. One must not take the lesser to harm the greater, nor take the lowly to harm the noble. Those who nourish the lesser parts become petty men. Those who nourish the greater parts become great men. Now suppose there were a gardener who neglected the valuable trees and instead nourished the sour plums and thistles, then he would be a base gardener. A person who nourished one of his fingers at the expense of his back and shoulders and did so without knowing it would be a wild and reckless person. Those who live only for food and drink are considered base by people, because they nourish their lesser parts at the expense of their greater parts. If people who live only for food and drink consider it no loss, then how could their belly be merely another foot or inch of their flesh to them?" (*Mencius*, 6A14). He also says: "The organs of the eye and ear do not reflect, and so they are obscured by things. . . . The organ of the heart does reflect, and when it reflects then it grasps things, but if it does not reflect it will not grasp things" (*Mencius*, 6A15). This is to say, eating and drinking are necessary, but if a person seeks after only food and drink, then he is a worthless person. People have a moral consciousness, and the value of human beings rests in this moral consciousness. Thus, people must have moral self-awareness, and this sort of moral self-awareness relies upon the reflective function of the heart.

Mencius affirms the value of human life, and so he requires mutual concern and respect among people. He says: "To feed someone without having any concern for him is to treat him like a pig. To have concern for him but show him no respect is to raise him as if he were a farm animal" (*Mencius*, 7A37). Thus, to treat people as people is Mencius' fundamental viewpoint.

Mencius discusses the question of "life" versus "righteousness." He believes that life is important, and righteousness is also important. However, if the two cannot both be had, then one should abandon life and choose righteousness instead. He says: "Life is something I desire. Righteousness is also something I desire. If I cannot obtain both, then I will abandon life and choose righteousness. Life is something I desire, but there is something I desire more than life, and so I will not act ignobly to get it [i.e., life]. Death is something I hate, but there is something I hate more than death, and so there are some problems one cannot avoid."(*Mencius*, 6A10) Moreover, he gives examples of "something I desire more than life," and "something I hate more than death" in saying: "A spoonful of food, a bowl of soup. If you get them you will live. If you do not get them you will die. But if I give them with an insult, then the people travelling on the roads will not accept them. Or if I give them with a kick, then even beggars will disdain them" (*Mencius*, 6A10). Those who are already seriously starving will not accept food offered in contempt. Life is of course important, but a person's character is even more important, and Mencius' famous saying that "I will abandon life and choose righteousness" (*Mencius*, 6A10) has had deep significance for the formation of the national spirit of the Chinese people.

The question of righteousness versus profit is intimately connected to the question of life versus righteousness. Mencius strictly distinguishes between righteousness and profit; he warns King Hui of Liang: "What need is there for your majesty to speak of 'profit?' Let there be only benevolence and righteousness" (*Mencius*, 1A1). He warns him further: "If superiors and inferiors contest for profit in their interactions, then the state will be endangered." Unlike the Mohists, what Mencius calls "profit" refers to personal profit. Moreover, Mencius sets up "profit" and "goodness" as opposites. He vigorously opposes pursuing personal profit, but he does not discuss public profit. He believes that the value of the Way and righteousness is higher than all material profit.

Furthermore, Mencius distinguishes between virtue and strength, saying: "He who borrows from benevolence by means of strength becomes a hegemon, and so the hegemon must possess a large state. He who carries out benevolence by means of virtue becomes a true king, and the true king does not have to await a large state. Tang succeeded with a territory of seventy *li*. King Wen succeeded with a territory of one hundred *li*. To make people submit by means of strength does not make their hearts submit, and so strength alone is insufficient. When one makes people submit by means of virtue, then the hearts within them are overjoyed and sincerely submit, just like the way Confucius' seventy disciples submitted to him" (*Mencius*, 2A3). Here he sets up as opposites "making people submit by means of strength" and "making people submit by means of virtue." In fact, when kings Tang and Wu "revolted" [against the tyrant leaders of their times], they did not merely have virtue, but they also had strength. So, Mencius does not completely look down on strength. He says at one point: "Wisdom can be compared to skill. Sageliness can be compared to strength" (*Mencius*, 5B1), and thus the sage can also be said to have strength. Nevertheless, he believes that the value of virtue is higher than the value of strength.

Mencius affirms the differences between things. He says decisively: "It is in the nature of things for them to be unequal. Some are worth twice, five times, ten times, a hundred times, a thousand times, or even ten thousand times more than others" (*Mencius*, 3A4). Things not only are thus different in their character, but their value is also different. Mencius clearly affirms the value of human beings, and within the realm of human life he moreover affirms the value of spiritual life.

THE DAOIST VIEW THAT "THINGS LACK NOBILITY AND BASENESS" AS A RELATIVISTIC THEORY OF VALUE

Laozi raises the question of the relativity of values. He believes that beauty and ugliness, good and bad, are all mutually codependent for their existence, and there is no absolute distinction between them. Laozi says: "All people under Heaven know the beautiful as beautiful, and thus there is the ugly. They all know the good as good, and thus there is the bad" (*Daodejing*, chap. 2). When people all know the beautiful as beautiful, then the ugly must already exist. When people all know the good as good, then the bad must already exist. He also says: "How great is the distance between beautiful and ugly?" (*Daodejing*, chap. 20). In fact, beauty and ugliness are not very far apart. Laozi moreover believes that favor and disgrace, noble status and disaster are all also relative. He says:

> Favor and disgrace are like a surprise. Noble status and great disaster are like a body. What do I mean by saying "Favor and disgrace are like a surprise?" Favor turns into disgrace, so when one gains it, it is like a surprise, and when one loses it, it is like a surprise. This is what I mean by saying favor and disgrace are like a surprise. What do I mean by saying, "Noble status and great disaster are like a body?" The reason I have great disasters is my having a body. If I have no body, what disasters will I have? (*Daodejing*, chap. 13)

To receive favor is in fact to receive disgrace, if one receives it but is surprised [by the reversal of fortune]. Glory and noble status are in fact great disasters, if one tries to undertake them with one's body. (Many of the old commentaries do not adequately explain this chapter. Only Wang Bi's commentary approximately grasps its true principle. Wang's commentary says: "Where there is favor there is sure to be disgrace. Where there is glory there is sure to be disaster. Thus, favor and disgrace are equal, and glory and disaster are united." He also says: "'my having a body' means 'because one has a body.'") Laozi furthermore gives evidence for the claim that "noble status and great disaster are like a body," saying,

"Although gold and jade fill one's halls, none can keep them. When wealth and nobility lead to arrogance, then one brings blame upon oneself" (*Daodejing*, chap. 9). If one is arrogant toward people because of one's wealth and noble status, in the end one is sure to encounter disaster.

Laozi believes that only casting off worldly nobility and baseness is the most noble thing. He says: "Blunt the sharp. Undo the divisions. Harmonize the brilliant. Unify the pointed. This is called the Mysterious Unity. In this way, no one can get close to you. No one can put you at a distance. No one can bring you profit. No one can bring you harm. No one can make you noble. No one can make you base. Thus, you are most noble of all under Heaven" (*Daodejing*, chap. 56). The meaning of the word "noble" as used in the two sentences "No one can make you noble," and "Thus you are most noble of all under Heaven" is different. The "nobility" of the former sentence is worldly nobility, and refers to obtaining royal honors. The "nobility" of the latter sentence refers to true value.

Zhuangzi develops Laozi's views and advances discussion of the relativity of value. Zhuangzi believes that right and wrong, good and bad, beautiful and ugly are all relative. Chapter two of the *Zhuangzi* discusses beauty, saying: "Mao Qiang and Li Ji are those whom people consider beautiful. But if fish see them they will retreat into the depths. If birds see them they will fly away high. If the deer see them they will bolt off. Of these four, who knows the correct looks for all the world?" It also discusses right and wrong, good and bad, saying: "As for the starting points of benevolence and righteousness and the paths of right and wrong, these things are all mixed up and jumbled together. How could I know to distinguish them?" He furthermore rejects differentiating right and wrong, good and bad. "What is right is not right. What is so is not-so." Chapter six of the *Zhuangzi* says: "Instead of praising Yao and condemning Jie, it is better to forget them both and transform oneself with the Way."[2] Zhuangzi believes that fundamentally there is no need to engage in value judgments.

Chapter seventeen of the *Zhuangzi* puts forward the claim that "things lack nobility and baseness." It states: "When one uses the Way to assess them, then things lack nobility and baseness. When one uses things to assess them, then each thing values itself and considers the others base. When one uses custom to assess them, then nobility and baseness do not rest with oneself. . . . When one uses their preferences to assess them, then one follows along with what they take as right and considers it right, and so all the myriad things are right. Or if one follows along with what they take as wrong and considers it wrong, then all the myriad things are wrong. If one understands that both Yao and Jie each considered himself right and the other wrong, then their preferences and tendencies will be clear." It says also: "When one uses the Way to assess them, what nobility is there? What baseness is there? This is called 'progressing to opposites.' . . . The myriad things are all one and alike. Which is lesser? Which is greater? . . . What is there to do? What is there not to do? They will originally transform of themselves." Looking at it from the perspective of the universal "Way," there does not exist a division between noble and base. "Progressing to opposites" is changing and transforming in the opposite direction. Nobility can transform into baseness, and baseness can transform into nobility, so that there is no division between nobility and baseness. "Transforming of themselves" refers to natural change. In asking "What is there to do? What is there not to do?" the point is that one need not deliberate over which things to choose and which things to reject, but should rather follow the natural flow in all matters. In fact, however, choosing and rejecting cannot be avoided. Chapter seventeen continues: "Those who understand power do not take the control of things to rest with themselves. . . . They are careful about what they decline and what they pursue, and so nothing can harm them." Thus, one must still have declining and pursuing, and one must avoid harm and disaster. In the end, Zhuangzi's theory of value falls into self-contradiction.

Zhuangzi also raises the question of truth and falsity: "Wherein does the Way contain 'truth' and 'falsehood'? Wherein do words contain 'right' and 'wrong'?" (*Zhuangzi*, chap. 2). He believes that what people ordinarily call knowledge is not true knowledge, but is rather only a tool for contesting with each other. "Knowledge comes from contesting with others. . . . Knowledge is the instrument of contesting with people" (*Zhuangzi*, chap. 4). Zhuangzi denies the value of ordinary knowledge, and he believes that true knowledge is intuitive knowledge of the Way.

THE VIEWS OF THE *COMMENTARIES ON THE YIJING* AND XUNZI ON THE STANDARDS OF VALUE

The *Commentaries on the Yijing* believe that the differentiation between nobility and baseness is decided by the natural order found in the height of Heaven and lowness of Earth. The "Appended Remarks," part one, says: "Heaven is lofty and earth is humble, and thus *qian* and *kun* are set. When the humble and the lofty are laid out, then the noble and the base are given their positions." Heaven is above, and Earth is below. Heaven is the most lofty and noble, and all things between Heaven and Earth have a certain position of nobility or baseness. The *Commentaries on the Yijing* believe that, between Heaven and Earth, there is the Way, and the *Commentaries* praise the usefulness of the Way, saying: "The alternation of *yin* and *yang* is called the Way. To continue these things is to be good. To perfect these things is to take them as one's nature. When the benevolent person manifests them, then it is benevolence. When the wise person manifests them, then it is wisdom. The common people make use of these things every day but do not know it, and thus the way of the gentleman is rare indeed. It is displayed in benevolence, hidden in activities, advances the ten thousand things but does not share the worries of the sage—this is the ultimate in abundant virtue and great works. To possess them richly is called great works. To renew them each day is called abundant virtue."[3] The opposition and unity of *yin* and *yang* is the fundamental regulation of things, and is termed "the Way." This Way nourishes the myriad things, and so it may be termed benevolent. That is the expression of this Way, and this Way possesses abundant virtue and great works, and the content of its great virtue and abundant works is in possessing things richly and renewing them daily. In taking "daily renewal" as its abundant virtue and "possessing them richly" as its great works, the *Commentaries* believes that this daily renewal and possessing richly are the highest values. This can be said to be a view about the standards of value. (In this passage, the subject of "is manifested in benevolence" and the following sentences is the Way. The "abundant virtue and great works" are praise for the Way, but are also praise for Heaven and Earth, because the Way is the Way of Heaven and Earth.) This is to believe that what has abundant content and is unceasingly renewed is what has value.

Xunzi affirms that human beings possess a value higher than that of other creatures. He says: "Water and fire have *qi* but not life. Grasses and trees have life but not awareness. Birds and beasts have awareness but not righteousness. Humans have *qi*, have life, have awareness, and moreover, have righteousness, and so they are the most noble things in the world" (*Xunzi*, chap. 9).[4] The reason why humans are most noble rests with the fact that they have righteousness. Xunzi claims that "human nature is bad," and so he is different from Mencius, who claims that "human nature is good." However, in admitting that righteousness is the unique feature of human beings, Xunzi is the same as Mencius. Xunzi believes that righteousness is a necessary condition for preserving a secure and stable life for human beings. He says: "There is nothing people value more than life, nothing they delight in more than security. For nourishing life and resting secure in enjoyment, nothing is more important than ritual and righteousness" (*Xunzi,* chap. 16). Just like Mencius, Xunzi also vigorously denounces people who only pursue material profit. He says: "To take following custom as goodness, to take wealth and goods as treasures, to take nurturing one's life as having achieved the Way—this is what the common people consider as virtue" (*Xunzi*, chap. 8). "Not studying or inquiring, lacking all correctness and righteousness, taking wealth and profit as what is exalted—such a one is a vulgar person" (*Xunzi*, chap. 8). He sets up and opposition between the Way and righteousness, on the one hand, and power and profit, on the other hand. "When one's intentions and thoughts are cultivated, then one looks down on wealth and noble status, and when one takes seriously the Way and righteousness, then one takes lightly kings and dukes, because one is mindful of what is on the inside, and so external things have little weight" (*Xunzi*, chap. 2). To take seriously the Way and righteousness and take lightly wealth and noble status is the common viewpoint of Confucians.

Xunzi believes that the highest standard of value is "completeness and perfection." In discussing learning, he says: "Make it complete and perfect, and only then is it learning. The gentleman knows that what is not completed and refined is not worthy to be considered fine. . . . The gentleman values his completeness" (*Xunzi*, chap. 1).[5] Completeness and refinement are thus the highest values. He also says: "One who accumulates goodness and completes and perfects it is called a sage. One seeks it and only then does one get it. One engages in it and only then does one accomplish it. One accumulates it and only then is one lofty. One perfects it and only then is one a sage" (*Xunzi*, chap. 8). This is Xunzi's view on the standard of value.

Xunzi also talks about the question of virtue versus strength. He says: "The gentleman relies on virtue. The petty man relies on strength. Strength is the servant of virtue" (*Xunzi*, chap. 10). Those who have strength should serve those who have virtue, because virtue is more noble than strength. However, he also believes that in ordering the state, one should give equal importance to virtue and strength. He says: "Make complete your strength. Make solid your virtue. If your strength is complete, then the feudal lords cannot weaken you. If your virtue is solid, then the feudal lords cannot diminish you" (*Xunzi*, chap. 9). If one fills out the strength of one's state and moreover uses virtue to make people submit, then this way one will "always be victorious" (*Xunzi*, chap. 9). Such a viewpoint is relatively more comprehensive.

THE LEGALIST THEORY THAT MORALITY IS USELESS

Just the opposite of the Confucians, who believe that morality is highest, Han Fei believes that morality is useless. He thinks that "benevolence, righteousness, kindness, and love" are not sufficient to bring order to the state. He says: "In persuading the rulers of men, the scholars of this age do not speak of taking advantage of severe and awe-inspiring power to subdue bad and disloyal ministers. Instead, they all speak only of benevolence, righteousness, kindness, and love. The rulers of this age think a reputation for benevolence and righteousness is a fine thing and do not investigate the truth of the matter. Thus, at worst their states are destroyed and they themselves perish, or at the least their territory is diminished and the ruler is disgraced. I will thus make clear that benevolence, righteousness, kindness, and love are not worthy of use, but instead that by means of severe punishments and heavy penalties one can order the state" (*Han Feizi*, chap. 14). Han Fei establishes morality and law as complete opposites. He also says: "Strength and order come from law. Weakness and chaos come from being soft. If the lord understands this, then he will set straight rewards and penalties and will not make displays of benevolence to his subordinates. Official position and salary come from accomplishment, and execution and punishment come from misdeeds. If the ministers understand this, they will exert themselves to the point of dying and not make displays of loyalty to the lord. If the lord grasps how not to be benevolent, and the ministers grasp how not to be loyal, then one can become king" (*Han Feizi*, chap. 35). He uses the way parents teach their sons as an example of the ineffectiveness of kindness and love. "Now suppose there were a worthless son. His parents' anger will not change him. His fellow-villagers' reprimands will not move him. His teachers' and elders' instruction will not alter him. . . . If you take up the officials' weapons, promote the common law, and seek out vile people, only then will he be frightened and change his behavior and switch his conduct. Thus, parents' love is not sufficient to teach their sons, but they must instead await the severe punishments of the local authorities, because the common people surely treat love with arrogance, but will heed awe-inspiring authority" (*Han Feizi*, chap. 49).

Here he is correct to use the worthless son's not heeding instruction to illustrate that relying on kindness and love alone is not sufficient to order the state. However, he completely fails to understand that moral education and law are mutually supporting, and so he completely dismisses the effects of moral education. Han Fei emphasizes practical effects, saying: "For words and deeds, one takes accomplishment and usefulness as their targets. . . . Now if in listening to words and assessing deeds one does not take accomplishment and usefulness as their targets, then even if the words are most keenly argued, even if the deeds are carried out most resolutely, then they are still recklessly offered proposals" (*Han Feizi*, chap. 41). "Thus, the enlightened ruler elevates practical affairs and gets rids of what is useless. He does not take as his way benevolence, righteousness, and those various arguments, nor does he listen to the words of the scholars." Han Fei regards benevolence, righteousness, and morality as completely useless. This sort of viewpoint may be called a "narrow utilitarianism."

Han Fei denies the value of morality, and only recognizes the value of power. In discussing the changes of history, he says: "The ancients exerted themselves to the utmost for the sake of virtue. In the Middle Ages, people pursued after wisdom. Nowadays, they contest for strength" (*Han Feizi*, chap. 47). He also says: "In highest antiquity people competed over the Way and virtue. In the Middle Ages, they pursued after wisdom and stratagems. Nowadays they contest over force and strength" (*Han Feizi,* chap. 49). What he means by "strength" is power, in the case of superiors, and brave fortitude, in the case of subordinates. Mencius gives great weight to virtue, and little weight to strength, but Han Fei exalts strength and denigrates virtue. Mencius still gives strength a proper role to play, but Han Fei thinks morality is completely trite and useless. Using Han Fei's views, the Qin state subjugated its six rivals and took control of the whole empire, but within two generations it was destroyed. History proved that Han Fei's extreme despotism is untenable.

DONG ZHONGSHU'S THEORY OF VALUE, "NOTHING OUTWEIGHS RIGHTEOUSNESS"

Dong Zhongshu reveres Confucius, and once again affirms the value of morality. He thinks that what is noble about people is their possessing morality. He says:

"Humans have received the mandate from Heaven, and so originally they vastly surpass the other various living things. Within the family, there is the proper intimacy between mother, father, older brother, and younger brother. Outside the family, there are the proper relations among lord and minister, superior, and subordinate. In associations and acquaintances, there is the proper treatment among the elderly, the senior, and the junior. In splendidly interacting with each other according to the proper form, in joyfully loving each other with displays of kindness—this is wherein people are noble" (*Hanshu*). Having morality is the special feature of people in which they are more noble than other creatures, and so the value of morality is higher than that of material profit. He also puts forward the claim that "in nourishing one's person, nothing outweighs righteousness"; "When Heaven produced people, it also caused them to produce righteousness and profit. Profit is the means to nourish their bodies, and righteousness is the means to nourish their hearts. If the heart does not obtain righteousness, then it cannot be joyful. If the body does not obtain profit, then it cannot be at ease. Righteousness is the proper nourishment for the heart, and profit is the proper nourishment for the body. No part of the body is more noble than the heart, and so no nourishment outweighs righteousness. . . . Thus, if a person has righteousness, then even though he is poor he can still delight in himself, but those who greatly lack righteousness, even if they are rich, cannot preserve themselves. I take this to show that the way righteousness nourishes people is in fact greater than profit and more substantial than wealth" (*Chunqiu Fanlu*, chap. 31). Material profit is for nurturing the body, and morality is for cultivating the spirit. Within the body, the spirit is most noble, and so morality has the higher value.

Dong Zhongshu puts forward another famous claim when he says: "The benevolent person makes his way correct and does not reckon upon profit. He cultivates the proper order and does not worry about accomplishments" (*Chunqiu Fanlu* chap. 32). These two sentences are quoted in the *Hanshu* biography of Dong Zhongshu as: "He makes his relations correct and does not reckon upon profit. He makes clear his way and does not calculate over accomplishments." These two quoted sentences later on exerted a deep and long-lasting influence, and became a common formula in debates over righteousness and profit.

WANG CHONG'S THEORY OF VALUE, "VIRTUE AND STRENGTH BOTH SUFFICIENT"

Wang Chong focuses on discussing the question of virtue versus strength. He believes that, in ordering the state, both virtue and strength are important. He says: "In the way to order the state, there are two things to nurture. One is to nurture virtue, and the other is to nurture strength. To nurture virtue is to nurture men of lofty repute, so as to show that you are able to respect the worthy. To nurture strength is to nurture retainers with great physical strength, so as to make clear that you are able to use soldiers. This is called having culture and martial affairs both properly arrayed, and having virtue and strength both sufficient. . . . One cannot rely on virtue alone to order the state, nor can one rely merely on strength to ward off enemies" (*Lun Heng*, chap. 29). On the one hand, one must honor morality, and on the other hand, one must cultivate actual strength. "Strength" here refers to brave fortitude. When Wang Chong is discussing strength, he sometimes also uses a broader meaning. For example, he says: "If people have knowledge and learning, then they have strength. . . . The court functionaries take managing affairs as strength. The Confucians take learning and inquiry as strength. . . .Thus, to be broadly learned and have comprehensive understanding is the strength of the Confucians. To be able to lift heavy objects and tear up hard things is the strength of brawny men" (*Lun Heng*, chap. 37). Brawny men have strength, and the Confucians also have strength.

Wang Chong discusses various different types of strength, saying: "To sow plants and cultivate grain is the strength of farmers. To do battle bravely and ferociously is the strength of soldiers. To build frames and make carvings is the strength of craftsmen and carpenters. To arrange records and compile books is the strength of official historians. To discuss the Way and debate government matters is the strength of worthy Confucians. All human ways of living have their particular strengths, but among the things they take as their strength, some are exalted and some are lowly. Confucius could raise up the portcullis of the north gate, but he did not pride himself on his strength, because he knew that the strength of bones and sinews is not as glorious as the strength of benevolence and righteousness" (*Lun Heng*, chap. 37). This is saying that bodily strength is strength, but mental strength is also strength.

Among the various different types of strength there is also a division between exalted and lowly. Wang Chong rates highly the power of knowledge and morality. He severely criticizes those people who "fill themselves with eating and to the end of the day do not apply their hearts to anything." He says: "When people are born they are endowed with a nature composed of the 'five constants.' They are fond of the Way and delight in learning, and thus they are distinguished from animals. Now some are not like this, but instead fill themselves with eating and entertain themselves with amusements. They ponder deep things and then seek to sleep. Their bellies are but pits for food, and their guts are but wine flagons, and thus they are just animals. The 'naked creatures'[6] number three hundred, and humans are the most superior. Among the natures coming from Heaven and Earth, humans are most noble, but what is noble is their knowledge and understanding. Now if one is benighted and obese, with nothing more that one likes or desires, then how is one any different from the rest of the three hundred 'naked creatures?' And can you call such a one superior and consider him noble?" (*Lun Heng*, chap. 38). Wang Chong advocates that virtue and strength are both important, but he also believes that morality and knowledge are the highest values.

SONG AND MING DYNASTY
NEO-CONFUCIAN AXIOLOGY

The Neo-Confucians of the Song and Ming dynasties continued the teachings of Confucian and Mencius, and they vigorously advocated the value of human life and the value of morality. They expounded the views of Confucius and Mencius, sometimes articulating them in a clearer, more easily understood manner. Among the Neo-Confucians, it was Zhou Dunyi who spoke most incisively on the value of morality. Zhou Dunyi says: "Yanzi had only a spoonful of food and a ladleful to drink, and he lived in a run-down lane. Other people could not endure his woes, but he did not change in his joyfulness. Wealth and noble status are what people love. Yet Yanzi neither loved them nor sought for them, but took joy in his poverty. What made his heart so unique? Between Heaven and Earth there is something which is most noble and most loveable, which can be sought after yet is different from those things. When one sees its greatness then one simply forgets about the smaller things" (*Tongshu*). He also says: "Between Heaven and Earth, that which is most exalted is the Way and that which is most noble is virtue, and that is all. That which is hardest to get is one's person, and within one's person what is hardest to get is simply for the Way and virtue to be present in one's person" (*Tongshu*). That is to say, worldly wealth and noble status are not what is most noble, but rather what is most noble is morality. Zhou Dunyi also says: "The gentleman takes being replete with the Way as nobility, and takes finding comfort in it with one's person as wealth. Thus, there is utterly nothing that he lacks, and he considers lightly official chariots and robes, and regards gold and jade as so much dust, because their weight simply adds nothing to those things [i.e., morality, what he takes as truly valuable]" (*Tongshu*). Although these words of Zhou are basically repeating the viewpoint of Confucius and Mencius, they are relatively clearer and more articulate, and can spur people to reflect deeply.

Shao Yong uses numbers to express the value of people. He says: "There are things that are worth as much as other things. There are things that are worth ten times other things. There are things that are worth a hundred times other things. There are things that are worth a thousand times other things. There are things that are worth ten thousand times other things. There are things that are worth a hundred thousand times other things. There are things that are worth a million times other things. If there is something which is born as only one thing among other things, but can become worth a million times other things, would this not be human beings? There are people that are worth as much as other people. There are people that are worth ten times other people. There are people that are worth a hundred times other people. There are people that are worth a thousand times other people. There are people that are worth ten thousand times other people. There are people that are worth a hundred thousand times other people. There are people that are worth a million times other people. If there is someone who is born as only one person among other people, but can become worth a million times other people, would this not be the sage? Thus, one knows that people are the greatest among things, and that the sage is the greatest among people" (*Huang Ji Jing Shi*). He also says: "Only human beings encompass all the myriad things, and are the quintessence of the myriad things. To use the example of the sounds of birds and beasts, each has one sound according to its own kind, but there is none which humans are not capable of. If you extend this to other matters, they are also all like this. . . . The life of human beings can truly be called noble indeed!" (*Huang Ji Jing Shi*). People's ability encompasses the myriad things, and so it is most noble.

Zhang Zai proposes explanations of the terms "possessing them richly" and "daily renewal" from the *Commentaries on the Yijing*. He says: " 'Possessing them richly' means it [i.e., the Way] is so great that nothing is outside it. 'Renewing them daily' means it is so long lasting that it never runs out" (*Zheng Shang*). He also explains "long-lasting" and "great" as follows: " 'Long-lasting' means that it has the purity of oneness. 'Great' means it has the wealth of encompassing things" (*Zheng Shang*). The "purity of oneness" and "wealth of encompassing things" means that it [i.e., the Way] is abundant yet not a jumbled mixture. These can be called "principles concerning the standard of value."

Cheng Yi says: "[In Mencius' saying that] 'Everyone has that which is noble in themselves,' the reason is that everyone can become a Yao or a Shun" (*Chengshi Yishu 25*). He also says: "That wherein the gentleman differs from the birds and beasts is that he has a nature composed of benevolence and righteousness" (*Chengshi Yishu 25*). People's value thus rests in their having moral awareness. Cheng Yi also says: "What the gentleman considers noble, the vulgar people of the world consider shameful. What the vulgar people of the world consider noble, the gentleman considers base" (*Chengshi Yishu 25*). This reveals the opposition between the axiology of the scholar and the axiology of the vulgar people of the world. What the vulgar people of the world pursue are sensual delights, goods and profit, wealth and noble status, and power. What the scholar pursues is a moral ideal.

Cheng Yi highly praises Dong Zhongshu's view on righteousness versus profit, saying: " '[The gentleman] makes his relations correct and does not reckon upon profit. He makes clear his way and does not calculate over accomplishments'— This is a point wherein Dong surpassed all the various other thinkers" (*Chengshi Yishu 29*). Later on, although Zhu Xi and Lu Jiuyuan would argue with each other over many scholarly questions, they both emphasized the distinction between righteousness and profit. I will not recount all those points here.

The Neo-Confucians of the Song and Ming periods regarded moral cultivation as greatly important, and they stressed "vigorously carrying it [i.e., morality] out with one's entire person." In their own lives, they achieved a relatively high level of cultivation. Neo-Confucianism [of those periods] is also called *Daoxue* [literally, the "Learning of the Way"]. From the beginning of the Qing dynasty, *Daoxue* has been criticized by many people, and moreover in recent years many people have denigrated the *Daoxue* masters as being "fake gentlemen." Indeed, many boosters of *Daoxue* did not live up to their words, and they can be called "fake gentlemen" and "false learners of the Way." However, many thinkers belonging to the school of *Daoxue* in fact led honest but poor lives, demonstrating resoluteness of intention, and so although it was hard for them to avoid being unrealistic, they were not simply fake or hollow. As Cheng Yi says: "What the gentleman considers noble, the vulgar people of the world consider shameful. What the vulgar people of the world consider noble, the gentleman considers base," and so it is understandable that they would encounter disparagement from some people.

WANG FUZHI'S THEORY OF VALUE, "CHERISH LIFE AND WORK AT RIGHTEOUSNESS"

Although Mencius advocates that one should "abandon life and choose righteousness," he does not deny the value of life, for he says that "Life is also what I desire." Laozi proposes: "Only one who does not act for the sake of life knows how to treat life as noble" (*Daodejing*, chap. 75). and thus he demonstrates a tendency to belittle life. (In fact, Laozi also speaks of "the way to live long and witness affairs for long time," and so his remark about "not acting for the sake of life" is merely another example of how "correct words seem paradoxical.") Buddhism regards life as suffering and seeks release from it. The Song and Ming dynasty Neo-Confucians emphasized the value of morality, but they did not regard the value of life with sufficient importance. In response to these circumstances, Wang Fuzhi proposes his teaching of "cherishing life." He says: "The sage serves people, and people serve life. Since there is already this person, one cannot but cherish his life" (*Zhouyi Zhuan 2*). People are living creatures, and so they should cherish their own lives. If one cherishes one's own life, then one should also cherish one's own body, and should oppose all viewpoints which deprecate the body. He criticizes the Daoists and Buddhists, saying: "If one debases the body, then one is sure to debase the feelings. If one debases the feelings, then one is sure to debase life. If one debases life then one is sure to debase benevolence and righteousness. If one debases benevolence and righteousness, then one is sure to turn away from life. If one turns away from life then one is sure to say that non-existence is what is real and to say that human life is simply delusion, and thus the deviant sayings of the two schools flourish" (*Zhouyi Zhuan 2*). Wang Fuzhi abundantly affirms the value of life.

However, life must accord with the Way and righteousness before it can have true value. Wang Fuzhi says: "One will treat one's life as noble, because life must be treated as noble. One will abandon one's life, because life must be abandoned [in certain circumstances]. . . . Life is for the sake of supporting righteousness, and so life may be viewed as noble. Righteousness is the basis for life, and so life may be abandoned [i.e., when living on would undermine righteousness, its basis]". (*Shangshu Yinyi 5*) One's life must exemplify the Way and righteousness, and only such a life can be viewed as noble. But when the occasion requires it, one should abandon life and choose righteousness.

Thus, Wang Fuzhi accurately explains the relation between life and righteousness. He furthermore proposes the claim that one should "work at righteousness." He says: "To establish the human Way is called righteousness. To generate useful things for people is called profit. If one casts out righteousness to bring in profit, then the human Way will not be established. If one casts out profit to bring in harm, then what is useful for people will not be generated. . . . At the juncture of profit and righteousness, there is a great difference between them. At the juncture of profit and harm, there is a close connection between them. Who understands that righteousness is sure to bring profit, and that profit cannot be [achieved by aiming at] profit? . . . There is no greater wisdom than this. One works at righteousness in order to keep harm far away, and that is all" (*Shangshu Yingyi 2*). Righteousness and profit are a unity of opposites, but they have a definite boundary between them. Profit and harm are also a unity of opposites, but they commonly change and transform into each other. If one concentrates on pursuing profit, one will frequently get harm. Only when one concentrates on acting with reverence for righteousness will one be able to avoid harms and disasters. Wang Fuzhi's views on the relationship between life and righteousness are inspired by Mencius' thought, but he speaks on them more thoroughly than Mencius does.

Axiologies in pre-modern Chinese philosophy mainly discuss two questions. One is the question of the types and levels of value. The other is the question of the fundamental standards of value. Regarding the types and levels of value, the Confucians emphasize that morality is the highest and supreme, and they believe that morality has intrinsic value, and thus they can be said to advocate a theory of intrinsic value. The Mohists affirm the importance of morality from the aspect of utility, and so they can be said to advocate a utilitarian theory of value. The Daoists point out the relativity of what the Confucians and Mohists call "morality," and instead seek a return to what is natural, and so they can be said to advocate a relativistic theory of value. The Legalists deny the value of morality and instead focus on practical results, and so they can be said to advocate a theory that morality is useless, or they might also be said to advocate a narrow utilitarianism.

Regarding the standards of value, Shi Bo of the Western Zhou and the early Confucians advocate that "harmony is noble," and take a pluralistic unity as the standard of value. Xunzi proposes his claims about "completeness and refinement," and the *Commentaries on the Yijing* proposes its claims about "possessing them richly" and "daily renewal," and thus it thinks that what has abundant content and ceaselessly renews itself is what possesses the highest value.

After the Western and Eastern Han periods, Confucian axiology assumed a position of dominance and became the guiding thought of Chinese culture.

Confucians affirmed the value of human beings, and emphasized the importance of morality, and this had a tremendous effect on the development of spiritual culture during the feudal period. However, the Confucians, and especially the views of the Neo-Confucians of the Song and Ming dynasties, exhibited severe biases in relation to the questions of righteousness versus profit, and virtue versus strength. From Dong Zhongshu to the schools of the Cheng brothers, Zhu Xi, Lu Jiuyuan, and Wang Yangming, all neglected the difference between public profit and private profit, and instead emphasized only the Way and righteousness, and thus exhibited a tendency to depart from what is realistic. Mencius and Xunzi both took virtue as important while treating strength lightly, but they still gave strength a certain proper place. Yet, later Confucians rarely spoke of the question of strength. The views of Mozi and Wang Chong affirming the importance of strength faded into obscurity, and most people pursued "sensual delights, goods, and profit," and "high official position and generous official salary," sinking into vulgar customs and paying no attention to the question of how to improve material culture. Thus, from the middle of the Ming dynasty, Chinese culture stagnated and gradually fell behind in comparison with the rest of the world, and this was partly because of socioeconomic reasons, but also had its intellectual roots.

In recent times, we often speak of "truth," "beauty," and "goodness" together. In ancient China, "beauty" and "goodness" were usually linked together, but "truth" for the most part appeared by itself. Truth is the value for knowledge, beauty is the value for art, and goodness is the value for conduct. These three belong to different realms. What the pre-Qin Confucians call "sincerity" is what the Daoists call "truth." From the Song and Ming periods on, "truth" became widely popular. Zhuangzi highlights "truth," but Zhuangzi looks down on ordinary knowledge. Both the Confucians and the Daoists regard experiential understanding (intuition) as the highest knowledge, and consider less seriously analytical understanding obtained through actual observation and measurement. Only the Mohists consider actual observation and measurement and analysis as important. The premature extinction of the Mohist School had a severely unfortunate effect on the development of natural science in China. The Confucians exalt ritual and music, and this had positive import for the development of art. The Mohists reject music, and neglect the value of art. In fact, science and art are mutually supporting.

The Confucians emphasize the nobility of morality, and they praise highly those men of purpose and benevolent people who "do not lower their purposes, and do not disgrace their persons." This indeed had a tremendously positive effect on the growth and development of the Chinese people. However, moral ideals and material profits are intimately related. If one neglects material profit for the people, then morality will become hollow preaching.

The questions regarding theories of value are extremely complicated. Although the theories of value in pre-modern China are not as abundant or as detailed as those of the recent West, they also have a distinctive content. The present essay has merely pointed out some typical views, but there are other concrete questions still awaiting further research.

NOTES

1. *Mozi*, chap. 48. [Translator's note: The exchange between Mozi and the Confucian turns on a wordplay which is hard to render in English. In ancient China, the words for "music" and "joy" were represented with the same character. Confucians often defined music as enjoyment using this same character, and that is how Mozi can accuse them of explaining the value of music in a circular manner.]

2. Translation adapted from Burton Watson. *The Complete Works of Chuang Tzu* (New York: Columbia University Press, 1968), p. 80.

3. *Yijing*, "Appended Remarks" (*Xici*), part one.

4. Translation adapted from Philip J. Ivanhoe and Bryan W. Van Norden, eds., *Readings in Classical Chinese Philosophy* (New York: Seven Bridges Press, 2001), p. 258.

5. Translation adapted from Ivanhoe and Van Norden, *Readings in Classical Chinese Philosophy*, p. 252.

6. According to Chinese sources, "naked creatures" refers to all animals which lack protective covering such as feathers, fur, scales, or shells. As a class, it includes worms and the like.

On the Idea of Axiology in Pre-Modern Chinese Philosophy

Kwong-loi Shun

In his intriguing paper, Professor Zhang Dainian argues that axiology, or theories of value, can be found in pre-modern Chinese thought even though the term "value" (*jiazhi*) is a modern term. According to him, different theories of value can be traced to various thinkers and schools of thought in the history of Chinese thought, including Confucian, Daoist, Mohist, and Legalist thinkers. If his claim were merely about different ethical views, in the sense of different views about how human beings should live, the claim would have been relatively uncontroversial. However, it is clear from his discussion that his claim is a stronger one. He speaks of value as something that pertains to different things, including truth, beauty, goodness, human life, morality, public benefit, human beings, and moral consciousness. He distinguishes between types of values, and speaks of economic or commercial value as well as describing truth, beauty and goodness as having value that pertains respectively to epistemology, art, and human conduct. He views value as something that can be compared as higher or lower; for example, he compares the value of morality to that of material benefits and the value of virtue to that of strength. He interprets different Chinese movements of thought in terms of different theories of value, for example, he characterizes the Moist as advocating a utilitarian theory of value, and the Daoist as having a relativistic theory of value.

These are very modern ideas indeed, and ascribing these ideas to pre-modern Chinese thinkers goes beyond ascribing to them different ethical views. On Zhang's interpretation, pre-modern Chinese thinkers have a reflective conception of value as something that pertains to different things, such as human life, morality, artistic objects, or merchandise. They distinguish value into types and compare value as higher or lower. Aside from the Daoists, their ethical views are

based on a comparative assessment of the value of various things; in the case of
the Daoists, their ethical view is based on a conscious higher order view about
the relativity of value. Interpreting Chinese thought in terms of theories of value
in this sense, I will argue, distorts our understanding of pre-modern Chinese
thinkers and leads us to lose sight of important elements of their ethical thinking, such as the way they seek to harmonize the different aspects of human life.

Since Zhang himself acknowledges that the term "value," or *jiazhi*, is a modern
term not present in pre-modern Chinese thought, what are his grounds for
thinking that pre-modern Chinese thinkers have theories of value? According to
Zhang, though the term "*jiazhi*" is a modern term, there are pre-modern terms
close in meaning to *jiazhi*, and he cites *gui*, meaning "noble" or "high status,"
as an example. He refers to *Mencius* 6A17, in which Mencius says that while
everyone desires high status (*gui*), what is truly of high status (*liang gui*) is not
high social ranks as ordinary people think, but the original heart/mind in oneself
that has an ethical direction and that can be cultivated and nourished. And he
takes this remark of Mencius' to show that Mencius believes that human beings
have a value that they originally possess.

What Mencius does with the term "*gui*" in this passage is a common move
in early Chinese thought. Starting with a term that has an ordinary usage and
that carries a certain respectability, a Chinese thinker would present his view of
what the term is truly applicable to as a way of steering the audience to a certain
perspective that differs from that of the ordinary person. Zhang himself mentions how Zhuangzi presents a view of what knowledge truly is as contrasted
with knowledge as ordinarily understood, and a passage he cites from the *Laozi*
also illustrates a similar move in relation to the use of *gui*. To highlight what on
his view a term is truly applicable to, an early Chinese thinker would often prefix
the term with "*liang*" (what is truly so). Another example besides *liang gui* is
liang bao, or what is truly to be treasured, found in a passage from the *Mozi* cited
by Zhang.

In the passage under consideration, Mencius is trying to steer the audience
away from the ordinary conception of high status as high social ranks, to a
conception of the ethical predisposition of the heart/mind as of truly high status.
The implication is that what human beings should devote themselves to is not
the pursuit of high social ranks but the cultivation of this ethical predisposition.
It does not follow, contrary to Zhang, that *gui* has the same meaning as "value"
(*jiazhi*), or that Mencius is making an observation about how human beings
have an original value. It will be an odd usage of the term "*gui*" to use it to
express what Zhang expresses with the expression "*jiazhi*" in his essay, as when
he speaks of commercial value or when he refers to the Daoist view of the
relativistic theory of value. Also, while Mencius is saying that there is a certain
ethical predisposition in the human heart/mind that should be cultivated, he is
not ascribing a value to human beings in the way that Zhang speaks of value as
pertaining to various things such as artistic objects or merchandises. In the

passage, *gui* still retains its ordinary meaning of "high status" or "nobility," though with the use of the expression *liang gui*, Mencius tries to steer the audience to a different way of viewing what is "truly" of high status.

It is very unlikely that pre-modern Chinese thinkers are concerned with theories of value in Zhang's sense. They do share certain common terminology that they use to express their ethical views. For example, they all present their teachings as teachings about *dao*, or the ideal way of life for human beings, and regard *de*, a term often translated as "virtue," as the quality or power in oneself that enables one to follow *dao*. But neither *dao* nor *de* is equivalent to the modern term "*jiazhi*," which Zhang uses to refer to the value of specific things. Instead, these terms are used in connection with a whole way of life that orders the various aspects of human life in a certain way. There are, of course, terms that refer to specific aspects of human life, such as "*ren*" (humaneness), "*yi*" (righteousness), "*li*" (material benefit or profit), "*fu*" (wealth), and "*gui*" (high social status). But none of these notions is close to the notion of value (*jiazhi*), since the desirability of each can be disputed. For example, Confucians dispute the importance that ordinary people attach to *fu* and *gui* and the emphasis the Moist put on *li*; the Daoists, however, dispute the Confucian emphasis on *ren* and *yi*. Sometimes, they would put their point by saying that what such a term truly applies to is not what their opponents think it applies to, as when Mencius proposes a conception of what is truly *gui* that is different from the ordinary conception. But this does not mean that any of these terms has the same meaning as *jiazhi*; what is happening is rather that these thinkers are drawing on the ordinary appeal of such terms to steer their audience toward a view of things different from the ordinary conception.

Zhang's interpretation that pre-modern Chinese thinkers build their ethical thinking on a comparative assessment of the value that pertains to things leads him to observations that arguably distorts our understanding of their thinking. Consider, for example, the way he describes the pre-modern Chinese conception of the value of truth, beauty, and goodness. According to him, the value of truth pertains to epistemology, that of goodness to conduct, and that of beauty to art. And though the character "*zhen*" (truth) is a later term, he thinks that the notion of truth is already embodied in related terms like "*xin*" (trustworthiness) and "*cheng*" (sincerity) that do occur in early texts. As for beauty and goodness, he cites the terms "*mei*" (beauty) and "*shan*" (goodness) in the *Lunyu* and the *Laozi* as terms incorporating these notions.

While pre-modern Chinese thinkers are concerned with the ideal way of life for human beings, their ethical thinking does not take the form of assigning value to things like epistemology and art and then making a comparative assessment of the value of these things. The cluster of terms that Zhang relates to truth do not focus on epistemology or knowing; instead, they are ethical terms whose focus is on certain qualities of human beings. For example, *xin* focuses on a faithful correspondence between the way one is and the way one presents

oneself outwardly, the latter often, but not necessarily, taking the form of verbal
expression. The emphasis is on the quality of one's being worthy of trust (hence
the usual translation "trustworthiness"), and not on epistemology. *Cheng*, on the
other hand, focuses on a certain "purity" in oneself, in the sense of the absence
of the slightest element within oneself that belies the way one should be and
thinks one is. For example, within a person who is in all appearance modest and
self-effacing, the slightest urge to show off, even without materializing in action,
shows a lack of *cheng*. *Cheng* is not a term of epistemology, but one among a
wide range of terms used by pre-modern Chinese thinkers to present their
ethical ideal.

This does not mean that these thinkers have no interest in what we now call
"knowing," or "truth"; they do have terms like "*shi*" (what is real) and "*qing*" (the
fact, what is genuinely the case) to express ideas close to what we nowadays call
"truth." And "*zhen*," as Zhang notes, is sometimes used in contrast with "*wei*"
(false appearance) to refer to what is really the case. However, the point is that
these thinkers do not operate with our modern conception of epistemology and
assign a value to knowing, and then compare this value to the value of other
things in the way that Zhang believes they do. Instead, their focus is on the
ethical life, and even terms like "*shi,*" "*qing,*" and "*zhen*" are imbued with ethical
connotations. For example, a person who is *zhen* is not an epistemologically
superior person, but an ethically superior person who lives a "genuine" life the
content of which is construed in different ways in different movements of thought.

The same is true of the term *mei* (beauty) as used in pre-modern Chinese
thought. Although Zhang at one point contrasts *mei* with *chou*, the modern
Chinese term for ugliness, the contrast in pre-modern Chinese texts is with
"*wu*," a term that is often used to mean "aversion" or "bad." This is clear from
all the passages from the *Laozi* and the *Lunyu* that Zhang cites, and what is of
particular interest is that these passages also link up *mei* with *shan* (goodness).
Mei is used in early texts to describe the phenomenon of people being drawn
toward certain things, this being contrasted with *wu*, one's having an aversion
to certain things. *Yu*, a term often translated as "desire," is also used in contrast
with *wu* to describe one's being drawn to things, but *mei* is unlike *yu* in that it
also connotes a more reflective appreciation of the things that one is drawn to.
Mei can be used in relation to the different senses—even food can be described
as *mei*—and it probably did not carry the same connotation of artistic appreciation that the modern conception of artistic beauty connotes. More importantly,
it is dubitable that pre-modern Chinese thinkers assign "value" to *mei* as such,
whether we describe this as artistic value or otherwise. Not only does the *Laozi*
passage that Zhang cites find problematic the judgment that certain things are *mei*,
the *Lunyu* passage also subsumes it under *shan* (goodness) in its implication that
what is important is not just *mei* as such but the kind of *mei* that is also *shan*.

Zhang's construal of pre-modern Chinese thought in terms of theories of
values also leads him to ascribe to it other ideas that, though common in

contemporary discussions, are arguably absent from pre-modern thought. Consider, for example, his claim that Confucians believe in the idea of the "value of human beings," an idea commonly found in contemporary discussions of deontology and of human rights. He cites Mencius' observation about *liang gui* (what is truly of high status) in the passage considered earlier and Xunzi's observation that what is *gui* (of high status) in human beings is that they have *yi* (righteousness). Taking *gui* to be the pre-modern equivalent of "value," Zhang interprets these observations to show that early Confucians believe in the "value of human beings." According to him, the moral consciousness of human beings that Confucians such as Mencius and Cheng Yi emphasize is that in which the "value of human beings" resides.

As we have seen, while early thinkers do use *gui* to steer their audience to a conception of what they regard as truly of high status, *gui* does not function in any way close to the modern term "value" (*jiazhi*). Zhang is correct in pointing out that Confucians emphasize the moral consciousness of human beings as what is distinctive of them, where this moral consciousness consists primarily in the capability to draw and abide by social distinctions. Furthermore, they view the ethical life as one in which human beings fully develop and exercise this capability. It does not follow, however, that they believe in some kind of value that inheres in human beings and that is superior to the value of other things. The view that human beings should fully develop and exercise their moral capability leaves open what the content of the ethical life is. The belief in the value of human beings and in its superiority to the value of other things, on the other hand, assigns a certain explanatory power to the notion of the value of human beings and leads to a view of the content of the ethical life as somehow privileging human beings. Zhang's belief in the explanatory power of the notion is seen from his observation that it is *because* Mencius affirms the "value of human beings" that he advocates mutual love and respect between human beings. And his view that human beings have a value superior to other things leads him to interpret *Mencius* 3A4 in terms of this idea, contrary to the point of the passage, which is primarily to reaffirm the need for social distinctions. This way of interpreting Mencius' thinking has arguably imposed on it a modern conception of value that is alien to early Confucian thought.

Since he interprets Confucian and Mohist thought as advocating competing theories of value, Zhang also interprets the Daoist opposition to these two movements in terms of a relativistic view of value. According to him, both Laozi and Zhuangzi view values as relativistic, and Zhuangzi even advocates an abstention from making value judgments and from making choices. This, according to Zhang, leads Zhuangzi into incoherence, because choices are inevitable for human beings.

Similar criticisms have been directed against crude forms of ethical relativism in contemporary ethics, but it is highly dubitable that early Daoist thought should be characterized in terms of a relativistic theory of value. Admittedly, both the *Laozi* and the *Zhuangzi* challenge the significance that people attach to ordinary evaluative judgments, and the *Zhuangzi* often does so by presenting descriptions of how things look differently from a different perspective, thereby casting doubt on the significance of one's initial evaluative judgment. However, the goal of this exercise is to lead the audience away from certain ordinary views of things, and away from the emotional vulnerability that follows from such views of things. The *Zhuangzi* is not advocating the elimination of choices, which Zhang rightly points out as incoherent, but is advocating loosening the hold of certain ordinary preconceptions so that one can respond spontaneously without being subject to the constraints of such preconceptions. The lesson that these texts teach is a practical one, rather than a theoretical account of the relativity of values as opposed to an objectivist view.

Zhang's interpretation of pre-modern Chinese thought in terms of reflective theories of value leads him to ascribe to them ideas arguably alien from their thinking, such as the categorization of value, the idea of the "value of human beings," or a relativistic view of value. More importantly, it leads him to present pre-modern Chinese thinkers as viewing the different aspects of human life as in competition. He talks about how these thinkers distinguish between "types" of value and assign these types to different "levels." According to him, different movements of thought are distinguished by the different ways they view the "levels" of the different types of values. After briefly surveying the history of pre-modern Chinese thought, he concludes that Confucians regard morality as having intrinsic value and place it at the highest level. Moists, on the other hand, give highest priority to utility, while Legalists regard morality as pointless and give highest priority to utility in a narrow sense. By contrast, the Daoists, in opposition to the Confucians and Mohists, regard all values as relative. This interpretation of pre-modern Chinese thinkers in terms of prioritizing different types of value misses an important element of their thinking, namely, their attempt to harmonize, rather than set in opposition, the different aspects of human life.

In presenting their views on the ethical life, these thinkers seek to both ground it in a conception of human nature and relate it to the kind of interests and concerns that motivate their audiences. They differ in their conceptions of human nature and of the grounding of the ethical life. They also differ in terms of the audiences they address; Han Feizi's focus on the way to govern is explained by his directing his teachings primarily to those in power. Still, they share the minimal agreement that the ethical life must be one possible for human beings and hence compatible with their nature, since otherwise their proposed ethical ideals will have little relevance to human beings. Furthermore, they also seek to link their proposed ethical ideals to the kind of interests and concerns that move their audience, since otherwise their proposal would have little practical appeal. Although they have different views of what the guiding consideration should be in the ethical life, they do not, contrary to Zhang, deny or downplay the significance of other considerations. Instead, they consciously seek to subsume these other considerations under the guiding consideration, in a way that all these different considerations are not in competition with each other but are harmonized within the proposed ethical ideal.

To see how Zhang's interpretation sets these considerations in competition rather than in harmony with each other, consider his interpretation and criticism of the way Confucians view the relation between "inner" qualities and "outer" manifestation, and between ethical cultivation and material benefits. According to him, Confucius' emphasis on *yi* (righteousness) over *li* (benefit, profit) shows that he regards the value of morality as higher than that of material benefits, or the spiritual needs of human beings as more important than their material needs. He makes a similar observation about how Mencius views morality as of higher value than any material benefit, claiming that Mencius not only opposes the pursuit of private profit but also neglects public benefit. This point he also puts in terms of how both Confucius and Mencius assign higher value to *de* (virtue) over *li* (strength). As he notes in his discussion of Mozi and Wang Chong, *li* can be used broadly to refer not just to physical strength but to external accomplishments. So, according to him, the Confucians' emphasis on *de* and comparative neglect of *li* is related to their emphasis on morality to the neglect of material benefits, and such a neglect is a fundamental flaw of Confucian thought.

Contrary to Zhang's interpretation, pre-modern Chinese thinkers do not see "inner" quality and "outer" accomplishments, or ethical cultivation and material benefits, as in competition. As mentioned earlier, in conceptualizing and presenting their ethical ideals, they consciously seek to link the proposed ideal to concerns that engage their audience. Since external accomplishments and material benefits are primary concerns of people of the times, whether those in government or those governed, they have to show how these considerations harmonize rather than compete with the proposed ethical ideal. This involves not just linking the ethical ideal to material benefits, but also showing how public benefit and private interest are not in competition with each other. For example, not only does Mozi emphasize public benefit as Zhang notes, but he also views public benefit and private interest as converging. Through an appeal to an overseeing Heaven (*tian*) and an assumption about the human tendency to reciprocate, Mozi also argues that one who performs altruistic acts will eventually be rewarded, whether by Heaven or by other human beings. The Moist position is that acting for the public interest is also to one's own interest, by contrast to the Yangist position, associated with Yang Zhu, that the public interest is promoted by each working toward his or her own interest.

Confucian and Daoist thinkers also see ethical cultivation as conducive to both public and private interest. Early Daoists advocate a state of existence in which one has minimal desires and no preconception about how one should respond to external situations. Such a state of existence is in one's own interest as it frees one from the strife and exhaustion of ordinary human life. The ruler should maintain such a state of existence among the people and in himself, and should minimize any active intervention in the life of the people. Such government through nonaction (*wuwei*) preserves order and harmony in society, and so is itself in the public interest. Thus, the state of existence advocated by the Daoists is not presented by them as competing with and overriding the considerations that engage the attention of the ordinary people; instead, it is conducive both to the public interest and promotes one's "true" personal interest. The deliberate effort to link up the proposed ideal with personal interest is particularly conspicuous in the *Laozi*, which is in part a political treatise. While the text advocates that a ruler should maintain his state in a condition of "weakness" in the sense of not building up military strength and not competing with neighboring states, it also presents this condition as one leading to true strength in the sense of one's ability to outlast the rivalry between the other states.

The relation of ethical cultivation to external accomplishments and public benefits is even more conspicuous in early Confucian thought. Confucius sees *de* (virtue) as the ideal basis for government, and the ruler with *de* will employ worthy officials who will attend to both the education and the material needs of the people. Likewise, for Mencius, the Confucian ideal of *ren* (humaneness) involves as an important element a general concern for the well being of others. A ruler should ideally govern through *ren*, and this involves caring for and providing for the people in a way that will draw their allegiance. So, contrary to Zhang, the importance of public benefit is emphasized rather than neglected by the Confucians. Neither do they totally neglect individual interest, even though they do oppose a preoccupation with personal profit. As long as one is not overly preoccupied with the pursuit of personal profit, but instead subsumes it under the proper ethical framework, it is respectable to act in ways that further ones own interest. Furthermore, ethical cultivation is itself to one's interest, as it leads to an incommensurable joy and contentment in one's life as depicted in Mencius' description of Confucius' disciple Yen Yuan. In the political realm, government through *de* or *ren* enables one to gain the allegiance of the people and become a true king. As made clear in the *Mencius*, this enables a ruler to accomplish his political aspirations in a higher form than what the ruler may initially be concerned with. For example, it enables the ruler to be "without enemies" (*wudi*), not in the ordinary sense of being invincible through military strength, but in the sense of gaining the allegiance of the people and thereby being without opposition.

To conclude, pre-modern Chinese thinkers do not work with terms close in meaning to the modern term "value" (*jiazhi*), and do not conceptualize the ethical life in terms of assigning values to the different aspects of human life and ranking their respective value. Instead, while they work with certain guiding considerations in their conceptualization of the ethical ideal, they also seek to subsume the different aspects of life under such considerations. Instead of giving higher value to human beings over other things, or to morality over material benefit, they see these different elements of the cosmic order and different aspects of human life as mutually interdependent and ideally in harmony. To read modern theories of value into their thinking leads us to lose sight of this distinctive feature of pre-modern Chinese thought.

THE CHINESE PATH TO POLYTHEISM

Zhao Dunhua

Translated by Miranda D. Brown

THE PROBLEM

Nowadays, most people agree that Chinese religion is polytheistic (with the exception of Buddhist adherents, who resist such a categorization). However, such a manner of speaking does not do justice to the independent nature of Chinese religion. This is because Chinese religion cannot be broken down in terms of objects of worship. Moreover, Chinese religions have not traditionally opposed polytheism to monotheism. In fact, the opposition between polytheism and monotheism does not have much meaning in the context of Chinese religion. However, here, we are not resisting the characterization of Chinese religion as polytheistic. The crux of the issue is rather to understand the semantic context in which such judgments occur.

"Polytheism" and "monotheism" are terms that were initially imported from the West. Using Judaic and Islamic faith traditions as their reference points, Western scholars categorized other religions as polytheistic. If there was one major deity worshipped within a group of deities, a religion was polytheistic. If each of the deities worshipped were mutually independent and their worship was not mutually exclusive, the religion was henotheistic. Western scholars believed that monotheistic faiths were superior to polytheistic and henotheistic ones. This notion led to another problem: How can we accept the hierarchy of value given to each of the faiths?

In this regard, there are two diametrically opposed theories. The first kind of theory, Progressive Theory, was best exemplified by Herbert Spencer, E. Burnet Tylor, J. George Frazer, and others. According to this theory, the degrees to which cultures evolve differ and are situated in different stages of civilized development.

They proceed through the three stages of primitivism, barbarianism, and civilization. What distinguishes these three stages of religion is whether its primitive or previous religion was polytheistic or henotheistic. According to Progressive Theory, each civilization (e.g., ancient India, Egypt, Babylon, ancient Greece) all started with a polytheistic stage. In the beginning, sorcery and totem also flourished. Ancient China was also this way. It was only the Jewish people who were able to create the henotheism that advanced nations would later use.

The second kind of theory, Degenerate Theory, was represented by William Schmidt, and others. It took as its starting point an explanation of henotheism. According to their explanation, the development of a religion does not start from a lower level and progress to a higher level. Rather, it begins from a high level and degenerates to a lower level. In the very beginning, religions were henotheistic. It was only afterwards when religion degenerated into polytheism that sorcery and totem appeared. In his twelve-volume *Der Ursprung der Gottesidee* (*The Origins of Concepts of Deity*), Schmidt made a famous attempt striving to demonstrate how the majority of primitive peoples worshiped an omnipotent father-like deity. This was the very first form of religion. Polytheism and ghost worship were only a manifestation of later additions and degeneration.

Progressive Theory and Degenerate Theory make the same assumption, namely, that all civilizations and ancient states had polytheism. Moreover, they assume that a majority of ancient polytheistic religions only had one major deity. They also assume that the other deities were under the control of the major deity and that they formed a systematic hierarchy. There were the Egyptian sun deities Re and Osiris, the Sumerian sky deity Anu, Babylonian religion's Marduk, ancient Greece's Zeus and Jupiter, Indian religion's Brahma and Siva, China's Heavenly Lord, and so forth. All of these represented primary deities in ancient polytheism.

With regard to the validity of the above, there are different explanations for both progressive and degenerate theories. Progressive Theory takes a psychological, sociological, and political/economic viewpoint in explaining how polytheist worship of a major deity was the beginning of a religion's promotion from a lower level. This move from primitive religious or the previous to polytheism and then to henotheism represents a progression from lower to higher levels. Opposing this is Degenerate Theory's explanation of how an original henotheism was transformed into polytheism. In this view, the main deity represented only a permutation of monotheism, that later was split into different names as objects of worship. Progressive Theory maintains that there is an evolutionary trajectory whereby objects of religious worship become increasingly elevated with a tendency toward increasingly less convergence. Degenerate Theory assumes degeneration with a tendency toward increasing divergence. We can say that the two theories are diametrically opposed.

Having gone through the analysis above, we wish to offer a theoretical contribution to the field of religious studies by questioning the evolutionary tendency in Progressive Theory with specific reference to the conventional judgment that Chinese religion is polytheistic. In order to raise this question, we can use what we know about how Chinese religion evolved, and thus divide its history into three stages. The first is prehistoric. The second is the Shang-Zhou period. The third is the Qin-Han period and what followed. It is the third stage that we understand the most about. As the historical evidence reveals, during this stage, people's reliance and belief in the high deity of traditional worship, "Heaven" or "Lord (*di*)," had abated. What was steadily increasing as a method of worship was the newly created tradition of the "Way of the Deities and Established Teaching" (*shendao shejiao*). After the Han dynasty, when the three teachings (Confucianism, Buddhism, and Daoism) were established, the objects of worship for each religion multiplied and the relationships became even more complicated. They largely were disseminated through popular religion. All of this reflects a trajectory of divergence in the polytheism of this period.

This essay does not propose to further explicate an already well-known phenomenon. Rather, the problem that we are concerned with here is the following: Was the tendency towards divergence during the third stage consistent with the tendency of the second (Shang-Zhou) stage? To put it another way, was there a single unbroken trajectory in Chinese religion from start to finish? If the answer is affirmative, then people probably have to make some reasonable assumptions, such as that a primitive henotheism existed at the start of the process of divergence. However, we do not presume to make too many assumptions about the nature of the first stage of religion. Moreover, we will restrict the focus of this essay to the second phase.

At present, the available materials tell us that the objects of religious worship during the Shang-Zhou period were the high deity, Lord on High or Heaven, the numerous ancestral and natural deities and that the main forms of religious activity were sacrifices and divination. This kind of religion had the characteristic traits of polytheism. Under the control of a main deity, each of the other deities formed a hierarchical order. Religious ceremonies also were conducted within a strict hierarchical system. This kind of religious form is already entirely familiar to us. At present, the problem is the following: How does this familiar form of polytheism come about? Or, alternatively, to use trajectories already observed in this essay, does this kind of religious form and development normally tend towards convergence or divergence?

According to conventional thinking, the high deity resulted from the promotion of an ancestral or nature deity from a relatively lower level, and its reification at a higher level. Moreover, the ancestral or nature deities were also perhaps a development from an even more basic level of animistic worship, totem worship, and sorcery. In short, the polytheism of the Shang-Zhou period represents an evolution from a relatively low level of primitive religion. The trajectory of evolution represents the convergence of objects of worship from low to high. Similarly, religious activities should also reflect this pattern of convergence through the systematization of its ceremonies in a hierarchic order.

This essay, however, will problematize the use of the term "convergence" in Progressive Theory. Moreover, it will seek to explain the autonomous and primary nature of the high deity and the dependent character of ancestral and nature deities. It will seek to explain how, at the same time, ancestral and nature deities did not evolve from the objects of lower levels of religious worship and activity but rather, they had their own autonomous origins and they determined the position of objects of even lower levels of worship and religious activity. If we are to use this notion of degeneration, then divergence means a process of transition from an order of few to an order involving many. Thus, the Shang-Zhou religion can be seen as the systematic divergence into polytheism. However, this notion of "divergence" is meant only to characterize Shang-Zhou religion. It still does not refer to the developmental trajectory from the distant past to Shang-Zhou times.

Does the polytheism of Shang-Zhou represent divergence from henotheism? Was there originally in the distant past a monotheistic religion? This is yet another problem since we can only conjecture about whether there originally was monotheism. Although this essay will strive to avoid making too many assumptions about the religious nature of the period prior to the Shang and Zhou, we think nonetheless that discussion of the nature of Shang-Zhou religion will be of use for treating this problem. As a result, in the conclusion, this essay will make some guesses about the nature of religion in the distant past based on the situation during the Shang-Zhou period. Moreover, we will offer a conjecture about the course that the evolution of the Shang-Zhou religion took. I hope that this will make some contribution to research on the religion of China in distant antiquity.

METHOD

In what follows we will consider whether the sources for understanding ancient Chinese religion can give us the evidence we require to challenge the evolutionary perspective of Progressive Theory. This essay will mainly rely upon oracle bone inscriptions and materials from the classics. However, we will not reject evidence from major archaeological discoveries. Even for the accounts left over from the ancient classics recorded by the Qin, archaeological evidence is still insufficient for providing us with facts that will inform us about religious beliefs and ceremonies. However, we cannot say that accounts without factual support are false. This way of arguing would be a logical fallacy: "arguing from ignorance" (arguing that things that we do not know about must not exist). We can only make this bare claim on the written evidence that we are making use of: that it has not yet been disproved by archaeological findings. The so-called Antiquity Doubters, on the other hand, have made the following claim on all written evidence: It must have supporting archaeological evidence. However, this kind of claim is impossible in practical terms. At present, archaeological evidence has disproved many of the theses of the Antiquity Doubters. This no doubt should bolster our confidence in the veracity of pre-Qin sources. At the same time, however, this in no way guarantees the veracity of sources which have not yet been disproved. Under these circumstances in which the archaeological evidence is insufficient, other kinds of evidence also have credibility. This includes comparisons between different sources, for example, comparing the written anthropological sources from present minority groups that have ancient folk legends. We can use these to verify pre-Qin accounts.

There are two classes of written sources for ancient Chinese religious concepts. One is the oracle bones and the other is the pre-Qin classics. The oracle bones record the sacrificial and divinatory activities of the Shang period. They mirror religious beliefs also shared in the *Shangshu, Chunqiu, Shijing, Zhouli, Zhouyi,* and so forth, works some of which are pre-Qin and some of which were compiled in the period between the Qin and Han. At present, most people argue that some of these classics reflect concepts that had circulated from the early period of the Western Zhou. These concepts bear a close relationship to the ones found in the oracle bone inscriptions. Both classes of sources, the oracle bone inscriptions and pre-Qin classics, are our major source of evidence for understanding Shang and Western Zhou religion. This period approximately spans the thousand years of between 1750 B.C. and 721 B.C.

In addition to the classics discussed above, there are other pre-Qin classics such as the *Guoyu, Zhuangzi, Shanhaijing,* and so forth, many of which contain folk legends about distant antiquity. Legends about distant antiquity are much less reliable than those sources for the Shang and Zhou periods. Naturally, these accounts cannot be treated as credible history. However, this is not to say that these legends were entirely fabricated. Antiquity Doubters of the past had come to this kind of judgment. However, recent archaeological evidence suggests that the period of the Five Emperors actually existed. The period of the Yellow Emperors correspond to the Yangshao and Dawenkou cultural periods. The Zhan Xu period correspond to the Longshan cultural period. The three periods of Yao, Shun, and Yu correspond the Longshan Central Plains cultural period. After having witnessed the debate between the Antiquity Doubters and their opponents, we should not read ancient historical accounts and legends simply as true or false, or try to peel away later additions to restore the meaning of the text from its corrupted form and semantic changes in order to read legends as real history.

An advantage to ancient Chinese written sources is the historical nature of their descriptive accounts from the Shang and Western Zhou, down to the Spring and Autumn as well as Warring States periods. This essay examines ancient Chinese religion by focusing on the Shang and Western Zhou (moving upstream and pushing down), to compare differences and similarities. Our aim is to make some generalizations about the actual trajectory of the evolution of Chinese religion. If we take the periods of the Shang and Western Zhou, the conventional hypothesis seeks to confirm a progression between their objects of worship and those of distant antiquity. This being so, if we can ascertain that ancient Chinese religion emanated from the lower level religion of an earlier period, then we ought to conclude that there was a convergence toward polytheism from a protoreligion or the previous religion. However, the trajectory could also have run in the opposite direction—meaning that ancient Chinese religion may have emanated from a more advanced religion (monotheism), which later split into polytheism. Even if the latter was the case, then the problem that remains is whether or not the previous religion was monotheistic or polytheistic. The solution, however, lies solely within the Chinese data, and may not be determined in advance by any theorist's presuppositions.

SOLUTION

Based on our preliminary description of Shang and Zhou rituals and objects of worship, we can split the problem of whether there was religious convergence or divergence into several component problems:

  a. Whether the supreme deity did, in fact, result from the convergence of ancestral spirits;

  b. Whether, in fact, the supreme deity did result from the convergence of nature deities;

  c. Whether, in fact, ancestral spirits and nature deities resulted from the convergence of lower-level objects of worship;

  d. Whether, in fact, beliefs about the supreme deity and the ancestral spirits were the result of convergence from the practices of sorcery.

Discussion of How the Supreme Deity is Not Equal and Did Not Originate from Ancestral Spirits

The oracle bones clearly demonstrate that in the Shang period, the objects of worship were the supreme deity and the Lord. At present, everyone is in agreement about this issue. However, the origins of the concept of the supreme deity remain an important problem. As a result, there are all sorts of different explanations for it. At present, one fashionable theory argues that the concept of "supreme deity" was an incarnation of the Shang's ancestral spirit. There are two ways of framing this "Ancestral Deity." The first speaks of the supreme deity as just being the Shang people's earliest ancestor or ruler.[1] The second speaks of the supreme deity as an abstraction of all ancestors. Moreover, the supreme deity is not any particular or concrete incarnation of an ancestral spirit.[2]

If we follow this "ancestor" theory, men of distant antiquity took their most powerful leaders as deities. Subsequently, as the tribe would expand, other peoples would also gradually begin to respect them as deities. Using etymological analysis, most people now believe that the "lord" (*di*) looks like the word for the base of a fruit (also *di*), which demonstrates that the base of fruits falls and produce other fruits. In addition, the *Shuowen* observes that the "lord is what faces the base of a melon fruit." Here, what is expressed is the idea of the tribe's origins. Wang Guowei has also examined this at length and has come to the conclusion that the lord "must have been the most prominent ancestor."

However, Chen Mengjia has explained "lord" in terms of the graph found in the oracle bones. In contrast, he has given a different explanation of Shang concepts of the supreme deity. He observes: "The Lord or supreme deity of the Shang period was the leader who administered nature. In his court, there were officials who were in charge of sending sun, moon, wind, and rain. The supreme deity ordered wind and rain, he sent down blessings and calamities, and using astrological omens, he expressed his grace and power. The early lords and kings could send their soldiers to ascend to Heaven, and at this time, the supreme deity sent down to the king blessings and calamities in order to indicate approval or disapproval. However, the supreme deity did not have a blood relationship to the king of men. The king of men had to go through the early lords and kings or other deities in order to make requests to the supreme deity for rain or fertile years or to make prayers for victory in battle."[3]

Chen Mengjia's work makes two major points for our understanding of Shang religious beliefs. First, the supreme deity and humans did not have direct contact. There was no kinship relationship between the supreme deity and the supreme deity who was the object of worship. However, worshippers could go through the mediation of a dead ancestor's spirit in order to obtain the blessings of the supreme deity. The Shang people worshipped their ancestors. This was because they believed that the spirits of their dead ancestors (the soldiers of the Lord) were the soldiers and retainers in the court of the supreme deity. As for sacrificing to natural deities, this was also because they believed that these nature deities were all the officials and functionaries of the supreme deity. They also believed that by relying upon and going through the aid of ancestral and natural deities, they could obtain news and protection from the supreme deity. Prayer and divination were how they sought out ancestral and natural deities. Second, the supreme deity was the highest leader and the ultimate arbitrator. The middle level (of the divine hierarchy) could grant human wishes, and the highest (among them) could intercede with the supreme deity to make a judgment. However, it was only the supreme deity who could make the final judgment and who had the greatest power. Thus, while there were for the Shang many objects of religious worship; nonetheless, they all revolved around a single, most high leader. The other objects of worship were the different means by which humans regularly communicated with the supreme deity, either as intermediaries or as aids.

The "primal ancestor" theory cannot explain why the Shang believed that their ancestors were the soldiers of the supreme deity, with whom they had no kinship relations. There are several different ways to explain the meaning of "Lord" in the divination records. While we can accept the explanation of "Lord" as resembling the bottom of the fruit, which shows that the character means the origins of the tribe, we cannot from this accept the conclusion that the Lord was supposed to be the first ancestor of the tribe. This is because if we say that the Lord gave the first ancestor his life, then he is the creator of that tribe. This is one problem. If we say that the supreme deity is supposed to have a kinship relationship with the tribe's ancestor, this would be another problem. Let us pursue this line of questioning one step further: Why do these kinds of problems develop for people who believe these legends? The most straightforward answer is: because there is a supreme deity who preceded the ancestors and the worship of the supreme deity is placed above that of the ancestors. In this instance, the Shang believed that a dark bird, according to Heaven's Mandate, produced their ancestor. The Zhou people believed that their ancestor was produced through the footprints of the Jiang spirit, Yuanjian. Nowadays, most people treat these sorts of legends as tribal folklore or silly legends. However, if we want to understand the problems and beliefs of the Shang and Zhou peoples, we can understand these stories. They believed these kinds of legends precisely because they wanted to avoid confusing the supreme deity with their own blood ancestors. The conclusion we can draw from this is the following: the original meaning of "Lord" is the one who brought about the creation of life. Moreover, Lord does not carry any connotations of blood kinship.

The character for Lord underwent a semantic change from being an appellation for the supreme deity to one for a human ruler. In early period oracle bones, the words for "Lord" and "supreme deity" were mutually exchangeable. In later period oracle bones, the ancestral spirits were also called "Lord." However, they were all used to accompany an ancestor's title, for example, "Lord Yi," and so forth. This was to be distinguished from the supreme deity who went simply by being called the "Lord." When we get to the period in which the *Shangshu* was compiled (probably during the Western Zhou), Lord had already become the appellation for human rulers. Lord Yao, Lord Shun, and so forth, were simply being called Lord while the highest spirit was being called the "supreme deity."

The shift in the meaning of the character Lord was the result of a conceptual change; in other words, the supreme deity gradually became confused with ancestral spirits. In the end, the term was appropriated by ancestral spirits. There is a probability that the conceptual change was a reaction to an evolution from henotheism to polytheism. We can use materials from Schmidt's book, *The History of Comparative Religion*, for evidence. After the beginnings of primitive culture or toward the end of that period, did the tribe's progenitor usurp the position of the highest deity? At times, this sort of usurpation could be friendly. In the very beginning, the father appears to be the earthly mediator of the highest deity. Because of this, the highest deity is pushed to the side. Moreover, the highest deity is gradually pushed into a kind of high and respected but empty position while the tribe's progenitor himself is transformed into the leader.

Although Schmidt himself did not research ancient Chinese religion, his thesis appears to be consistent with the evolution in Shang and Zhou religion that we have described. During this period, was the ancestral spirit not only at first an earthly mediator for the supreme deity? And was it not that there was a change whereby he became the highest object of worship? Did not the supreme deity become a high but distant bright Heaven?

Because the supreme deity that the Shang people worshipped was a concrete object of worship, some people have conjectured that the supreme deity was a conglomeration of all the ancestral spirits. Others have argued that from this corporate ancestral spirit there emerged an abstract concept. For example, K. C. Chang has argued: "There was no clear-cut distinction to be drawn between the supreme deity and the ancestors from the divinatory materials. Moreover, one gets the sense that the 'lord' was very likely a joint or a reified conception of the ancestors."[4]

The reification thesis misses the absence of a concrete, kinship relationship between the Shang people and the supreme deity. Moreover, it cannot explain why the supreme deity was not the direct object of worship and why the supreme deity did not receive sacrificial offerings. If we were to consider the corporate ancestors as an object of worship, then the supreme deity would be the most frequent object of worship for the Shang. The consequence (of this thesis) would be to greatly oversimplify the complexity and diversity of the sacrifices recorded in the data. These, in actuality, provide evidence to the contrary: The Shang people did not trouble themselves with the ranks of their ancestors, and they rarely concerned themselves with their "corporate body."

What is more important is this: The Shang people had one kind of name, *xie*, for their sacrificial rituals. The ancient pronunciations for *xie* and *qia* were interchangeable. A *qia* sacrifice was just a ritual sacrifice for ancestors. If the supreme deity was an incarnation of the ancestral spirits or a reified representation of them, then the object of worship for the *qia* sacrifice would have been the supreme deity and not all of the ancestral spirits. In actuality, in the oracle bones' references to the "Lord," there were sacrifices made to the supreme deity. Later, men called this sacrifice *"di."* There were many grades and varieties in the sacrifices of the Shang people and those grades were rigorously maintained. They would not confuse the objects of sacrifice. The Shang people made clear the distinction between their sacrifices to the supreme deity and their *qia* ancestral sacrifices. This has already been clearly demonstrated. In their minds, the supreme deity was not equivalent to the corporate ancestors.

Discussion of the Supreme Deity as Not the Result of the Convergence of Nature Deities

There are some people who try to resolve the problems in the "ancestral spirits" thesis by making recourse to the "nature deities" thesis. For example, while he correctly pointed out that the Shang people believed that the supreme deity had no kinship relationship to them, Chen Mengjia nevertheless argued that the supreme deity was perhaps "Bright Heaven." In addition, he explained the supreme deity as an "agricultural deity" to whom people would frequently pray for rain. In each of the divinatory records, phrases such as "Lord orders wind," "Lord orders rain," and "Lord orders snow," and so forth, would appear in response to the fact that the Lord's major power lay in his control over wind and rain.[5] Such explanations accord with current and general tendencies to anthropomorphize nature in creation legends. However, this is not at all in accordance with our explanation of Shang beliefs. To make the supreme deity of the Shang people equivalent to a nature spirit is inconsistent with the hierarchies in Shang religious concepts. This would also be inconsistent with Shang concepts of heavenly deities.

In the eyes of the Shang people, the supreme deity was useful not only because he controlled wind and rain, but also because he administered heavenly omens. Humans all encountered major occasions that required them to pray to the supreme deity. Those who ruled the Shang and the Zhou, when encountering matters great and small, had to "make inquiries" about each step. Their reaction is often regarded as superstition. However, was it not also a reflection of their beliefs about the omnipotence of the supreme deity? Of course, many of the prayers humans would direct to the supreme deity were related to agriculture. However, this was not because the supreme deity was an agricultural deity. This is just because the Shang and Zhou were agricultural nations.

Ancient Chinese religion considered the supreme deity, or the Lord, as the highest deity, and below this highest deity there were two classes: the ancestral spirits and nature deities (including the Heaven spirit and the earth deity). Within the Shang and Zhou systems of polytheistic religious worship, there was first the supreme deity, then the ancestral spirits, then the nature deities, and then finally the myriad deities (for example, the kitchen deity, the gate deity, etc.). First, the ancestral spirits were originally the first kings, and the nature deities were from officials who had served under the first, or original, dynasty. This is seen in an account from the *Zuozhuan* (Duke Zhao, year 19). There, Cai Mo observed that the deities of the five cycles and of the altars of soil and grain (*sheji*) had originally been five officials. This clearly demonstrates that the objects of sacrifice were ancient men who had made contributions to the state and people. Second, the hierarchy of sacrifices made to ancestral spirits ranked as higher than those made to nature deities. The oracle bone inscriptions record that the most important sacrificial ritual was for ancestral spirits. In the *Zhouli*, the sacrifices were distinguished by size, and according to Zheng Xuan's commentary, the objects of the great sacrifices were those of the *sheji*, the five sacrifices, and an assortment of small sacrifices.

If we say that the ancients distinguished between their ancestors and the supreme deity, then we cannot from this conception of the ancestral spirits arrive at a concept of the supreme deity. By the same token, how could they arrive at the concept of the supreme deity from a relatively low-level nature spirit? One basic principle of creation legends is that concepts about the hierarchy of deities are a reflection of human hierarchies. However, if it were the ancient officials or heroes serving as nature deities that produced the supreme deity, would it not be the case that they had usurped the positions of the ancient kings serving as ancestral spirits? Because of this, the "nature deities" thesis as creation thesis is self-contradictory.

The "nature deities" thesis and concept of the highest deity may also be related as follows: the supreme deity was the highest of the celestial deities and was the master of all natural phenomena. Because of this, the nature deities converged into the highest deity. But in fact they were the supreme deities of the Shang and Zhou (that is, the Lord on High and Heaven) a single object of worship? If the two were not the same, then what relationship existed between them? There is no definitive answer to this question. However, the discussion has already taken on the following trajectory.

First, we should see whether we can divide the object of worship into a celestial spirit, human ghosts, and earth deities and see if we can make the supreme deity equivalent to Bright Heaven. These are concepts that belong to the period after the Zhou. As K. C. Chang has correctly pointed out, the "supreme" in the graphs, *shang di* (supreme deity) did not in fact neither express his position, nor does it reveal whether the supreme deity was a celestial spirit or a supreme deity situated in the heavens above. According to the evidence in the divinatory records, the supreme deity is not at all made to be in the sky or made to have an abstract relationship with Heaven.[6] Li Jia has also observed that "the earliest meaning of "supreme deity" was that of the earliest deity or the head spirit; it did not yet mean the Lord in the heavens above—seeing the supreme deity as the Lord in the heavens was a later meaning."

In its earliest occurrences, the supreme deity was not equivalent to Heaven. Calling the highest deity Heaven seems to have been a Zhou convention. In the oracle bones, which have been excavated in recent years from the Zhouyuan, it is already clear that the Zhou people already had begun to call their highest deity Heaven.[7] However, in the Shang oracle bones, the evidence clearly demonstrates that the highest deity was never called Heaven. Moreover, there is further evidence to the effect that the Shang did not venerate Heaven. According to the *Shiji's* "Basic Annals of the Shang," the Shang King Wuyi made human figurines of wood and called them the "Heavenly spirits." He gambled with them and ordered people to act for them; if the Heavenly spirits failed to win, he would humiliate them and make a leather pouch filled with blood. He would look up and shoot at it, declaring that he was "Shooting at Heaven." Relying upon contemporary notions of respecting Heaven as the highest master, Sima Qian criticized Wuyi as "deficient in the Way." However, we know that the Shang treated the supreme deity with extreme fear. In the oracle bone inscriptions,

Wuyi often made records of his supplications to the supreme deity. He worshipped the supreme deity to an extent that he did not venerate the heaven deity. Does this not directly prove that in the eyes of the Shang people, the supreme deity was not equivalent to Heaven?

As the power of the Zhou tribe grew, the appellation of Heaven became more widespread while the supreme deity gradually became more and more confused with Heaven and evolved into Heaven. Relying upon this trajectory of the supreme deity being replaced by Heaven, Guo Moruo judged that all places within the *Shangshu* where Heaven is treated as the highest deity should not be considered part of the original text. According to him, these were the products of the Zhou who added on materials according to the prevailing ideas of their time. For example, in these places, "Lord" was routinely used as an appellation for the human king, for example, Yellow Lord, Lord Ku, Lords Yao, Shun, and Yu, and so forth. At most, "Lord" was an appellation previously used for no person that subsequently became a reference to human kind. This use was entirely different from its use in the oracle bones.

While the compilation of the *Shangshu* occurred during the Zhou dynasty, (1045–256 B.C.) the accounts about the three Lords Yao, Shun, and Yu very likely took shape before then. If we examine the New Text version of the *Shangshu* (in order to avoid debates about its authenticity, we will not discuss the Old Text version of the *Shangshu*), our general impression about it is this: The appellation of the supreme deity had from very early on been preserved in the classics. In the later classics, however, the use of Heaven to express the idea of the highest deity became increasingly commonplace. In the first chapter of the *Shangshu*'s "Yaodian," in no instance is Heaven used for the highest deity. In it, "August Heaven" refers to a heavenly omen. In the "Yushu," and in every chapter of the "Xiashu," Heaven most often refers to Heaven's Mandate. Thus, it does not necessarily refer to an appellation of the highest deity. In the Shang-Zhou transition, Heaven and Lord were used interchangeably, both of them forms of address for the highest deity. Only during the Western Zhou period, (1045–771 B.C.) did the use of Heaven as an appellation become increasingly predominant.

Examining the evolution of "supreme deity" into Heaven within the *Shangshu*, we can make a guess as to why men of the Zhou period were not very likely to have added the appellation of the supreme deity or to have called the highest deity the Lord on High (Yu shu). For such an appellation would have been inconsistent with the trends of their time. The concept of Lord on High very likely was not the invention of the Shang people and was probably a legacy that they inherited and perpetuated from their predecessors. The Shang people called the Lord on High the "Old Lord." The *Shijing* (Shangsong's Xuan niao) observes: "Long ago the Lord ordered martial Tang . . ." Does this not clearly show that the appellation of Lord on High was from the distant past? During the Shang and Zhou periods, the habit of calling the highest deity "the Lord" was simply preserved. After the Zhou dynasty, the highest deity was called "Heaven" and ancestral spirits were called "Lord," and the human king was called the "Son of Heaven." After the Qin dynasty, there was another development: the human king was called the "Lord."

Changes in prevailing appellations reflected changing concepts. This relates to what Schmidt pointed out regarding how ancestral spirits usurped the position of the highest deity and how the highest deity became increasingly removed from the affairs of the human realm. This is comparable to the evolution of ideas about the Lord on High. The meaning of Heaven is slightly lacking in human character and is more natural or ethical in character. The Lord on High for the Shang people was the master of all things and was inscrutable. Moreover, the Lord on High had no kinship relationship with the Shang and could only be reached through the intercession of ancestral spirits. In the "Zhou shu," however, the concept expressed about Heaven was mainly from the perspective of ethics or the heavenly mandate. Heaven's intentions followed and changed with those of humans. After being subject to learning and ethics, humans could come to understand the Mandate of Heaven and put into practice the Way of Heaven. Thus, in the "Zhou shu," the Lord on High that the Zhou people faced was not as fearsome or awe-inspiring as the one that we find in the oracle bones. When we reach the period of the Warring States, (475–221 B.C.) what remained of the concept of Heaven was mostly of an ethical or natural character. In the periods from the Qin-Han (221 B.C.–A.D. 220) and afterwards, Heaven became the symbol for the highest master. It remained the object of state worship. Nevertheless, Heaven already lacked its original meaning as the highest deity who had absolute power and a human character. The relationships between Heaven and the Lord on High, the Lord on High and the Emperor, all became increasingly ambiguous. During this period, sacrifices and rituals were subject to decline.

What the examination above has revealed is that the concept of the Lord on High had evolved between the Shang and the Western Zhou periods (ca. 1600–256 B.C.). The concept of the highest deity became weak. In other words, the concept and its appellation became increasingly complicated. However, its usage increasingly abated. Thus, this development in thought reflects the trend towards polytheism in ancient times.

Discussion of Ancestral Spirits and Nature Deities as Not the Result of Convergence from a Relatively Low-Level Conception of the Soul

In ancient times, *gui* and *shen* were used interchangeably. Both referred to the soul: "The *yang hun* became *shen* while the *yin po* became the *gui*" (*Zhengzi tong*). From this, we can translate *gui* or *shen* correctly as "spirit." Yet, to translate *shen* in ancient texts as "deity" is misleading, and might cause foreigners to mistake ancient Chinese worship of *gui* and *shen* for something comparable to westerners' worship of a deity. In actuality, we can say that there was only one deity that was worshipped in ancient China and that was the Lord on High or Heaven, as we have previously discussed. Moreover, to translate *shen* and *gui* as spirit, we must also make a distinction between this meaning and the idea of the soul or spirit usually associated with theories of animism. In both, the largest difference lies with the fact that the first has form and the latter lacks form. Those things that lack form can be nowhere and can be seen by men as only the efficaciousness of the being they worship. However, during the Shang and Zhou dynasties, the worship of *gui* and *shen* revolved around the Lord on High or Heaven. This is how ancient Chinese polytheism is characteristically different from animism.

The objects in the worship of *gui* and *shen* can be further subdivided into *gui*, Heavenly *shen*, and earthly deities. As the accounts about Cai Mo in the *Zuozhuan* and about Zhan Qin from the *Guoyu* reveal, the *gui* and *shen* that were worshipped in this period were all *gui* and *shen* with human forms. However, in the classics, there is also an account where there are *gui* and *shen* that have animal forms or that are half human and half beast. What kind of relationship did these sorts of objects of worship bear to the *gui* and *shen* with human forms in ancient religion? Were they objects of worship? And how did they become objects of human worship in each period? Animism theory provides a rather systematic answer to this problem. It argues that in the earliest primitive worship, life was closely tied with animistic spirits. This was totemism. Later, worship was focused more commonly on nature deities. In the final stage, the human soul itself was worshipped. From this, there was a progression from low to high. This is a systematic explanation. However, it is entirely inconsistent with the situation in ancient Chinese religion that we find in the classics.

We can subdivide the kinds of *gui* and *shen* that are half human and half beast found in ancient Chinese classics into two categories: monsters and men of the past (this includes ancestral spirits). Our examination clearly shows that, during the Shang and Zhou periods, these two were not the objects of ancestral worship. However, during the Spring and Autumn periods and the Warring States period, they gradually evolved into objects of folk worship. To summarize, this transformation reflected diverging objects of worship and a trend towards convergence.

With respect to monsters, we can see that during the Spring and Autumn periods, they were traditionally regarded as "treacherous." Moreover, they were not worshipped as *shen*. In the "Quli" chapter of the *Liji*, it is clearly stated that "when one sacrifices to that to which one should not sacrifice, this is what is called an excessive sacrifice; excessive sacrifices are without blessings." Confucius also observed, "if it is not your *gui* but one sacrifices to it, this is dangerous" (*Lunyu*, "Wei zheng"). When King Zhao of Chu was ill, there was someone who observed that through the worship and veneration of He Bo, the calamity could be wiped out. However, King Zhao refused. Confucius praised him, saying: "King Zhao of Chu understood the Way" (*Zuozhuan*, Duke Ai, Year 6). Nevertheless, such stories, also illustrate how the practice of worshipping the monsters as efficacious *shen* had become entirely popular by the Spring and Autumn and Warring States periods. This is also illustrated in Mozi's view on *gui* and *shen*, which mostly reflected folk religious beliefs. He also included the worship of monsters along with the worship of hill and water, *shen* and *gui*, and Heavenly *gui*. Moreover, he also believed that human *gui* could become fierce *gui*, and they, too, should receive sacrifices in order to avoid their harm. This kind of attitude was also utilitarian. It only involved the attainment of advantage and the avoidance of trouble—regardless of whether the *gui* and *shen* were fetishized. We can also see that Mozi's view was a reaction against Confucius' attitude. With regard to Confucius' lighthearted comment about "being respectful to the kitchen stove," Mozi's followers responded with a utilitarian attitude: "If one collects fault with respect to Heaven, then he will be without any blessings" (*Lunyu*, "Ba xiao"). What Confucius retained was an awe of Heaven and respect of ancestral traditions. He nevertheless acknowledged monsters, but he did not worship them. With this analysis of how different kinds of *shen* and *gui* were viewed during the Spring and Autumn periods and Warring States period, we can see that while the worship of monsters was a reflection of the flourishing of folk religion in this period, it was also strictly incompatible with Shang and Zhou religion.

In the classics of the Spring and Autumn and Warring States periods, ancestral spirits frequently were depicted as having the form of animals or half human and half beast. Contemporary explanations treat this as the products of imaginary legends. Or, they are treated as the legacy of totemistic worship practices from distant antiquity. We would argue that both kinds of explanations are only partially correct. It is correct to treat as legendary these images of ancestors, which are depicted as animals or half human and half beast. However, we cannot rely upon these later concocted legends and must rely on actual historical foundations that bear a relationship to ancient totemism. However, totemism was not a religion, protoreligion, or previous religion based on the worship of nature or animals. Rather, it was a kind of expression of the tribe's common protolanguage and previous language. Only later in the course of the devolution of religious objects did the totem finally become an object of worship. Below, we will conduct a necessary discussion of these conclusions.

If we speak just of its meaning, totem is a people's or a primitive tribe's clan emblem or marker. In order to understand the nature of totem, we must understand a totem's symbolic meaning. At present, there are two kinds of explanations. The first sees totem as being an animal or natural thing that has a kinship relationship with ancestors. The second sees totem as expressing a kind of classificatory relationship between humans and nature. Again, both of these explanations are half correct. If we combine both kinds of explanations, we arrive at an explanation that sees totem as a classificatory relationship that originally expressed kinship. Primitive people required such classificatory tools in order to put into practice exogamy. Thus, the totem appears to have been a clan's surname. Having a surname, they then could avoid same surname marriages. In actuality, the earliest surnames were animal ones or ones whose characters had the female radical component. For example, Emperor Yan was surnamed Jiang. The character for "Jiang" came from the combination of *yang* (sheep) and *nu* (woman). The Yellow Emperor was surnamed Ji. Within the character for Ji is *yi*, which in the bronze inscriptions is written as *si* (two dogs back to back). In the middle, there is a representation of a four-legged animal with ears and a tail.[8] In the oracle bone inscriptions, the ancestor of the Eastern Yi, Emperor Jun, was written in the form of a bird. After characters took shape, people added the woman radical component to the totem figure to form a surname. The reason is this: People of the same surname cannot intermarry. A people's totem followed that of the mother who gave birth to them. This is observed in the *Guoyu*'s "Saying of Jin," which observes: "The surname is how we make distinctions in marriage; those of the same surname don't marry, thereby avoiding discord among sons and grandsons." Totems, thus, were linked with ancient surnames. However, it would not be entirely correct to say that the meaning of totem just involved marriage taboos. Rather, it expressed blood relations.

With respect to totems in animal form or those who were half human, half animal, or the legends about ancestral spirits who were formed from the combination of animal forms—this is how these stories were invented. During the Spring and Autumn and Warring States periods, writing had already been basically standardized and increasingly became widely used. And, it was exactly during this period of the compilation of classics that ancestral spirits attained the form of animals. In the *Shanhaijing*, there are a great number of half human, half animal deities; in other classics, there are also such accounts. These reflect the production of these sorts of legends. The *Mozi* observes that Lord Mu of Zheng encountered Ju Mang, a spirit with the face of a human and the body of a bird. The *Guoyu* recounts that Lord Guo saw in a dream a spirit with the face of a human, white fur, and tiger claws. The guesses men made during the Spring and Autumn periods about these animal forms were very likely made according to primitive totems. From this perspective, we can see that legends about the spontaneous birth of Gaozu emerged in order to explain the puzzle of why there is a kinship relationship between these animals and people. Moreover, when this puzzle emerged, it resulted from regarding ancestral spirits as animals. In short, we can say that the origins of legends in which ancestral spirits take animal forms did not originate from totem worship of distant antiquity. Legends did not come directly out of totems. Moreover, within the course of evolution from totemic symbols to writing, semantic changes were produced.

Now that we have separated totems from legends and separated totem from religious beliefs, it is not difficult to explain the evolution in religious beliefs held by ancient men. Based on the evidence just presented, the earliest power of totem resided in its ability to express kinship relationships within a clan. Totem was the marker of clans, and its function was similar to that which surnames performed for later men. Totem was for men of distant antiquity, the capital Self, the collected self. It is exactly because it had such an important function that totem became an object of worship. However, totem worship was not for certain the earliest form of religious activity. Its existence coincided entirely with the worship of the ancestral spirits or highest deity. Comparing it with what comes later, the religious power of totem worship was comparatively weak. However, the power it exerted in society was comparatively strong. Its principal function was to strengthen the solidarity or collective sentiment of the clan or the primitive tribe, thereby increasing social cohesion.

Ancestral worship had a similar power. However, it had a particular relationship with the highest spirit. Because of this, what totem lacked was the power to bless sons and grandsons. It also lacked the power of ancestral spirits to command nature or human affairs. Even if we rank the worship of the highest deity, the worship of ancestors, and the worship of totem in a hierarchy from high to low, we could not establish a hierarchy of priority. The three are entirely mutually inclusive and not in conflict. Most of the objects of worship are the highest deity and ancestral spirits, while the ancestral spirits are responsible for the relatively lower-level nature deities. The highest deity lacks human form while the ancestral spirits do have human form. Ancestral spirits and nature deities do not result from the development of animal or animistic forces. They merge only after the development of writing. Ancestral spirits and totem are mutually interchangeable. At the same time, only when ancestral spirits usurped the actual position of the highest deity were humans able to worship deities with animal forms. This kind of later religious phenomenon reflected the increasing interchangeability of objects of worship and a trajectory of devolution and divergence.

Discussion of Why Ancient Religion is Not the Result of Convergence from Witchcraft

Some Progressive Theorists, who deploy the power of sociological perspective to examine the origins of religion, mistake the earliest form of religion as witchcraft. They use remnants of shamanistic traditions that persist to the present as a case in point, treating shamanism as a representative form of primitive religion. But was ancient Chinese religion a development from witchcraft? Can we or can we not relegate it to the category of shamanism? With respect to this concept of shamanism, there are two kinds of explanations. Normally, we say that shamanism is a folk religious custom that is a remnant from distant antiquity. In particular when we speak of shamanism, we point to divination practices. As we will make clear below, to not discuss that brand of shamanism is to not discuss the origins and basic characteristics of ancient Chinese religion.

There is a kind of historical source that can make clear the trouble that witchcraft encountered in the religion of distant antiquity. The *Guoyu*'s "Sayings of Chu" recounts the speech in which Guan Shefu explained "cutting off the passage way of Heaven." According to this text, in ancient times, the common people and spirits did not mingle. The common people were able to be loyal and trustworthy, and the spirits were able to possess bright virtue. The work of the common people and the spirits were different. They were respectful and not profane. Coming down to the decline of Shaomeng, the nine tribes disordered virtue, and the common people and deities mixed and mingled. They could not order things. Husbands would put out the food offerings and the household would become the scribes of witches. They lacked the essential rules. The offerings the common people offered were deficient and they did not come to know the blessings [of the spirits]. Winter sacrifices were enjoyed without measure. The common people and the spirits occupied the same position. The people were profane and made alliances. They lacked seriousness and fear. The spirits then took human customs as rules. Subsequently, Zhuan Xu ordered that the Nanzheng Zhong would administer spirits and the Huo Zhengji would administer the common people. He caused them to return to the old principle and for the common people and the spirits not to mutually invade or mingle. This is what was called the "separation of the path to Heaven."

Guan Shefu also tells us that in ancient times there were specialists in sorcery and witchcraft. The status of these sorcerers and witches was that of commoners: "The common people's brilliant essence is in not being disloyal; when they are this way, then the luminous beings come down. When they reside in a man, he is called a sorcerer; when they reside in a woman, she is called a witch." We can see from this portion of Guan Shefu's speech that the belief that "the common people and deities should not intermingle" was a tradition originating from distant antiquity. This tradition, by the time of Shaomeng, had already been destroyed by the nine tribes. However, in Zhuan Xu's time, a revival of the tradition was encouraged.

However, to speak of the tradition as either destroyed or revived is not entirely accurate. This is because ancient Chinese religious traditions did represent a single, coherent tradition. As Mr. Xu has pointed out, because archaeology has made plausible the theory of "three great tribal organizations of ancient times," consisting of the Huaxia, the Eastern Yi and the Miaorong, each of which was continually in conflict and in harmony with the other two. Yet it was these that formed the arteries of the cultural traditions of the Xia, Shang, and Zhou. Later in the northern and southern cultural spheres of the Spring and Autumn periods, we must acknowledge that to a large degree, there were two diametrically different religious traditions; one in which "the common people and the deities did not intermingle," and one in which "the common people and the deities intermingled and mixed" persisted. The Chu culture had the flavor of deep sorcery worship. We can see this in Qu Yuan's "Li Sao." In the customs of minority groups from the south, we can also see this. However, sorcery had not yet appeared in the Central Plains culture. After the Qin-Han, sorcery and witchcraft sunk to the depths of a "despicable craft."

Our conclusion is that in distant antiquity, sorcery had been a folk custom in the Central Plains. Sorcerers were not those individuals mainly charged with things such as sacrifices and ancestral rites and they were less so the objects of worship. We cannot deny the importance of the likelihood that sorcery had originated in the south. However, its use was just what the Central Plains culture had to avoid and restrict. The result was that sorcery and sorcerers did not serve an important role within the religious traditions of the Central Plains area. For this reason, we cannot treat sorcery as the origin of the religion that had begun in the Shang or Zhou periods (one important part of the traditions of the Central Plains).

Sorcery and the ancient religions diverge greatly in this way: sorcery venerated and worshiped the souls of deities, while in ancient religions, the Lord on High or Heaven was worshipped. The "luminious being" which descended upon the body of the sorcerer or sorceress was not equivalent to the Lord on High or Heaven. The "luminous being" was not equivalent even to the ancestral spirits. Such were perhaps a relatively low-level human ghost or natural anima. The low-level of the object of worship probably can be explained by that the fact that sorcerers belonged to the realm of folk custom, that they were not part of orthodox ceremonies or rituals, for they originated from the "common people," and sorcery was not an official duty.

However, "sorcerer" later became an official duty. The main task for sorcerers was divination by stalk and milfoil. This was because the goal of divination was to guess the intentions of the Lord on High. Because humans could not directly communicate with the Lord on High, they required an intermediary to get the upper levels to descend. Moreover, they believed that the sorcerers and sorceresses who had the power to communicate with the deities should act as intermediaries. From this, the sorcerers functioned as diviners. Nowadays, many people have many mistaken ideas about divination. For example, they confuse it with sorcery. Associating it with sorcery, they imagine it to be shamanism. After it became prevalent in the Shang and Zhou periods, divination became a distinctive characteristic of ancient religion. Because of this, there are some people who judge that ancient Chinese religion belonged to a category of shamanism. This kind of hypothesis is circuitous and there are many difficulties and unclear aspects to it. To put it simply, there are at least three places where divination and sorcery are different.

First, the aims are different. Nowadays, many people's understanding of the character of sorcery has been deeply influenced by Sir James George Frazer's book, *The Golden Bough*. According to Frazer's definition, the goal of sorcery is to use spontaneous force to influence nature's course. Divination does not appear to share this kind of intention with sorcery. Its goal is not to change the course of nature but to know in advance the course it will later take in order to determine whether a course of action is right or wrong and to decide how to act.

Second, the objects of belief are different. Sorcerers did not have to believe in a highest deity; they only had to believe in a supernatural force. In other words, the highest deity would also have to use spontaneous force and also had to be able to be mobilized by sorcerers. Divination was established on the foundations of absolute belief in the highest deity. With regard to human affairs, divination functioned as adjudication, because the diviners expressed the intentions of the Lord on High. The Lord on High could not obey the assignments of humans. On the contrary, humans absolutely had to obey the divine intentions of the Lord on High. The "Jiyi" chapter of the *Liji* observes: The diviner held the tortoise shell in his arms and faced south. The son of Heaven in his dragon-robe and squared topped cap faced north. The Son of Heaven, no matter how much he knew, invariably proceeded to get a judgment about the matter at hand. This indicates that he did not go his own way and that he honored Heaven. This was devout religious belief.

Third, the function of sorcerers was different. Sorcerers represented the major body of sorcery. They had the ability to communicate with souls, to call upon the wind and rouse the rain. There was nothing they were unable to do. Divination also required sorcerers and witches to act as intermediaries in communicating with the deities. However, there were limits to what the sorcerers did. They were not only unable to change the intentions of the Lord on High, but they also were unable to make a definitive interpretation of the meanings of the stalks. Moreover, the king himself had to make the final judgment about whether the stalks were auspicious or inauspicious. According to statistics, over a hundred thousand oracle bones have already been excavated. With the exception of twelve, all of the divinatory words say, "the king divined, observing . . ." Not only that, but those divinatory words such as "the king cast the stalks," and "the king divined" frequently occur. This illustrates how the king frequently replaced diviners and how they themselves made promises in their inquiries. Chen Mengjia has guessed, based on this trajectory in which the names of diviners occur less and less frequently than in the later period, that a majority of the oracle bones did not record the names of the diviners.[9] This reveals that the king functioned as the adjudicator in the course of making divinatory queries.

The fact that the sorcerers did not make judgments in the course of divination is another way that demonstrates how divination was not sorcery. Divinations were appeals to top intermediaries, ancestral spirits (who were the "soldiers to the Lord") in the vicinity of the Lord on High. The human king had a kinship relationship with his ancestral spirits and thus, it was easier for him to obtain the blessings of his ancestral spirits. The intermediary that the diviner communicated with bore a kinship relationship to the deities and was not merely someone with a special ability to communicate with the deities. Those who were charged with the responsibilities of making divinatory queries were very likely members of the king's own household. Their kinship ties were characteristic of their responsibilities. As one would expect, the most important characteristic of the member of the king's household charged with divination was his ability to communicate with the deities. Perhaps because in actual practice attempts to communicate with the deities were ineffective, those believed in distant antiquity to possess the ability to communicate with the deities were gradually, in the course of divination history, dispensed with. Possessing a kinship tie became more important for communicating with the deities and, in the end, became the only channel of communication. In response to this, it was important for the king, who bore the closest kinship relationship to the ancestral spirits to become a diviner—to the point that he became the only adjudicator.

In light of these findings, we can suggest several inferences. One cannot, based on the fact that divination flourished, classify Shang religion as a primitive religion (sorcery or shamanism). On the other hand, if we carefully examine how divination reflected religious concepts, we can also discover that divination revolved around beliefs about the highest deity and ancestral spirits and developed from certain special kinds of prayers and ceremonies. Divination carried the content of prayers and was the result of written accounts.

CONCLUSION

Having completed the analysis above, we may venture the following conclusions:

First, the conception of the highest deity and the Lord on High was not an invention of the Shang people but represented a religious tradition from a prior period. At this time, we know little about this historically prior religious tradition and we do not know how the concept of the highest deity came into being. We also do not know whether the highest deity or the Lord on High was in fact the earliest object of worship. However, we can know that totem worship flourished in this historically prior period and that animism and sorcery did not affect the high position of the highest deity. They coexisted with the worship of the highest deity or were an unrelated social custom.

Second, Shang and Zhou religions focused on the highest deity with the assistance of ancestors and nature deities and so on. This polytheistic system was closely related to the religious concepts of the historically prior religion where "humans and the deities did not intermingle" and "the passage to Heaven was severed." From this, the Lord on High did not bear a kinship relationship to humans, and humans could not directly communicate with the Lord on High. They required the intercessions of other deities to mediate for them in order to get those on high to descend. Ancestral spirits and nature deities had these kinds of goals and bases. They worked as the a priori kings and lords and bore a kinship relationship to humans. Polytheistic worship focused on the worship of the highest deity.

Third, an important object of sacrifice during the Shang and Zhou periods were the ancestral spirits. However, the highest ceremonial forms were reserved for the worship of the highest deity, thereby expressing feelings of overwhelming gratitude for the highest deity and religious sentiments of awe. The divinatory practices that flourished during the Shang and Zhou periods were religious ceremonies intended as prayers directed at the highest deity. They cannot be characterized as protoreligious customs such as "animism," sorcery, shamanism, and so forth.

Fourth, during the Shang and Zhou periods, the worship of the highest deity was transformed from the worship of the Lord on High to the worship of Heaven. The universal and ethical characteristics of Heaven became more pronounced. Moreover, the human quality and power of the highest deity began to disappear. Humans' sense of dependency on the highest deity, their sentiments of awe, and other religious feelings also diminished. These trajectories shaped the ethico-religious perspective and philosophical views about the relationship between Heaven and Man during the Spring and Autumn periods and Warring States period.

Fifth, during the Spring and Autumn periods and Warring States period, divergence occurred in the objects of worship as they were disseminated and multiplied. The boundaries between ancestral spirits and the highest deity became blurred. Ancestral spirits became the highest objects of sacrifices. Deities of the *gui* and *shen*, lacking human form, emerged in large quantities. They were confused with ancestral and nature deities. The structured hierarchy of polytheism was ruined and disorganized. There was a differentiation in the worship of myriad deities that lacked a common highest deity. This polytheism increasingly took the form of henotheism.

Sixth, before the Shang and Zhou periods, and even until the Spring and Autumn periods and Warring States period, the evolutionary trajectory of Chinese religion was that of divergence. Whether or not we acknowledge it to have been originally monotheistic, polytheistic, or henotheistic, it was a religion that moved from high to low. Now, a diverging trajectory that moves from high to low must be regarded as devolutionary. Although Chinese religion's major form was polytheistic, nevertheless it did not entirely devolve into polytheism. It went through three stages: first, in the historically earlier period, through the worship of the highest deity, though it was not at all a primitive henotheism, we can at least say that it was something approaching henotheism because it was a relatively simple worship focused on the highest deity. Second, religion during the Shang and Zhou periods reached maturity and had a typical, systematic polytheism. Third, after the Warring States period, there remained something approaching monotheism as well as the heavily documented polytheism.

NOTES

1. Wang Guowei has made a detailed study on this topic. He comes to the conclusion that the Lord "must have been the most distinguished of the Shang ancestors."

2. Wang Guowei, "Yin Bucizhong Guojian Aiangong Xianwang Kao," in *Guantang Julin* (Beijing: Zhonghua shuju, 1991), 2: 412.

3. Chen Mengjia, *Yinxu Buci Zongshu* (Beijing: Zhonghua shuju, 1988), p. 580.

4. K. C. Chang, *Qingdong Shidai* (Beijing: Sanlian shudian, 1983), p. 264.

5. Chen Mengjia, *Yinxu Buci, p.* 574–580.

6. Chang, *Zhongguo Qingdong,* p. 264.

7. Xu Xitai, *Zhouyuan jiaguwen zongshu* (Beijing: Santai chubanshe, 1987).

8. See Wang Xiaodun, *Yuanshi xinyang he Zhongguo gushen* (Shanghai: Shanghai chubanshe, 1989), p. 39–40.

9. Chen Mengjia, *Yinxu buci zongzhu* (Beijing: Zhonghua shuju, 1988), pp. 202, 205.

Monotheism in the Philosophy of Religion

A Response to Professor Zhao

Stephen T. Davis

In "The Chinese Path to Polytheism," I see Professor Zhao as trying to situate the Chinese data on ancient religion within the broad context of religious studies. He believes the available evidence, meager as it necessarily is, supports the strong possibility that in Chinese religion, monotheism antedates polytheism. That is, while the question of the origin of religion remains a matter of speculation, the worship of "the Lord on High" and "Heaven" (in the Shang and Zhou periods) cannot be explained as evolutionary developments away from anything like ancestor worship, animism, or shamanism. Indeed, the evidence Zhao adduces points in the other direction, namely, that in ancient China polytheism developed out of monotheism.

Let me make a preliminary and general point before discussing Zhao's argument. I believe his paper provides a fascinating and to me hopeful glimpse of the development of the philosophy of religion in contemporary China. As we all know, since the early 1980s, China has shown an increasing degree of openness to international academic dialogue. And I believe Professor Zhao's argument tacitly demonstrates the extent of the departure, among Chinese academics, from the Marxist philosophy of religion that once predominated discussions of religion in the People's Republic of China and that aimed at trivializing religion. I believe Zhao's paper is an impressive witness to the new freedom for philosophical inquiry in China, and especially to the possibility of using a diversity of philosophical methods for explaining China's religious history.

My problem as a commentator is that as a philosopher of religion in the Western "analytic" tradition, I know little of two of the fields that Professor Zhao's essay is located in—ancient Chinese history and ancient Chinese religion. Fortunately, I am familiar with scholarly debates about the origins of religion. So there are some points in Professor Zhao's fascinating paper to which I can respond (helpfully, I hope), but the central thrust of his paper is far from my area of expertise.

Let me make three main points.

First, I wonder whether Professor Zhao should consider more deeply how much ground the term "monotheism" can cover. The argument of his paper largely ignores the various nuances—at least some of which are relevant to his core argument about ancient Chinese religion. Let me list several possible religious viewpoints:

1. Atheism—no God, gods, or divine reality exists. This is the opinion of many educated people today, both in the West and in the East, and especially in those places in the East that have been strongly influenced by Marxist thought.

2. Monism—there is only one reality; all differentiation is only apparent or illusory. There are several religions or philosophies that espouse radical monism. Advaita Vedanta Hinduism is certainly an example.

3. Esoteric Monotheism—other things exist beside the one God, but God is the sole underlying reality of all things.

4. Metaphysical Monotheism—one and only one undifferentiated God exists; other things depend for their reality on God but are realities different from God. Judaism, Islam, and many other religions espouse this theory.

5. Trinitarian Monotheism—the one and only God exists in three persons. This is the orthodox Christian view.

6. Metaphysical Henotheistic Monotheism—many gods exist, but one of them is more powerful or more perfect than the others, and is to be worshipped. Some scholars of the Hebrew Bible hold that this was the view of God held by the preexilic Hebrews.

7. Cultural Henotheistic Monotheism—many gods exist, all or many of them roughly equal in power or perfection, but one of them is singled out by a given culture for worship.

8. Polytheism—many gods exist, and all of them, or at least a certain number of them, need to be correctly worshipped.

Now my point in listing these eight views is that *all* the religious theories listed here between 1 and 8 can be and often are referred to as "monotheistic."

So the trichotomy that Professor Zhao uses in his paper—monotheism/ henotheism/polytheism—is, in my view, not as helpful as it might be. I recognize that several of the above distinctions are related specifically to Western religions, and so are not directly relevant to ancient China. Still, my point is that there are many things that can be meant by the term "monotheism." Accordingly, Professor Zhao's trichotomy is too blunt an instrument to help us make crucial decisions about the history of the human practice known as religion, in China or elsewhere. Since there are very many religious phenomena that can legitimately count as monotheistic, the term "monotheism" cries out for careful definition.

My worry is that what was true even in the 1960s when this debate raged is still true today. Few scholars today would accept the "progressive/degenerate" dichotomy as helpful in deciding the fascinating question of the origin of religion. The terms of the debate as it was carried on in the days of Sir James George Frazer and Wilhelm Schmidt are no longer widely accepted.

I do not believe that any sophisticated analyst of religion today would accept a teleological account of what religion is, as Professor Zhao seems to do. Rather than seeing some sort of evolutionary movement from primitive to modern religions, I believe most scholars would argue that what we see in various places and over times are the various dimensions of the broad, "family-resemblance" type concept of religion. Apart from theological commitments, why say that one is "higher" or "more evolved" than another?

It is also puzzling that Professor Zhao seems to take religious symbols literally. This is crude for several reasons, not the least of which is this: many atheists find certain religious symbols to be meaningful, even uplifting and inspiring. Many advocates of one religion find certain of the symbols from another religion meaningful, even uplifting and inspiring. Many religious believers interpret certain of the symbols of their own religions non-literally or nonrealistically. That is, they take their deep significance to lie in what they point to or help us aspire to rather than what they literally say. To many people, the sense rather than the reference of certain religious symbols is what is important.

Of course many religious people do take religious symbols literally. But as an illustration of what I mean, I will mention an Asian philosopher of my acquaintance who is himself a practicing Vinshnavite Hindu. He interprets the crucial reincarnation/karma doctrine of that religion (as he says) "nonrealistically." He does not literally believe that he or anyone else will be reborn after death into a new life with karmic consequences intact. He interprets the reincarnation/ karma doctrine of his religion as a powerful symbol and reminder of the need for people to live with justice and compassion here and now.

Third, let me say something about the ancient monotheism thesis itself. Here we naturally think of the debates that surrounded the impressive work of Father Wilhelm Schmidt (1868–1954). A crucial text is the condensed version (translated into English as *The Origin and Growth of Religion: Facts and Theories* [New

York: Methuen, 1931]) of Schmidt's twelve-volume work, *Der Ursprung der Gottesidee* (Munster: Pub, 1912–1955).

I do not claim that Professor Zhao's argument depends on the work of Schmidt or even that he agrees with Schmidt's thesis, except possibly as it applies to archaic China. As I understand him, Professor Zhao is not arguing about the origin of religion per se; he is arguing merely that Chinese religion in particular did not begin (as is often assumed) with polytheism. Nevertheless, Professor Zhao's conclusions are consistent with Schmidt's, and will be warmly received by his present-day supporters.

Schmidt thought he could prove (in keeping with Genesis) that religion began with monotheism, and then degenerated into polytheism. Now Schmidt's conclusions were regarded by some "evolutionary" scholars as being driven less by the available evidence and more by Roman Catholic dogmatic considerations. (And it is indeed a teaching of Catholicism that the religion of the earliest humans was monotheistic, and that polytheism is a degeneration of the original and revealed monotheistic religion.) But I do not regard that *ad hominem* argument as a serious criticism of Schmidt, let alone of Zhao, who is not arguing for (or against) Schmidt's thesis.

Still, a few comments about Schmidt's argument may be helpful: (1) his works on this topic showed evidence of enormous erudition and amazingly wide learning; (2) he offered impressive conceptual work in providing criteria for the temporal stratification of cultures; and (3) he showed great skill and agility in exposing gaps in the evidence cited by "evolutionists," as well as fallacies in their arguments. Nevertheless, it has seemed to many scholars to be impossible for us to know how religion began. Professor Zhao seems to agree.

My own view, for what it is worth, is as follows: (1) I agree that there was widespread ancient belief in what Schmidt called "High Gods," or "Sky Gods," on whom humans were said to depend and to whom humans were said to be obligated; (2) I agree that the classical "evolutionary" theory of the development of religion (espoused, among many others, by Sir James Frazer) rests on feeble evidence. This is the theory (or type of theory) which says that religion began with magic (this was Frazer's view), or perhaps with shamamism, totemism, or ancestor-worship, and moved from there to animism, and from there to polytheism, and from there to henotheism, and from there finally to monotheism; and (3) turning to Professor Zhao, although again I am no expert in this area, I am convinced by his argument that archaic Chinese religion, as depicted in the evidence and records that he considers, was apparently quite close to some versions of monotheism.

But I think we simply have to admit that there is very much that we do not know in this area. One of those items is how widespread monotheistic tendencies were in the ancient world. I am sure that Professor Zhao would agree with me at this point. The claim that religion began with pure monotheism and that polytheism was a degeneration of monotheism cannot, in my view, be proven. It is something we will probably never know, given the paucity and opaqueness of the evidence. And one difficulty for Schmidt-like theses is the often-noted fact that monotheistic religions usually seem to have been "founded" by one or more individuals—people like Moses, or the ancient Hebrew prophets, or Jesus, or Mohammed.

Nevertheless, I admire Professor Zhao for his courage and energy in taking on this difficult question. And I completely agree with him that the debate between the "Progressivists" and the "Degenerativists" is outmoded, and that the weight of available evidence is slightly less favorable to the Progressivists. I commend his essay to the scholarly world. Perhaps it can help revive a fascinating and important debate that has been largely dormant for over a generation.

The Discussion of Mind and Nature in Zhu Xi's Philosophy

Chen Lai

Translated by Robert W. Foster

HEAVENLY ENDOWED NATURE

The concept of nature (*xing*) has different meanings in Zhu Xi's philosophy. The first meaning refers to the principle of Heaven and Earth received by people and things. Compared to the physical endowment, upon which it depends for a place to exist, it is sometimes simply referred to as the Heavenly Mandate (tianming). Compared to the nature of the physical endowment (*qizhi zhi xing*), it is then called the "original nature" *(benran zhi xing)*. The second meaning refers to the nature of the physical endowment of people and things. Sometimes it is used to refer to both the nature of people and things; sometimes only to the nature of people. In rare circumstances, he adopts the view often found in Hu Hong's works, taking nature to be the principle of Heaven and Earth. These must all be given more careful examination in concrete issues. Here we will focus the discussion to that in Zhu Xi's philosophy of nature that is most connected to the important and fundamental nature of the Heavenly Mandate, which is the idea that nature is principle.

The two Cheng brothers once proposed that "nature is principle." In terms of theories of human nature, the meaning depends upon stressing that human nature is in complete accord with moral principles and is completely consistent with the universal laws of the cosmos. However, in the scholarship of the Chengs, although they usually spoke of this "nature and Heaven's Way," thereby establishing some connection between nature and principle, the unity of nature and principle is only a natural unification of Heaven and human, without the later

75

substantive view that the endowed heavenly principle is nature. Zhu Xi's philosophy holds that there is principle and *qi* in the universe,[1] that everything produced by people and things receives the *qi* of Heaven and Earth for physical form and the principle of Heaven and Earth for innate nature. In this way, Zhu Xi's view that nature is principle is a bit more advanced when compared to the Chengs'. Qian Mu has pointed out that Cheng Yichuan's discussion of nature essentially explains Mencius's ideas. In Yichuan's thought, nature and principle "are not descended from the cosmic realm"; yet, in Zhu Xi's scholarship, the common principle within Heaven and Earth descends into the human physical form, then the form becomes what is called nature: "the cosmic realm and the human realm are directly connected."[2]

This idea is based in Zhu Xi's dissatisfaction with the inability of the traditional Confucian theory of the goodness of nature to build some direct connection between nature and the heavenly Way. He said: "Mencius only spoke generally of nature's goodness, and rarely spoke of that which makes nature good. Certainly there are sayings like 'one *yin* and one *yang* are called the Way,' and 'that which maintains it is good,' and 'that which fulfills it is nature,' but these are only saying that nature is the Heavenly Way."[3] He also said: "Mencius never once sought for the original cause, never once said what was first. He only said 'that which fulfills it is nature."[4] Here, "that which maintains it is good" refers to the principle of Heaven and Earth; "that which fulfills it is nature" denotes the nature of people and things. Zhu Xi held that Mencius' theory of good nature lacked an ontological source or grounding to elucidate nature; in the theory of principle he "little understood what came first." Therefore, he was not able to articulate the necessary connection between the nature of people and things and the principle of Heaven and Earth. Zhu Xi believed that the reason nature was good neither depended upon merely being able to derive a clear explanation from tracing back the activities of moral sentiment (if it was as Mencius said, then if one followed these emotions, one could be good), nor did it depend upon merely deriving from the natural connection between nature and the heavenly Way.

The most important philosophical source upon which Zhu Xi based his view that nature is the endowed heavenly principle is the line "one *yin* and one *yang* are called the Way; that which maintains it is good; that which fulfills it is the nature" from the "Xici Zhuan" section of the *Yijing*, which at that time was believed to have been written by Confucius. According to Zhu Xi's explanation, "that which maintains it is good" indicates the heavenly principle flowing through Heaven and Earth; while "that which fulfills it is nature" indicates the nature that is fulfilled by being the heavenly principle endowed into the physical body of each person and thing. The next source is the statement in Zhou Dunyi's *Taijitu shuo*: "when the reality of the Non-ultimate and the essence of *yin* and *yang* and the Five Phases come into mysterious union, integration ensues."[5] Zhu

Xi believed this meant that all things were formed by the union of the essence of the two and the five, and the reality of the Non-ultimate—the essence of the two and five being the two forms of *qi* [*yin* and *yang*] and the Five Phases. Non-ultimate denoted the principle of Heaven and Earth. Based on this view, nature is merely a part of the complete principle with a special mode of existence. If the principle of Heaven and Earth is like a great wave-capped sea, then human nature is like sea water poured into a container: the contents are the same. If we say the two are different, it is because in their forms of existence, principle and nature have distinctions in moving according to *qi* and being restricted by *qi*. Zhu Xi said:

> that which maintains it is good; that which fulfills it is nature: this principle is always good throughout Heaven and Earth. It is never not good. When living things obtain it, then we can start to call it nature. It is only this principle. In Heaven it is called mandate (*ming*). In people it is called nature.[6]

> Nature is simply principle. It is the overall name for the manifold principle. This principle is also simply the common principle amidst Heaven and Earth. Only after it is endowed does it become mine.[7]

Zhu Xi believe the principle flowing through Heaven and Earth was what the "Xici Zhuan" of the *Yijing* said to be "that which maintains it is good," and that the principle endowed into and residing in the human body was "that which fulfills it is nature."

> "That which maintains it is good," is precisely the beginning of the flow of heavenly principle; it is what people and things embody and begin [to live]. "That which fulfills it is nature," is then saying that this principle has a place in which to reside. Therefore, in terms of being a human or a thing, it determines which is ignorant and which brilliant. This being so, when it does not have a body, this nature is the principle of Heaven and Earth, this is how it becomes the nature of people and things.[8]

The nature of people and things is merely a part of principle. Compared to the whole of principle compared to the principle flowing through Heaven and Earth, it has only a partial and specially formed existence. Zhu Xi himself took the above-mentioned analogy as "'that which maintains it is good' is common, while 'that which fulfills it is nature' is individuated. There is only one principle of the Way; one does not say 'this is it, that is not.' It is like a fish in water: the water in its belly is simply [the same as] the water around it."[9]

Zhu Xi believed that, from the perspective of people and things, the natures of people and things are all received from Heaven. From the perspective of Heaven, one could say the Mandate of Heaven gives or bestows it upon the innumerable things. Zhu Xi said: "[Cheng] Yichuan called that which Heaven endowed the mandate, and what things received the nature. It is the same principle. Speaking of it as that which Heaven bestows upon things, we call it the mandate; we call it the nature when speaking of that which people and things receive from Heaven. It is simply that the perspective from which we are speaking is different."[10] In this way, through the idea of endowment Zhu Xi linked the *Zhongyong* passage "the heavenly mandate is called mandate" with Yichuan's explanation "what heaven endows is called mandate, what things receive is called nature."

Although Lixue established a direct link between nature and the Heavenly Way, this type of link stemmed from an artificial construction, so in the concrete content of explaining this link one cannot evasively adopt a far fetched interpretive method. According to Zhu Xi's formulated logic, people's moral innate nature springs from the principle of Heaven and Earth, but it is not the same as speaking of naturalness and its standards are completely moralized. For Zhu Xi, the notion of "the principle is unitary, its manifestations numerous" advocated dispensing with those unrefined methods of explanation. According to Zhu Xi's theory, nature and the heavenly Way "are like a long connected thing. Its flow is the heavenly Way and people obtain it as nature. The primacy, prosperity, beneficence, and fortuitousness of *qian* [the prime male energy] is the heavenly Way. People obtain it as the benevolent, righteous, proper, and wise nature."[11] He further maintains: "My benevolence, righteousness, propriety, and wisdom are Heaven's primacy, prosperity, beneficence, and fortuitousness; in general, all that I have comes from it."[12] He continues:

> people's natures all come from Heaven, and the transformations of Heaven's *qi* must work through the Five Agents. There the natures of benevolence, righteousness, propriety, wisdom, and trustworthiness are the principles of water, fire, metal, wood, and earth. Wood and benevolence, metal and righteousness, fire and propriety, water and wisdom: each has that which it controls. Only earth has no position and so serves as the core of the other Agents; thus trustworthiness also has no position and so serves as the core of the other four agents.[13]

In different categories and domains, the universal laws of the cosmos have different manifestations. Benevolence, righteousness, propriety, and wisdom are the various manifestations of the principles of primacy, prosperity, beneficence, and fortuitousness of the Five Agents, therefore they are both appropriate and necessary. If one were to say that this aspect of Lixue, insofar as it seeks the constant natural roots of moral categories for a specific person in human history, is totally misunderstanding the historical and class-based character of morality, then this may be overly critical of what the ancients were saying. What is undeniable is that Lixue is the starting point of the moral norms of a specific period (feudal China), using some one-sided link to the natural order as their proof in order to maintain the institutional systems and evaluative criteria of contemporary society. Speaking from moral philosophy itself, this theory unarguably strengthens the a priori color of human nature transcending society and humankind.

PHYSICAL ENDOWMENT

The question of human nature was originally meant to explain the form of the good and evil character of people, to explain the basis of people's good and evil actions. Does the idea that "nature is principle" fully solve this issue? In Zhu Xi's view it did not. He said: "If we only say benevolence, righteousness, propriety, and wisdom are nature, then why are there those born into the world without [these virtues]? It is simply that their physical endowment is so. If we do not discuss that physicality, this principle of the Way is not thorough, and so 'is not complete.' If we are only discussing the physical endowment, that source of good and evil unquestionably can only be this principle of the Way, and all is 'unclear'."[14] He also said: "Humans' natures are all good, however, some are born good and some are born evil: this is because their physical endowments differ."[15] In other words, the idea that the endowed principle that is nature is only talking about people having inherent, good qualities; however, it has no means of explaining the origins of the evil qualities. If the evil qualities are only formed with the lure of acquired material desires, then there is no way to explain the existence of innately evil people upheld by Lixue. In Zhu Xi's opinion, evil qualities also have an innate source. Yet this innate evil can be transformed by moral cultivation. In this way, for the sake of the completion and clarity of Lixue's theory of human nature, at the same time that one uses principle to explain the innate, a priori goodness of people, one must also create an explanation for the innate influences that are not good; this is the theory of the physical character, or physical endowment.

Among the pre-Qin philosophers, Mencius believed evil was completely acquired, with no innate connection. Zhu Xi said: "Mencius' theory is to only say human nature is good, but it is problematic when dealing with that which is not good. In other words, initially there is nothing that is not good, but afterwards there is that which is not good. If this is so, then it seems that discussing nature and not discussing physicality is somewhat incomplete."[16] Yet since the Han dynasty, most Confucian thinkers tended to believe that, aside from the sages, human nature contains, to varying degrees, the roots of evil action. Dong Zhongshu considered emotions to be the "avaricious nature"; Yang Xiong also said that the good and evil of the nature are mixed; while Han Yu who still held that most people's human nature always contained elements in opposition to the four virtues. In the Song dynasty, the theory of physicality was commonly used to explain the constitution of people and things. Almost all thinkers used physicality to explain human natural dispositions and characters, including the differences in moral qualities and the origins of their production. Zhu Xi, when advocating the idea of physicality, clearly showed that while admitting that there were naturally good and naturally evil people, [his predecessors] strove to find the answer to the problem in the innate aspect, and that this route was clearly wrong. Zhu Xi said:

> Mencius' recognition that nature is good only understands the greater foundation, but he did not consider that the source of good and evil that follows this is the so-called physical endowment different in everyone. Later people did not see it, so many different confused theories of good and evil arose and competed. Master Cheng's theory is rather close. He thus said, "to discuss nature and not discuss physicality is incomplete; to discuss physicality and not discuss nature is unenlightened; thus neither is correct." Although this was so, and the combined discussion of nature and physicality was completed, this idea stems from Zhou Lianxi's [Zhou Dunyi] Great Ultimate claiming that there are inequities in *yin-yang* and the Five Agents. From this idea, the Two Chengs extrapolated the development of the nature of the physical endowment.[17]

He also said:

> When Master Zhou appeared, he began to once again push the theory of the Great Ultimate, *yin-yang*, and the Five Agents to explain that when people and things are born their nature is the same, but according to the source of their physical endowment their transformations and interactions are correspondingly different. When Master Cheng appeared, he again began to explain that nature is principle and along with Master Zhang [Zai] all believed in the theory of the nature of the physical endowment. Thereafter, the goodness of the nature did not impair the [notion that] the physical endowment had that which is bad, while the badness of the physical endowment ultimately also did not confuse the nature's necessary goodness.[18]

Zhu Xi pointed out that from Zhou Dunyi to the Two Chengs the issues that Lixue's theory of physical endowment sought to resolve was, on the one hand, to clarify the existential differences in human character, while on the other, to stress the explanation that the badness of the physical endowment is the source of people's evil qualities.

The physical endowment is not the nature of the physical endowment. Physicality refers to the physicality of *yin-yang* and the Five Agents, while endowment refers to the set form derived from the coalescing of physicality: "physicality coalesces as the endowment, and the nature is therein."[19] Furthermore, "Physicality is that initial bequest, the endowment is the completed form; it is similar to the minerals comprising metal and the sprouts of trees. It is also said that there is only one *qi* for *yin-yang* and the Five Agents, that it circulates between Heaven and Earth, with the refined becoming human and the coarse becoming things. The most refined of the refined become sages and worthies, the coarse within the refined become the ignorant and unworthy."[20] The physical endowment refers to physical matter and the specific bodies it forms. According to Zhu

Xi's view, through an unceasing process, the *qi* of *yin-yang* and the Five Agents does not stop accumulating and producing each type of physical form, and that the bulk of material from which physical form accumulates can be divided into refined and coarse *qi*. The former takes purity, perspicacity, and refinement as its special qualities. The latter takes turbidity, bias, and impurity as its special qualities. From this, the former's accumulated physical body is human, while the latter's is a thing. To use the differences in the material comprising the physical endowments of humans and things to explain the differences between humans and things is a fundamental idea in Lixue's cosmology. Zhu Xi said: "Humans and things are born together between Heaven and Earth. Inherently they have the same principle, but the received *qi* has differences. If one receives the pure and refined, then one is human; if something receives the turbid and biased, the one is a thing." [21] He also said: "Speaking from the singular *qi*, then people and things all receive this *qi* and are born; speaking from the refined and coarse [aspects], then people obtain this *qi*'s correct and penetrating [qualities], while things obtain this *qi*'s biased and obstructed [qualities]."[22]

In Zhu Xi's view, purity or turbidity, bias or rectitude are only being generally discussed; however, in each individual person some are relatively pure, some are relatively turbid. Although this difference does not influence people in terms of being human, it does result in the innate differences in morality and intelligence among individuals. He said: "The various theories of purity and turbidity and bias and rectitude are based in the language of *Zhengmeng*, and further developed in Lü Boshi's *Zhongyong xiangshuo*. Yet these are still based upon the necessary linguistic division between the worthy and wise and the ignorant and unworthy. If we speak generally, then people are pure and things are turbid; people are correct and things are biased. To further delineate this, the wise are the purest of the pure, the worthy are the most correct of the rectified, while the ignorant are the most turbid of the pure, and the unworthy are the most biased of the rectified. And Hengju's [Zhang Zai] saying that things have that which is near to the nature of humans is also this [division of] the most pure of the turbid and most correct of the biased."[23]

Of course, this process is a completely natural, unconscious, and purposeless process. Zhu Xi pointed out, "this stems from the midst of the great source, it seems to be patterned, but there truly is not something bestowing upon them. Where is there someone above apportioning this?"[24] He further stated: "Living *qi* flows, appearing in a cycle. From the outset we do not say that its full *qi* is apportioned to humans and one grade lower is given to things. It is only that the allotment accords with that which is obtained."[25] He stressed that the *qi* allotment's complex variety and differences were completely "commensurate by chance and are not ranked."[26] "Commensurate by chance" means that because the contexts of different times and places are different, the *qi* of Heaven and Earth encountered at the time of people's births are completely different. Zhu Xi said: "Moreover as Heaven and Earth revolve, there are innumerable beginnings without exhaustion.

This can be seen in that when the sun and moon are clear and bright and when the natural circumstances match what is correct, those born receive this *qi*; and since the *qi* is pure and bright, complete and full, it necessarily makes a good person. If the sun and moon are dim, and cold and hot are inverted, these are the perverse *qi* of Heaven and Earth. If a person receives this *qi*, how can there be any doubt that he will be a bad person? The reason people study is precisely because they want to transform this *qi*, yet it is extremely difficult to transform."[27]

The Two Chengs once believed the theory that "to discuss nature and not discuss *qi* is incomplete; to discuss *qi* and not discuss nature is unenlightened." Lixue advocated discussing the two aspects of Heavenly Mandate and physical endowment in regard to their functioning in people, and so is able to completely explain the generation of and differences in the good and evil qualities of people. However, looking at it from theoretical results, it is not easy and simple to maintain a balance when discussing both *qi* and nature. If one emphasizes discussing nature, "then why have there only been several sages and worthies since antiquity?" If one emphasizes discussing *qi*, "then everyone trusts his initial endowment and does not cultivate his actions."[28] Discussing nature is emphasizing that each person has the ability to become a sage or a worthy, yet if one cannot develop a reasonable explanation for this ability's difficulties in the face of changing reality, then this ability becomes illusory; therefore, in terms of Confucians' theory of human nature, developing the notion of the physical endowment was necessary.

If we are to fully discuss the physical endowment's influence on people, then the physical endowment not only determines each person's intelligence and character, but it moreover also determines life's social opportunities and fate, such as poverty or wealth, longevity or early death, and so forth. However, here I have not prepared a wide-ranging discussion of all the influences of the *qi* allotment.[29] The reasons for the differences between the heavenly material comprising a person and the degrees of character and intelligence is extremely difficult. Ancient philosophy's use of *qi* to explain is understandable. In fact, when Zhang Zai brought up the physical endowment, it was originally used to explain the natural dispositions of strength, weakness, and sluggishness. Cheng-Zhu theory developed this to explain the source of good and evil intrinsic qualities, but this cannot provide a truly valuable explanation of the formation of a person's intrinsic moral qualities.

THE HEAVENLY MANDATE AND THE PHYSICAL ENDOWMENT

Every individual thing is the "coalescence," the "combination" of the Heavenly Mandate's nature and the physical endowment. Heavenly Mandate and physical endowment are not separate and cannot be separated. Zhu Xi said: "Heavenly Mandate and physical endowment flow together; when there is Heavenly Mandate, then there is physical endowment. If one is lacking, there cannot be living things. So if there is Heavenly Mandate, there must be this *qi* that can bear this principle. If this *qi* were lacking, then how does this principle find a place to reside?"³⁰ Here Heavenly Mandate refers to the nature of Heavenly Mandate (*tianming zhi xing*), which is the nature-principle (*xingli*). This is to say, Heaven bestows upon the innumerable things principle and *qi* at the same time. Regarding the production of any real, concrete thing, it is not possible for one of the two to be lacking. "The nature of the Heavenly Mandate would have no place to reside if there were no physical endowment. Like a ladleful of water, if there is not something to contain it, the water does not have a place to stay."³¹ This place to reside refers to "that which fulfills it is nature." Furthermore, "It is not possible for nature to be endowed separately from *qi*. When there is *qi*, the endowed nature exists therein; without *qi*, the endowed nature has no place in which to adhere."³² According to Zhu Xi's philosophy, the principle of Heaven and Earth can only be called "principle"; the principle endowed into the bodies of people and things can be called "nature." Because of this, in discussing it in relation to a specific physical body, when there is not yet this *qi*, this form, the principle of Heaven and Earth still exists; however, the nature is certainly seemlessly joined with the physical endowment. Stressing this point on the one hand opposes the Buddhist doctrine of the independent existence of the nature, and on the other hand makes clear that the nature of every individual person and thing necessarily receives the functioning of a physical body.

The Heavenly Mandate and physical endowment are not mixed together. The nature-principle and physical endowment not only are not separate, moreover, they are not blended. This is precisely what was discussed in the *Taijitu jie* and was later reemphasized by Zhu Xi's "*yin-yang* refers to its original body, it is not said to be blended with *yin-yang*." The combination of principle and *qi* in a real thing, according to Zhu Xi, is not like salt dissolved into water to make one body. Instead, the image is oil combined with water, which still maintains its identity as oil. From the larger perspective, the oil and water are combined into one body, but in fact the oil still is not "blended" with this water. Therefore, this type of "mysterious union" also is not mysterious: "though located in the *qi*'s midst, the *qi* is itself *qi*, the nature is itself nature, they are not intimately blended with each other."³³ "Principle and *qi* are certainly two entities, but looking at them in a thing, then the two entities are thoroughly combined and cannot be divided each into its own place, so there is no impairment to two entities each acting as one thing."³⁴

The physical body covers the nature-principle. As already pointed out, Zhu Xi believed that the physical allotment comprised the source of the evil qualities of people: "The reason that there are good and bad people is only because the physical endowment's allotment of each has the pure and the turbid."³⁵ As for the concrete manner by which the *qi* allotment influences human qualities, Zhu

Xi had different theories. As stated in the preceding section, the differences in
the beauty or evil of the initial body of the physical endowment (if the perverse
qi of Heaven and Earth are embodied, then one is evil) directly determines a
person's good or evil qualities. Yet as many places in Zhu Xi's philosophy recognize, when speaking of people, most important in the physical allotment's
fulfillment as the source of evil is the obstruction of the original nature arising
from the turbidity, thus influencing a person's good innate character as manifested in many ways. Zhu Xi once used a lantern as an analogy: "There is this
flame, which is the original nature, which is always brilliant. The physical endowment is not the same. It is like a lantern using a thick paper to dim it, then
the flame is not very bright. If one uses a thin piece of paper, the flame is
brighter than the one with thick paper. If one uses gauze to dim it, the flame
is bright again. If one removes the lantern, then the flame's whole form can be
seen. This principle is just like this."[36] Regarding everyone, their natures are fully
complete, but there are full and partial manifestations: "It is only because the
physical endowment is different that partiality is demonstrated."[37] Zhu Xi often
used the analogy of a jewel to develop the same idea. Both analogies are to clarify
that the innate differences in human moral character are completely determined
by whether or not the pure or turbid physical endowment blocks the manifestation of the nature-principle. As for the difference between humans and animals, aside from the turbid and partial bodies of animals blocking the
nature-principle, the original nature-principle with which they are endowed is
also partial and incomplete.

There is one question that must be raised concerning the relationship between nature-principle and the physical endowment. It is that in Zhu Xi's philosophical view of the generation of people and things, are the two statements that
"principle and *qi* are united" and "principle is bestowed according to *qi*" the
same? Luo Qinshun once pointed out, "I still have my doubts about the three
lines 'the ultimate of non-truth mysteriously unites and coalesces with the essence of the two [*qi*] and the five [agents].' Generally, there must be two entities,
only then is it possible to speak of uniting. Are the Great Ultimate and *yin-yang*
two entities? If insofar as their being entities they truly are two, then before they
unite where does each exist?"[38]

Zhu Xi once said: "The means by which people are born is simply the
unification of principle and *qi*."[39] "This body's existence between Heaven and
Earth is simply the coalescence of principle and *qi*."[40] "Principle and *qi* unite, so
there are people."[41] "That people have life is simply from nature and *qi* uniting."[42] "Truth is principle; essence is *qi*. When principle and *qi* unite then they
are able to fulfill forms."[43] These statements frequently cause people to believe
that prior to the concrete production of people and things, principle and *qi* seem
to each have independent existences, and that it is only when people and things
are produced that they unite as one.

However, Zhu Xi also said: "When this *qi* coalesces, principle is present therein." And "Only where *qi* has coalesced is principle present therein."[44] Furthermore, "Heaven uses *yin-yang* and the Five Agents to transform and produce the innumerable things; *qi* to complete their forms, and principle to bestow therein" (*Zhongyong zhangju*)."[45] Finally, "If we discuss the bestowing, then there is this *qi* and only after is principle accordingly supplied. Thus, if there is this *qi*, then there is this principle; if there is no *qi*, there is no principle; if this *qi* is plentiful, then principle is plentiful; if this *qi* is scant, then principle is scant."[46] According to these statements, principle is originally within *qi*; when *qi* coalesces into a body, principle accords with it to reside in the physical form. Principle comes to reside in the physical endowment due to its previously according with the flowing transformations of *qi*.

According to the logical unfolding of Zhu Xi's thought, in the first stage it ought to be that principle is prior to *qi*. In the second stage, *qi* is produced, and principle is also within *qi*. In the third stage, concrete things are produced. Everything unifies both principle and *qi* in its own body; at this stage there are concrete things ceaselessly being produced and annihilated, there is also *qi* that has not yet coalesced into things and principle that has not yet come to reside in people or things. Because of this, due to the internal logic of Zhu Xi's philosophy, in the second and third stages, principle and *qi* are both united without separation and are not existing independently. In the section of this paper regarding principle and *qi*, the discussion about whether or not principle is separate from *qi* and acting alone is precisely an expression of this question of action or quietude. Because of this, according to the internal logic of Zhu Xi's philosophy, one cannot say that prior to the production of things principle and *qi*, each independently flows through the universe, and that it is only when a specific form coalesces that [principle] is added into the *qi*. Of course, in Zhu Xi's view, the principle "added to" the *qi* flowing through the universe is different from its "residing" through descending into the physical endowment, because the latter "is then bound by the physical endowment."[47] In fact, in Zhu Xi's system, that principle and *qi* unite, and that principle is bestowed according to *qi*, are not different. Therefore, when one examines a specific person or thing, each is constituted from principle and *qi*; but regarding the process by which people and things are constituted, prior to the production of concrete things, principle also does not act independently without anything upon which to adhere. Zhu Xi himself said: "At no time does the rise and fall of *qi* cease; principle simply adheres to *qi*."[48] Therefore, regarding the expression of Zhu Xi's theory of the relationship between principle and physical endowment, one ought to notice: first, that this expression does not mean that principle is not initially prior to *qi*; second, nor does it mean that prior to the production of concrete physical forms, principle is in a condition of existence without anything upon which to adhere. Though these two aspects derive from Zhu Xi's various theories, they very easily cause people to create misinterpretations.

THE NATURE OF THE HEAVENLY MANDATE AND THE NATURE OF THE PHYSICAL ENDOWMENT

Those who discuss it often believe that in Zhu Xi's philosophy, human nature is equally formed from the nature of the Heavenly Mandate (*tianming zhi xing*) and the nature of the physical endowment (*qizhi zhi xing*). This viewpoint is to a great extent derived from believing that the nature of the physical endowment is the fundamental nature of the physical body (like the avaricious nature). We can still examine whether or not this analysis fits with Zhu Xi's thought. The nature of the Heavenly Mandate refers to the received principle of Heaven and Earth—this is without question. Here we will focus the discussion on the following issues: what, ultimately, is the nature of the physical endowment? In Zhu Xi's philosophy, is the nature of the physical endowment the acquisitive, hasty nature of the physical endowment, or is it not? Why did Zhu Xi stress that the nature of Heaven and Earth is not external to the nature of the physical endowment? We will also further examine the key discussion of Zhu Xi's view of "the nature's fundamental substance" stemming from the relationship between the nature of the Heavenly Mandate and the nature of the physical endowment.

As stated before, due to the dual influences of the embodied principle and *qi* received by all people and things, one cannot say that the manifest nature of people or things is determined purely by principle or purely by *qi*. In order to clarify that human nature has received the conditions of both principle and *qi*, it not only must have the concepts of Heavenly Mandate and physical endowment, but it also must have the concept of human nature that synthetically reflects the influences of principle and nature: this is the concept of the nature of the physical endowment.

The Two Chengs originally stated that "it is not easy to speak of what proceeds 'people are born in quietude'; when one speaks of nature, then it is already not the nature." According to Zhu Xi's understanding, "prior to 'people being born in quietude,' they do not yet have physical form, principle has not yet been received, so how can one call it nature."[49] This is to say, the statement "prior to people being born in quietude" means that each individual person and thing has not yet been produced. As stated before, when people and things have not yet been born, "that which follows them is good"; principle still has no specific location. Only at the stages of "that which completes them is nature" and "after people are born into quietude," when principle resides in a specific physical form, is it able to become the nature of people and things. Therefore, "prior to people being born into quietude" there is no nature to speak of; it is only "after people being born into quietude" that one can speak of nature. This being the case, how does one understand "when one speaks of nature, then it is already not the nature"? The *Yulei* records:

> Someone asked about the section regarding "prior to people being born in quietude." [Zhu Xi] responded, "When Mr. Cheng spoke of nature, there was the

original nature and there was the nature of the physical endowment. People have this physical form, which is the nature of the physical endowment. The "nature" in "when one speaks of nature" is speaking of the blending of the physical endowment with this original nature. The "nature" in "then it is already not nature" is the original nature.[50]

Initially, "that which maintains it is good" could only refer to principle; while "that which completes it is nature" could be called "nature." However, once there is the physical form, and principle has a residence, the nature manifested by actual people and things then derives from the influence of the physical endowment, and already is not the nature of the original principle. Zhu Xi said:

"Prior to people being born into quietude" is when people and things have not yet been born. When people and things have not yet been born, one can only call it principle; speaking of when nature has not yet been obtained, refers to "in heaven it is called mandate." "When speaking of the nature, it is already not the nature" is saying that when one calls it nature, this is only after people have been born; this principle is already in the physical body and it is not completely the original substance of nature. Therefore it is said, "it is already not the nature." This refers to "in people it is called nature." In general, when people have this physical form, then this is when this principle first exists in this physical form and is called nature; when speaking of nature, then it already is connected to the living and combined with the physical endowment, and cannot be the original substance of nature. However, the original substance of nature is also never blended. It is important for people to understand this: its original substance is never once separate, nor is it ever blended.[51]

The letter in response to Yan Shiheng also points out:

"People are born into quietude" is when it is unmanifested; "prior" is when people and things have not yet been produced, and so one cannot call it nature. One calls it nature after people have been born, when this principle is in the midst of the physical form and is not completely the original substance of the nature. However, its original substance is never external to this. It is important for people to understand that it is not blended into this.[52]

These ideas are all saying that when people and things have not yet been produced, the principle of Heaven and Earth cannot be called "nature"; it can begin to be called nature after the principle is residing in a specific body. Yet once the principle enters the physical body it cannot avoid receiving the "corruption" of the physical endowment; thus, every real and direct human nature is not nature's original aspect (nature's original substance). Many times Zhu Xi explained this viewpoint. He said:

"It is not easy to talk about, because there is no nature to speak of; it is not nature, because already it is blended with the physical endowment."[53] "After birth, what is called the nature has the *qi* allotment blended in, and is not the nature of principle."[54]

"When one speaks of nature, there is some physical endowment therein."[55]

"Human nature is originally good. When it descends into the physical endowment, then it is gradually corrupted into badness. Though gradually corrupted into badness, yet the original nature still is as of old therein."[56] "If the physical endowment is evil, then it draws the nature into badness as the nature is added to the physical endowment. If this physical endowment is bad, then it goes bad with the nature."[57]

In the various passages noted above, Zhu Xi clearly exhibits a philosophy in which every real and direct human nature is not the original substance of nature. This, in regard to that which everyone manifests and uses, is not real human nature of nature's original substance; it is "the nature of the physical endowment." In this sense and strictly speaking, regarding concrete, actual people, one cannot simply say nature is principle; one can only say nature's original substance is principle. Therefore he said, "nature's original substance is only principle,"[58] "Nature's original substance is the seed of humanity, righteousness, propriety, and wisdom,"[59] "What is difficult to speak of is the original substance of nature,"[60] and "Mencius said that the original substance of nature is good."[61]

Only when one understands the above theories can one understand that "discussing the nature of Heaven and Earth is only speaking of principle; while discussing the nature of the physical endowment is speaking of principle and *qi* combined" as Zhu Xi said;[62] then one can understand why Zhu Xi called the nature of Heaven and Earth the "original nature." Therefore, though the nature of the Heavenly Mandate spoken of in Zhu Xi's philosophy with regard to people, stresses the inherent basis of morality, what he called the nature of the physical endowment is neither simply pointing to the various qualities of *qi*—such as being healthy or avaricious—with regard to humankind, nor is it simply pointing to what later people referred to as the sensory desires of the "nature of the physical drives."[63] From the perspective of "the original substance of nature," the nature of the physical endowment is the transformed condition of the original nature, referring to the nature-principle receiving the physical endowment's corrupting influence. The original nature is the nature of the physical endowment's original condition and is neither concomitantly established with the nature of the physical endowment, nor is it external to the nature of the physical endowment; rather, together with the nature of the physical endowment it forms the nature of human nature. However, since it uses both principle and *qi*, the nature of the physical endowment reflects the interplay of moral rationality and sensory needs; it is not a nature solely determined by the consciousness of physical drives.

If one looks at it from the same level, one cannot say that there is an original nature external to the nature of the physical endowment. Zhu Xi constantly refuted the view that held that people had two types of nature established at the same time. He said, "the physical endowment is made of *yin-yang* and the Five Agents; the nature is the complete substance of the Great Ultimate. If we discuss the nature of the physical endowment, then this complete substance simply descends into the physical endowment. It is not that there is another nature."[64] "Generally, the original nature and the nature of the physical endowment are not two divided things."[65] Further, "The nature of the physical endowment is simply the nature of Heaven and Earth; it is just that this nature of Heaven and Earth passes through there. The good nature is like water; the nature of the physical endowment is like pouring it into soy and salt: the flavor is the same."[66] The nature's original substance is like water; the nature of the physical endowment is like salt water; water is the original substance of salt water. From this, when speaking of the nature of the physical endowment and the original nature in relation to humans, its meaning is similar to primary and secondary qualities. After people are born in quietude, the directly manifested human natures are all the nature of the physical endowment, incapable of not being blended with the physical allotment.

Based upon this view, Zhu Xi certainly opposed the view of Yu Fangshu, Xu Zirong and others that "there is only the nature of the physical allotment and there is no original nature."[67] Zhu Xi's letter responding to Xu Zirong says, "and if you said that a withered thing only had the nature of the physical endowment and no original nature, this would be extremely laughable. If this were so, then this thing would have only one nature, but humans would have two natures. This is unseemly, perhaps it is because you do not understand that the nature of the physical endowment is only this principle descended into the physical endowment, and so it accords with the physical endowment to itself create a nature. This is precisely what Master Zhou called each unique nature. If initially there was no original nature, then from where does this nature of the physical endowment come?" All natures of the physical endowment come from the transformation of the original nature. Therefore, there cannot be a nature of the physical endowment that is unrelated to the original nature or is completely independent of the original nature.

As for Zhu Xi's own development of his theory concerning the nature of the physical endowment, based upon a passage recorded by Jin Quwei, Qian Mu once believed that at the time Zhu Xi believed the idea of the nature of the physical endowment was not necessary. Jin Quwei's passage is: "[someone] asked why the nature seems to be two things in *Reflections on Things at Hand*? [Zhu Xi] answered, everyone always misunderstands this idea. When we speak of nature this is not so. Human nature is initially good. When it descends into the physical endowment, then it is gradually corrupted into the bad. Though gradually corrupted into the bad, yet this original nature as of old is still present. It completely depends upon the students putting forth effort. Now, though people are said to have the original nature, they also have the nature of the physical endowment, and this greatly impairs principle."[68] In fact, what Zhu Xi was here opposing was only seeing the two as both being established in human nature; he was not opposing the idea that people have the nature of the physical endowment. Precisely what is expressed here is the idea noted above that original nature is the original substance of the nature of the physical endowment. According to the *Yulu xingshi*, Jin Quwei recorded this in the second year of the Hengxi reign period [1175–76], when Zhu Xi was forty-six years old. If the above passage recorded by Jin Quwei really is from Hengxi 2,[69] then we can say that the foundation of the above-mentioned thought concerning the nature of the physical endowment and the original nature was already formed.

One facet of the view of the original substance of nature refers to the nature of Heaven and Earth that is the original condition of every direct and real human nature prior to receiving the gradual corrupting influence of the physical body. Another facet, due to Zhu Xi's understanding of principle, is essentialization, and so also stresses that principle is in the midst of the physical endowment, yet is "not blended." Hence, he said: "When one speaks of nature, then one moves into there being life and combination with the physical endowment, but it cannot be considered the original substance of nature. Thus, the original substance of nature has never been blended in; people must understand this point, their original substance has never been separated, it has never been blended."

Views similar to those of Yu Fangshu, Xu Zirong and others that the nature of the physical endowment is only understood as the property of *qi*, also has a basis in the development of Lixue. The nature of the physical endowment spoken of by Zhang Zai is the avaricious nature of *qi*. And what the Two Chengs called the "nature of the physical endowment" is the nature of *qi*. However, if this is so, people would seem to have two types of human nature, so this is clearly a theory that the nature has two sources. In Zhu Xi, the nature of the physical endowment is determined by being derived from the transformation of the nature of Heaven and Earth; nature-principle is the original substance of the nature of the physical endowment. Because of this, if examined philosophically, Zhu Xi is still explaining human nature from both aspects of principle and *qi*. At this level of meaning, one can say that it is still a dualistic theory. However, in the theoretical formulation there are differences from the Two Chengs. In Zhu Xi's philosophy, the original nature is a concept that is one level deeper than the nature of the physical endowment. Thus, original nature is determined to be at two levels and does not result in two human natures. In this regard, it can also be said to take the form of a single source with many levels.

In understanding the facet of Zhu Xi's thought dealing with the nature of the physical endowment, one ought to carefully distinguish among the several concepts of physical endowment, the nature of the physical endowment, the heart-and-mind (*xin*) of the physical endowment (even the emotions of the physical endowment).[70] Most importantly, the physical endowment is a material concept, referring to a specific physical body. The nature of the physical endowment, then, refers to the human nature formed by the nature of Heaven and Earth receiving the corrupting influence of the physical endowment. The heart-and-mind of the physical endowment refers to the "human heart-and-mind" as opposed to the "heart-and-mind of the Way." Zhu Xi once said, "the human heart-and-mind is the mind of the physical endowment."[71] The human heart-and-mind is strongly rooted in the physical endowment, yet the heart-and-mind of the physical endowment is different from the nature of the physical endowment. According to Zhu Xi's philosophical guidelines, what is reflected in the nature of the physical endowment is not merely the functioning of *qi*, and so the heart-and-mind of the physical endowment only refers to the heart-and-mind of the conscious sensory desires determined by the physical endowment.

NATURE AND EMOTIONS

When discussing Zhu Xi's ideas of manifested and unmanifested, there is already a general distinction regarding the relationship between nature and emotions. Here, aside from a concise recapitulation of the fundamental relationship between nature and emotions, I will also add a supplement.

In explaining Mencius's "the heart-and-mind of compassion is the beginning of benevolence; the heart-and-mind of shame is the beginning of righteousness; the heart-and-mind of respect is the beginning of propriety; and the heart-and-mind with a sense of right and wrong is the beginning of wisdom," Zhu Xi said:

> Compassion, shame, respect, sense of right and wrong are emotions. Benevolence, righteousness, propriety, and wisdom and nature. The heart-and-mind unites the nature and emotions. The beginnings are the tips of a thread. Because of the manifestation of the emotions, nature's original state can be seen; it is as if there is a thing in the middle and the thread is seen on the outside.[72]

Zhu Xi believed that nature is the innate essence of psychological activities, while the emotions are the external expressions of this type of essence, and that one can, by means of the various visible external emotions, grasp the internal essence that is inside and invisible. The invisible internal essence is said to be "unmanifested," while the visible external emotional expressions are said to be "manifested."

In Zhu Xi's philosophy, aside from other stipulations, such as nature is the embodied principle, and is the basis of morality, an important stipulation is that nature is the basis of the emotions. The ideas of nature and emotion, unmanifested and manifested, stress that emotions take nature as an internal basis, that nature takes emotions as external expressions. The unmanifested-manifested relationship between nature and emotions is clearly the relationship between substance and function; thus "nature is the substance, and emotions are the function."[73] Emotions have periods when they are still not yet manifested, so nature does not always have expression. Therefore, the process of going from nature's unmanifestness to emotions' manifestness is one of moving from quietude to activity. Regarding the meaning of this process, nature's relation to emotion can be said to have the sense of "origin" or "root."[74]

By beginning from the foundational standpoint that nature is good, Zhu Xi not only fully absorbs previous people's theories of nature and emotions as substance and function and of nature manifesting as emotion, he moreover adopts the concrete clarification of the above-mentioned theory of stimulus-response. Zhu Xi's *Yushan jiangyi* says:

> Generally these four (benevolence, righteousness, propriety and wisdom), are within the human heart-and-mind, and are the original substance of nature. When they are unmanifest, they are unclear, lacking a visible form; when they are manifest and functioning, then benevolence is compassion, righteousness is shame, propriety is reverence, and wisdom is a sense of right and wrong. When they manifest according to the event, each having connections to its source so they are not confused with each other, then they are called emotions.[75]

When Zhu Xi responded to Chen Qizhi's letter, he developed the explanation of the relationship between nature and emotions found in the *Yushan jiangyi*:

> In the unmanifestness of the four beginnings, though silently unmoving, there is order and structure within each. They are not muddled and completely lacking anything. So when stimulated by something external, the internal responds. With the stimulus of a child falling into a well, then the principle of benevolence responds and the compassionate heart-and-mind is formed. With the stimulus of passing by temples and courts, then the principle of propriety responds and the heart-and-mind of reverence is formed. From the numerous principles completely held within, each is clearly distinct, so when in contact with the external, it responds according to the stimulus.[76]

This means that moving from the unmanifest nature to the manifest emotions must generally require the contact of an external thing as the criteria. When an external thing and a human being come into contact, speaking relative to nature, there is a "stimulus." With regard to that stimulus, nature spontaneously creates a reaction, which is the "response." The reaction created by nature is then expressed as a specific emotional manifestation. A child falling into a well is the stimulus, the benevolent nature acts and bears the emotion of compassion, which is the response. This type of stimulus-response process is precisely the process whereby nature acts as emotion. Thus, Zhu Xi said: "Whenever an affair comes up, there is a principle to respond to it."[77] With this theory, Zhu Xi believed that when an external thing enters the scope of human consciousness, subjectively it must evoke a corresponding psychological response, and this psychological activity, in fact, takes human nature as its basis.

Finally, there is an issue that must be discussed regarding Zhu Xi's theories of nature and emotions. Chinese philosophy fundamentally considers the emotions to be happiness, anger, sorrow, fear, love, hate, and desire. Therefore, an important meaning of "emotion" is human emotional activity, considering the seven emotions to be the concrete content. However, when developing the *Zhongyong*'s theory of the emotions being unmanifest and manifest, Lixue advocated "when there is thought, it is manifested," striving to incorporate the content of thought into the "emotions." Zhu Xi also stressed that "the heart-and-mind is the residence of the spirit ruling the whole body. The nature is thus the various principles received from Heaven and held in the heart-and-mind. When manifested as conscious thought, it is all emotion. Thus, it is said that the heart-and-mind unifies nature and emotion."[78] According to these ideas, "emotions" already are not limited to the general emotional activities of happiness, anger, sorrow, and delight, and they moreover encompass various thought processes. Of course, regarding the seven emotions themselves, emotional activities create external forms and often have some concrete thought within. There is no contentless, pure happiness, anger, sorrow, or delight. Aside from this, according to Zhu Xi's thought, there are good and bad emotions. Thus, the scope of "emotion" is not limited to the good conscious thoughts of the four beginnings; rather, it should also include the various bad conscious thoughts that take the seven emotions as their external form. In this way, there are at least three meanings for emotion in Zhu Xi's philosophy: the first is as the four beginnings directly manifested by the nature-principle; the second generally refers to the seven emotions; the third encompasses various forms of concrete thought.

However, this being so, there is a rather large problem in Zhu Xi's philosophical theory of the nature and the heart-and-mind. According to Zhu Xi's philosophy, "nature manifests as emotions, the emotions are rooted in the nature." If we look at this idea in particular, the four virtues correspond to the four beginnings, which is self-explanatory. However, according to Zhu Xi's theories, the seven emotions are also the manifestations of nature (as in the *Zhongyong zhangju*). From the idea that "when there is thought, it is manifested," the various concrete thought processes also are all manifestations of nature. Whether the seven emotions are, or are not, matched with the four beginnings,[79] people still manifest evil emotions and thoughts. Are these emotions ultimately manifesting from the original nature? If one says that these emotions are also manifested from the four beginnings, then good nature is manifested as evil emotions, and the substance and function are in no way the same; this is clearly a huge contradiction. Another expression of this contradiction stemming from the emotions having good and evil stirrings is that Zhu Xi's idea of the nature and emotions as substance and function often is an inverse proof for the theory of nature being good. According to Zhu Xi's way of thinking, emotions are the expression of nature; this being so, from the universal existence of the emotions of the four beginnings in the average person, one can truly understand that all humans have the nature of the four beginnings. However, there are good and evil emotions, so by the same means, one could say that due to humans having various bad emotions we know that humans also have a corresponding bad nature. Thus, Zhu Xi's use of this method of using emotions to prove the nature is less than universal and falls into contradiction.

One way to resolve the contradiction is to narrowly define the manifested emotions of the nature; as stressed by several later Confucians, the happiness, anger, sorrow, and delight spoken of in the *Zhongyong zhangju* in fact only refer to the four beginnings, and are not saying that all seven emotions are to be considered manifestations of the nature-principle. Another way is that the four beginnings and the seven emotions divide principle and *qi*. Zhu Xi once said, "the four beginnings are the manifestations of principle, while the seven emotions are the manifestations of *qi*."[80] If we affirm Zhu Xi's statement that the emotions (of the correspondence of nature and emotions to substance and function) are only referring to the four beginnings and are not referring to the seven emotions, then we must resolve the question of from whence the seven emotions are manifested. Dividing the four beginnings and seven emotions into principle and *qi* is, in fact, examining the emotions by separating the heart-and-mind of the Way and the human heart-and-mind into the manifestations of principle and *qi*. However, moral sentiments like the four beginnings can also take the form of the seven emotions and comprise one segment of the seven emotions. Thus, it is difficult to generalize that the seven emotions are the manifestations of *qi*. In fact, there is another way. If we broadly define emotion as all the emotions, then unmanifested nature cannot be the original nature comprised of benevolence, righteousness, propriety, and wisdom, but ought to be the nature of the physical endowment. Because the nature of the physical endowment in Zhu Xi's philosophy embodies the function of principle and also embodies the function of *qi*, the nature of the physical endowment has both good and evil, and because of this it can be made to embody them at the same time. However, this is not something Zhu Xi ever said. *Zhuzi yulei* contains a line which suggests this meaning: "when happiness, anger, sorrow, and delight are not yet manifest, there is only obscurity. The so-called natures of the physical endowment are all therein. Happiness, anger, sorrow, and delight are only emotions."[81]

Of course, what has been said above only refers to the various logical means if one wants to resolve the contradiction in Zhu Xi's theory of nature and emotions. Zhu Xi never truly resolved it this way. Even if there was only one passage in Zhu Xi's philosophical works regarding dividing the four and seven into principle and nature, it would be too insufficient to say that Zhu Xi already held this idea. In fact, in Zhu Xi's theory that the emotions are manifested from nature, the emotions encompass the four beginnings and the seven emotions. Although in this view there are contradictions and difficulties regarding embodying both, yet, to a certain degree, it contains a reasonable, positive component, which comes from affirming that the emotions are based in the nature; thus, we certainly cannot accept complete asceticism and to a certain degree we affirm the place of the emotions. Zhu Xi both time and again criticized Li Ao's philosophy of extinguishing the emotions, and strove to revise the *Dao xue*'s line of thinking that if the heart-and-mind had emotions, then one could not obtain its true "correct heart-and-mind"; both of which is based upon this.

NOTES

1. Translator's note: *qi* is one of the few Chinese terms that has not been rendered into English. The term encompasses too many levels of meaning. Translating it as physical material might be closest when considering it is here contrasted with Zhu Xi's use of principle (*li*).

2. See *Zhuzi xinxue'an*, chapter 1.

3. *Zhuzi yulei*, juan 28, recorded by Pan Shifeng.

4. *Zhuzi yulei*, juan 4, recorded by Huang Yigang.

5. Translator's note: following W. T. Chan's translation in *A Sourcebook in Chinese Philosophy* (Princeton: Princeton University Press, 1963), p. 463.

6. *Zhuzi yulei*, juan 5, recorded by Chen Heng.

7. Ibid., juan 117.

8. Ibid., juan 74, recorded by Cheng Duanmeng.

9. Ibid., juan 98, recorded by Ye Hesun.

10. Ibid., juan 95, recorded by Cheng Duanmeng.

11. *Zhuzi yulei*, juan 28, recorded by Xi Gaiqing.

12. Ibid., juan 60, recorded by Pan Shifeng.

13. Zhu Xi, "Da Fang Binwang san," *Zhu Wengong wenji*: juan 56.

14. *Zhuzi yulei*, juan 4, recorded by Pan Shifeng.

15. Ibid., juan 4, recorded by Teng Lin.

16. Ibid., juan 4, recorded by Huang Xun.

17. Ibid., juan 59, recorded by Chen Chun.

18. Zhu Xi, *Mengzi huowen*, juan 11.

19. *Zhuzi yulei*, juan 1, recorded by You Jingzhong.

20. Ibid., juan 14, recorded by Lin Ke.

21. Zhu Xi, *Mengzi huowen*, juan 1.

22. *Zhuzi yulei*, juan 4, recorded by Shen Xian.

23. Zhu Xi, "Da Li Minshu, no. 7," in *Zhu Wengong wenji*: juan 62.

24. *Zhuzi yulei*, juan 4, recorded by Chen Heng.

25. Ibid., juan 94, recorded by Zhou Mo.

26. Ibid., juan 55, recorded by Lin Kuisun.

27. Ibid., juan 4, recorded by Deng Lin.

28. Ibid., juan 4, recorded by Li Hongzu.

29. See Zhang Liwen, *Zhuzi sixiang yanjiu* (Chinese Social Sciences Press, 1982), chap. 9, sect. 2

30. *Zhuzi yulei*, juan 4, recorded by Huang Xun.

31. Ibid., juan 4, recorded by Ye Hesun.

32. Ibid., juan 94, recorded by Chen Heng.

33. Zhu Xi, "Da Liu Shujing wen, no. 2," in *Zhu Wengong wenji*, juan 46.

34. Zhu Xi, "Da Liu Shujing wen, no. 1."

35. *Zhuzi yulei*, juan 4, recorded by Jin Quwei.

36. Ibid., juan 64, recorded by Chen Wenwei.

37. Ibid., juan 64, recorded by Chen Wenwei.

38. Luo Qinshun, *Kunzhi ji*, juan 2.

39. *Zhuzi yulei*, juan 4, recorded by Shen Xian.

40. Ibid., juan 3, recorded by Huang Yigang.

41. Ibid., juan 60, recorded by Pan Zhi.

42. Zhu Xi, "Da Cai Jitong, no. 2," in *Zhu Wengong wenji*, juan 44.

43. Zhu Xi, "Da Liushu jing wen, no. 2"

44. *Zhuzi yulei*, juan 1, recorded by Shen Xian.

45. Ibid., juan 1, recorded by Dong Zhu.

46. Zhu Xi, "Da Zhao Zhidao, 2," in *Zhu Wengong wenji*, juan 59.

47. *Zhuzi yulei*, juan 94, recorded by Zhou Mo.

48. Ibid., juan 4, recorded by Liao Deming.

49. Ibid., juan 95, recorded by Zheng Kexue.

50. Ibid., juan 95, recorded by Ye Hesun.

51. Ibid., juan 95, recorded by Zhong Zhu.

52. Zhu Xi, "Da Yan Shiheng , no. 1," in *Zhu Wengong wenji*, juan 61.

53. Zhu Xi, "Da Liu Taozhong wenmu," in *Zhu Wengong wenji xuji*: juan 9.

54. *Zhuzi yulei*, juan 95, recorded by Ye Hesun.

55. Ibid., juan 4, recorded by Huang Gan.

56. Ibid., juan 95, recorded by Jin Quwei.

57. Ibid., juan 95, recorded by Shen Xian.

58. Zhu Xi, *Mengzi huowen*, juan 10.

59. Zhu Xi, "Da Lin Dejiu," *Zhu Wengong wenji*, juan 61.

60. Zhu Xi, "Da Huang Shangbo, no. 4," in *Zhu Wengong wenji*, juan 46.

61. *Zhuzi yulei*, juan 4, recorded by Yu Daya.

62. Zhu Xi, "Da Zheng Zishang, no. 14," in *Zhu Wengong wenji*, juan 58.

63. The division of "the nature of righteousness and principle" and "the nature of physical drives" first appeared in Zhu Xi's disciple Chen Zhi's (*zi* Qizhi) *Muzhong ji*. One can refer to *Song-Yuan xue'an*, juan 65, "Muzhong xue'an."

64. Zhu Xi, "Da Yan Shiheng, 1," in *Zhu Wengong wenji*, juan 61.

65. Zhu Xi, "Da Fang Bomo, 3," in *Zhu Wengong wenji*, juan 44.

66. *Zhuzi yulei*, juan 4, recorded by Shen Xian.

67. See the section "Comparison of Principle and *qi*" in the chapter "A Discussion of Principle and *Qi*," in *Chen Lai zixuan ji* (Guiling: Guangxi Normal University Press, 1997).

68. *Zhuzi yulei*, juan 95, recorded by Jin Quwei.

69. In fact, not all of the recordings by Jin Quwei in *Zhuzi yulei* are from Hengxi 2.

70. In Korea's Yi dynasty, Yi T'oegye and others held that the seven emotions derived from *qi*, that the four beginnings derived from principle, and also separated the emotions into original emotions and emotions of the physical endowment.

71. *Zhuzi yulei*, juan 78, recorded by Gan Jie.

72. *Mengzi jizhu*, juan 3.

73. *Zhuzi yulei*, juan 5, recorded by Shen Xian.

74. Translator's note: Here Chen Lai refers the reader to another chapter in the original work, *Zhu Xi zhexue yanjiu*, that deals specifically with the issue of manifested and unmanifested.

75. *Zhu Wengong wenji*, juan 74.

76. Zhu Xi, "Da Chen Qizhi," in *Zhu Wengong wenji*, juan 58.

77. *Zhuzi yulei*, juan 37, recorded by Li Fangzi.

78. Ibid., juan 98, recorded by Zhou Mo.

79. Zhu Xi once had the idea that the seven emotions were allocated to the four beginnings; yet he also had the idea that the seven emotions could not be allocated to the four beginnings (for both see *Zhuzi yulei*, juan 87). The emotions of the seven emotions ought to belong to the emotional activities in a psychological sense; while the emotions of the four beginnings belong to moral awareness and moral emotional activity. In fact, every morally aware activity could take any of the seven emotions as its emotional form. It is very difficult to say which emotion definitely corresponds to which awareness.

80. *Zhuzi yulei*, juan 53, recorded by Fu Guang. During Korea's Yi dynasty, there was once a debate between Yi T'oegye and Ki Kobong on dividing the four beginnings and seven emotions into principle and *qi* based upon this. See my "Yue lun Chaoxian Lichao ruxue Li Huang yu Qi Dasheng de xing-qing li-qi zhi bian" (A general discussion of the Confucian debate between Yi Hwang and Ki Kobong on nature and emotions, principle and *qi* during Korea's Yi dynasty), in *Beijing daxue xuebao* (Beijing: Peking University Press), 1985, no. 3.

81. *Zhuzi yulei*, juan 4, recorded by Huang Xun.

WHAT IS LIVING AND WHAT IS DEAD IN THE CONFUCIANISM OF ZHU XI?

Bryan W. Van Norden

PREFACE

Chen Lai's "The Discussion of Mind and Nature in Zhu Xi's Philosophy" was originally a chapter in his book, *Zhu Xi Zhexue Yanjiu* (*An Investigation of the Philosophy of Zhu Xi*), however it is presented here outside of its original context. In addition, this essay deals with philosophers and concepts that are well known to its original Chinese audience, but will be unfamiliar to almost all westerners. Consequently, I am providing this brief preface to introduce it to English-speaking readers.

Zhu Xi (C.E. 1130–1200) is regarded by many as the greatest Chinese philosopher of the last two millennia. He established what became the orthodox view of *Dao xue,* the School of the Way, better known in the West as "Neo-Confucianism." According to *Dao xue,* there was an original Chinese ethico-political *Dao* (or Way), that had been passed down by the sage kings of antiquity, to Confucius, to his disciples, then to Mencius, who stated explicitly that "human nature is good." The Way was then gradually lost, and the "barbarian" teachings of Buddhism (which arrived in China in the first century C.E.) became the leading philosophical, ethical, and cultural movement. Centuries later, the *Dao* was rediscovered by Confucians who led a cultural and political counteroffensive against Buddhism. In responding to Buddhism intellectually, it was necessary for these *Dao xue* philosophers to make clear what they took to be the *Dao* of the ancient Confucians, and how it differed from that of the Buddhists. This was a complicated task. To begin with, they were confronted with a large set of texts. Some—like the *Yijing*—were already canonical within Confucianism; others—like the *Mean*—were increasingly respected within Confucian circles. These texts used a variety of terms and phrases in what seemed like a completely unsystematic way, such as "mind," "nature," "principle," "*qi*." How were these terms and these texts to be reconciled? These needs were answered by two of the greatest thinkers in *Dao xue*, Cheng Yichuan (also referred to as Cheng Yi, C.E. 1033–1107) and his brother Cheng Mingdao (also referred to as Cheng Hao, C.E. 1032–1085), who formulated the metaphysical and ethical basis of *Dao xue*.

According to this metaphysics, every concrete object is a composite of *li* and *qi*. The standard translation of *li* has come to be "principle," although this is somewhat misleading, since it suggests an individuated rule that can be explicitly formulated. *Li* is the structure or pattern of the universe. The *li* in itself is not individuated; it is completely present in each and every thing that exists, and it is an inherently good pattern. *Qi* is something like a self-moving and spontaneously generating matter that makes up the "stuff" of things. *Qi*, in itself, has very few properties. It is spatially located and comes in varying degrees of "clarity" and "turbidity." Since the *li* is the same in everything, it is the *qi* that individuates entities, distinguishing one thing from another. Furthermore, the properties of kinds of entities are determined by the inter-action between the *li* and the relative "clarity" of a thing's *qi*. The more "turbid" a thing's *qi*, the less of the *li* it manifests. Inanimate objects have the most turbid *qi*. Plants have *qi* that is less turbid; this is reflected in the fact that plants have properties and capacities that inanimate things do not. Non-human animals have perception (and Zhu Xi also thought they manifest some ethical virtues), because they have even clearer *qi* than plants. Humans, as a group, have the most refined *qi* of all creatures, resulting in the fact that they have mental and ethical capacities beyond those of other animals. The relative clarity of the *qi* further distinguishes within each kind of entity. Thus, sages have clearer *qi* than do fools. As Chen Lai observes, the *qi* we are born with has a significant effect on the extent of our virtuousness. However, it is also possible (through education and activities such as meditation) to refine one's *qi*, thereby achieving a greater level of virtue.

The power and flexibility of this metaphysical system answered many of the theoretical needs of the *Dao xue* movement. For example, human "nature," in itself, is pure *li*. However, we can distinguish this from the *li* as it is manifested in a particular person's *qi* (which may be turbid or clear).[1] By means of such distinctions, one can, with sufficient inventiveness, reconcile every claim in the classic Confucian texts with every other. For example, Confucius said that hu-mans are by nature close together, which seems different from Mencius's claim that human nature is good. However, Cheng Yi explained that Confucius was talking about human nature as it is manifested in particular individuals. Our manifested natures are similar (we all are, after all, humans) but they are also distinct, depending on whether our *qi* is very clear or turbid. Mencius, in contrast, was talking about human nature in itself, which is indeed purely good. Similarly, when the *Mean* (a text much favored by followers of *Dao xue*) states that what is meant by "nature" is the Heavenly Mandate, this, too, is completely consistent with what Mencius says. Both are talking about the *li* in itself. However, the language of the *Mean* emphasizes the fact that this *li* is "bestowed on" particular entities, while the language Mencius uses emphasizes the fact that this *li* is within each person. The *Dao xue* view can also diagnose the error in heterodox views. For instance, when Xunzi (an early critic of Mencius within Confucianism) said that human nature is bad, his mistake was that he one-sidedly focused on human nature as it is manifested in most people, thereby ignoring the importance of human nature in itself.

One of Zhu Xi's major contributions to *Dao xue* was to develop a detailed educational curriculum, founded on the Four Books—the *Greater Learning,* the *Analects* of Confucius, the *Mencius,* and the *Mean.* This was a significant shift in emphasis away from what had previously been the canonical group among Confucians, the Five Classics.[2] The Four Books books, along with Zhu Xi's extensive commentaries on them, became the basis of the civil service examinations in China, and remained so for the next six hundred years. In his commentaries (as well as in his extensive and energetic teaching and correspondence), Zhu Xi explicated and defended the world view of the Cheng brothers (especially Cheng Yichuan). How original, then, was Zhu Xi? One of Chen Lai's arguments in his paper is that Zhu Xi's view is a significant advance over that of the Cheng brothers.

The subtlety that makes the *Dao xue* world view so flexible can also make it difficult to understand the precise connections among some of its own claims and terms of art. Part of the project of Chen Lai's paper is to clarify the subtle nuances of meaning of some of the key terms in the philosophy of Zhu Xi. For example, what exactly is the relationship between *li* and *qi* in a particular entity? Chen Lai observes that, on the one hand, *li* and *qi* do not exist independently in the universe. This is a point on which all followers of Dao xue agree. However, Zhu Xi also stresses that *li* and *qi* are not "intimately blended." Rather, *li* and *qi* somehow maintain their identities as distinct entities. Chen Lai illustrates this by saying that *li* and *qi* are united, not like salt in water, but like water and oil.

The seemingly esoteric issue of how *li* and *qi* are related became one of the central issues within *Dao xue.* In fact, the two major schools within *Dao xue* divide, in part, over just this point. Zhu Xi's view became known as *Li xue,* the School of Principle. His contemporary Lu Xiangshan started what became known as the *Xin xue,* or School of Mind, wing of *Dao xue.* But perhaps the most famous, and certainly most charismatic, figure in the *Xin xue* movement was Wang Yangming. I take up some of the issues dividing these schools in my following comments.

COMMENTS ON CHEN LAI'S "THE DISCUSSION OF
MIND AND NATURE IN ZHU XI'S PHILOSOPHY"

Angus Graham suggested that, although Zhu Xi

> Polished the system he inherited from his predecessors [such as Cheng Yi and
> Cheng Hao], bringing out its dualism by clarifying the relations between Principle
> and Ether *qi*, and exploring the implications of the identification of Principle and
> the Supreme Ultimate, he added nothing significant of his own. The truly creative
> figure in the movement [i.e., *Dao xue*] is Cheng Yi.[3]

Chen Lai holds a very different view, arguing that "Zhu Xi's view that nature is
principle is a bit more advanced when compared to the Chengs'." In particular,
Chen Lai identifies several features that are characteristic of Zhu Xi's thought:
everything "receives the *qi* of Heaven and Earth for physical form," everything
receives "the principle of Heaven and Earth for innate nature," and "endowed
heavenly principle is nature." Graham has passed away, but if he were still alive,
he might point to the following comments from the Cheng brothers as evidence
for his view that Zhu Xi's metaphysics is substantially present in the thought of
the former philosophers:

> It would be incomplete to talk about the nature of man and things without includ-
> ing *qi* and unintelligible to talk about *qi* without including nature.[4] (Cheng Hao)

> There is no nature that is not good. Evil is due to capacity. Man's nature is the
> same as principle, and principle is the same from the sage-emperors Yao and Shun
> to the common man in the street. Capacity is an endowment from *qi*. *Qi* may be
> clear or turbid. Men endowed with clear *qi* are wise, while those endowed with
> turbid *qi* are stupid.[5] (Cheng Yi)

> Things and the self are governed by the same principle. If you understand one, you
> understand the other, for the truth within and the truth without are identical. In
> its magnitude it reaches the height of heaven and the depth of earth, but in its
> refinement it constitutes the reason of being in every single thing.[6] (Cheng Yi)

Graham would, I think, acknowledge that there are differences in details and
in emphasis between the Cheng brothers and Zhu Xi, but he would suggest
that we can see Zhu Xi's substantive view already present in the teachings of
the former.

Chen Lai also addresses the issue of whether nonhuman animals receive a
complete endowment of *li*:

> As for the difference between humans and animals, aside from the turbid and
> partial bodies of animals blocking the nature-principle, the original nature-
> principle with which they are endowed is also partial and incomplete.

Chen Lai here takes a stand on an issue that vexed even Zhu Xi's own disciples. The disciples found that Zhu Xi says different things about this topic in different places. In some texts, Zhu Xi seems to suggest that nonhuman animals receive only partial endowments of principle. At other times, he suggests that every animal receives the same principle, but the clarity of a creature's *qi* determines how much of this principle is manifested. One of Zhu Xi's disciples composed a brief essay, outlining what he took to be Zhu Xi's views:

> [In your *Collected Commentaries on the Mengzi*] you say that man and things are similar with respect to *qi* but different with respect to principle, in order to show that man is higher and cannot be equaled by things. In your *Questions and Answers on the Greater Learning*, you say that man and things are similar with respect to principle but different with respect to *qi*, in order to show that the Great Ultimate is not deficient in anything and cannot be interfered with by any individual.[7]

Zhu Xi commends the student for explaining this point more clearly than Zhu Xi had himself. On another occasion, Zhu Xi answered a disciple's question about the endowment of principle in things by saying, "You may consider it complete or you may consider it partial. From the point of view of principle, it is always complete, but from the point of view of material force, it cannot help being partial."[8] This may seem like waffling, but I think Zhu Xi's view is actually quite careful, and depends upon distinguishing between principle in itself and principle as manifested in a particular thing's *qi*. Principle in itself *is* complete in each thing: each human, each cat, each dog, each plant, and each mote of dust possesses complete principle. However, the turbidity of a thing's *qi* determines the extent to which this complete principle manifests itself. Depending upon what our purpose is in speaking, and what we wish to stress, we may say that principle in a thing (that is, principle in itself) is complete, or we may say that the principle of a thing (that is, the manifested principle) is partial.

In the remainder of my comments, I want to discuss two issues that are suggested by Chen Lai's paper, although he does not directly address them: (1) is the *Dao xue* interpretation of the development of Confucianism accurate? and (2) does *Dao xue* have anything to offer as a living philosophical position?

DID ZHU XI GET CONFUCIUS AND MENCIUS RIGHT?

Chen Lai cites the brilliant historian of Chinese philosophy, Qian Mu, who "has pointed out that Cheng Yichuan's discussion of nature essentially explains Mencius's ideas." Qian Mu's statement is ambiguous, though. Consider the following two statements: "Thomas Kuhn explains Kepler's laws of planetary motion" and "Newton's physics explains Kepler's laws of planetary motion." In the former sentence, the historian of science Thomas Kuhn is said to "explain" Kepler's laws by making clear to us the significance these laws had *for Kepler and his contemporaries*: what they meant *for them*, why they were regarded as plausible *by them*, and so forth. In the second sentence, Newton is said to "explain" Kepler's laws by giving an account *in terms of Newton's own physics* that explains why Kepler's laws are approximately correct. As Kuhn explains, Kepler was led to the discovery of his laws by "his frequently mystical Neoplatonic faith."[9] Newton's theory of gravitation provides an alternative explanation of why, for example, the planets move (as predicted by Kepler's views) in ellipses. However, the terms of Newtonian dynamics (especially as related to the conception of inertial motion) are alien to Kepler's world view.[10] Consequently, Newton's "explanation" of Kepler's laws is not one that could have been acknowledged by Kepler.

The question I want to raise is this: what sort of explanation has Zhu Xi provided of the views of Mencius (and Confucius, and others) on human nature? I believe that Zhu Xi saw himself as explaining Mencius and Confucius in terms that the latter two could acknowledge as simply more elaborate and explicit versions of their own views. However, I want to argue that, in reality, Zhu Xi's relationship to Mencius was more like the relationship of Newton to Kepler. One of the key issues on this point is the meaning of the term *li*. As we have seen, *li*, for followers of *Dao xue*, is something like the structure of the cosmos, found complete in every concrete thing that exists. *Li* is a central and frequently recurring term in *Dao xue*. Furthermore, as Chen Lai makes clear, a variety of other terms are taken to ultimately refer to *li*. Let us contrast this with what we find in some early Confucian texts.

The term *li* occurs precisely zero times in the *Analects* of Confucius. It does show up repeatedly, though, in Zhu Xi's commentary on that text, beginning with his comments on the second passage in Book 1 of the *Analects*. *Li* occurs a grand total of seven times in all of the *Mencius*. These occurrences are in only three passages. In 5B1, *li* occurs four times in the compound expression *tiaoli*, which simply means "orderly." In 7B19, *li* occurs in the expression *li yu kou*, which means, "to be fluent in speech" (literally, orderly in regard to mouth). Obviously, neither of these passages suggests the metaphysically loaded use of *li* found in the writings of the *Dao xue* philosophers. The only other occurrences of the term in the *Mencius* are in 6A7, where we find:

> What is it that hearts prefer in common? I say that it is fine patterns *li* and righteousness. The sages first discovered what our hearts prefer in common. Hence, fine patterns *li* and righteousness delight our hearts like meat delights our mouths.[11]

It is conceivable that Mencius has in mind here *li* in the same metaphysical sense that *Dao xue* uses. However, there is nothing in the passage to suggest that reading. And, as we have seen, the other uses of *li* in the text are completely distinct from Zhu Xi's use.

So what does *li* mean for early Chinese thinkers? I think we find a paradigmatic early use of *li* in the writings of the Daoist Zhuangzi, where he describes
a cook who carves up an ox with amazing skill. Describing how his knife moves
through the ox, the cook says,

> I rely on the Heavenly patterns *tianli*, strike in the big gaps, am guided by the large
> fissures, and follow what is inherently so. I never touch a ligament or tendon,
> much less do any heavy wrenching! A good butcher changes his chopper every year
> because he chips it. An average butcher changes it every month because he breaks
> it. There are spaces between those joints, and the edge of the blade has no thick-
> ness. If you use what has no thickness to go where there is space —oh! there's
> plenty of extra room to play about in.[12]

Here *li* seems to refer to the natural structure or pattern of the ox carcass. Something like "structure" or "pattern" is the general sense this term has in early texts.
This is much less metaphysically loaded than *Dao xue*'s conception of *li*.

My interpretation is not original. In the Qing dynasty, the brilliant philosopher and philologist Dai Zhen provided essentially the same critique of the
"Song Confucians" and their interpretation of earlier Confucianism.[13] He wrote:
"In the doctrines of the Six Classics, Confucius, and Mencius, and even in the
biographies and multitudinous documents (of ancient history), the word 'principle' is seldom seen."[14] Why, then, did the followers of *Dao xue* give the term
such prominence? Dai Zhen argues, "'The Song Confucians' came and went
with Daoists and Buddhists, and thus mixed in Daoist and Buddhist explanations when formulating their doctrines."[15]

In support of Dai Zhen's hypothesis, consider how the term *li* is used by
some later Buddhists. The slogan of the Hua-yan Buddhists is "all is one, and
one is all."[16] One is all, because any one (seemingly) individual thing is connected to everything else through a net of causal interconnections. The Buddhists take this to imply that no thing has a genuine individual nature.[17] And
since no thing has an individual nature to distinguish it from other things, all
is one. The Buddhists illustrate the causal interconnectedness of things using an
image from Hindu myth: *Lord Indra's net.* At the intersection of every two
strands in Indra's net is a jewel so bright that it reflects every other jewel in the
net. The jewels stand for (seemingly) individual things, and the strands of the
net stand for the causal connections among them. Looking for a philosophical
term to describe this net of interconnectedness, the Buddhists seized on *li*. We
can see both why this was an obvious term to pick (after all, the term did mean
"pattern"), but also how the Buddhist use of the term is wedded to their particular metaphysics. This metaphysics, remember, developed in China long after
the death of Confucius and Mencius.

The Buddhists held that seeing that one is all and all is one helped a person
to overcome attachment to particular people and things. The *Dao xue* Confucians

did not want to go that far, since attachment to one's own family members has always been a central component of Confucian ethics. The genius of the Cheng brothers was to combine the Buddhist notion of *li* with the concept of *qi*, a notion that was stressed by their relative, Zhang Zai, and their teacher, Zhou Dunyi. *Qi*, as the Chengs conceived it, was what individuated the universal *li*. As Chen Lai explains, this proved to be a remarkably fruitful combination of ideas, which answered a number of theoretical needs of the *Dao xue* Confucians.

So we can give a narrative that connects the teachings of Confucius and Mencius to the doctrines of the *Dao xue* Confucians, via the doctrines of the Hua-yan Buddhists. But the narrative suggests that the *Dao xue* view would be very unfamiliar to Confucius and Mencius.

My original analogy was that Zhu Xi is to Mencius as Newton is to Kepler. We commonly think that Newton's interpretation captured what was right about Kepler's views, but did it in a more encompassing and sophisticated form. Can the same be said about Zhu Xi's interpretation of Mencius? This depends on two things: how much of what is insightful in Mencius's view has Zhu Xi had to sacrifice, and how plausible is Zhu Xi's view on its own terms?

Regarding the first point, Dai Zhen charged that the *Dao xue* interpretation failed to do justice to several insights. In particular, Dai Zhen argued that Zhu Xi's conception of *li* led to a denigration of physical desire that was not characteristic of Mencius. I'm not going to focus on this issue, though. Instead, I want to say something about the second general issue: the plausibility of Zhu Xi's views on their own terms.

ARE ZHU XI'S OWN VIEWS PHILOSOPHICALLY VIABLE?

By what standards should we evaluate the *Dao xue* world view? It would be a mistake, I think, to evaluate it only by the standards of modern science. The *Dao xue* world view does not operate by the same standards of evaluation as modern science, and it does not have the same goals as modern science. For example, unlike modern science, *Dao xue* does not stress predicting and explaining empirical phenomena, nor does it stress testable results or mathematical models.[18] When faced with a case such as this, Peter Winch has argued that we cannot judge the nonscientific view to be mistaken or nonrational.[19] On Winch's view, to claim that *Dao xue* is inadequate or unwarranted as a scientific theory is a category mistake, like claiming that a quarterback was checkmated. Charles Taylor has made what I take to be a strong argument in response to Winch, though. Taylor would say that, while the *Dao xue* standards and goals do not correspond fully with modern science, they do overlap to some extent.[20] Consider, for example, the prediction and explanation of empirical phenomena. Although this is not the primary focus of *Dao xue*, and although *Dao xue* appeals to justificational standards alien to modern science, it is also true that the doctrines of *Dao xue* were interconnected with claims and theories that *did* make empirical predictions and did offer explanations. Consequently, it is a challenge to *Dao xue* that modern science has had remarkable success in explaining and predicting (1) the natural phenomena to which *Dao xue* doctrines originally applied;[21] and (2) a range of phenomena with which the *Dao xue* philosophers were unacquainted, and regarding which the explanatory power of *Dao xue* is, at best, unproven.[22]

These facts do not, by themselves, render *Dao xue* obsolete. The situation is similar, in outline, to that of Aristotelianism. Aristotle's philosophy has many aspects. Some of his views are in conflict with modern physics, astronomy, and biology. Part of the scientific revolution involved the rejection of these Aristotelian ideas. For many thinkers, this led to a wholesale rejection. However, today, many philosophers believe that it is possible to isolate Aristotelian insights on ethics and metaphysics from his mistaken views on natural science. Alasdair MacIntyre and Martha Nussbaum, for example, have tried to defend versions of Aristotelian ethics divorced from what the former called his "metaphysical biology."[23] Likewise, there has been a revival of interest in Aristotelian metaphysical ideas on substance and essence. Perhaps something similar could be done with *Dao xue*. Consequently, I shall say a little about both the metaphysics and the ethics of a *Dao xue* that is purified of outmoded proto-scientific ideas.

Metaphysics

We can think of each entity as having two aspects: a common aspect (corresponding to the *li*, a pattern common in all things) and a particular aspect (corresponding to the *qi*, the particular constitution of a thing).[24] The common pattern only exists in particular things, is the same in each thing, and is present in each and every thing that exists. However, the way in which the pattern is manifested in a particular thing is determined by the particular constitution of that thing. We can apply the common aspect/particular aspect distinction to any thing, situation, or process that is a possible subject of thought or discussion. Consequently, there is no privileged ontology, in the sense of one correct way of dividing up reality into kinds and entities. For instance, I can apply the common-particular distinction to myself, or to the relationship between my wife and me, or to a molecule in my body, or to any other thing I can think of.

The common pattern is normative, but in a way that has some explanatory power. For example, we can explain why a family is dysfunctional by appealing to the stresses induced by failure to follow the normative structure supplied by the pattern. An analogy may help here. Imagine a manifestation of the pattern as being like the elasticity of a spring in a machine. The elasticity of the spring determines that it can function effectively through a certain range of movement. However, the elasticity also limits the spring in certain ways: if the spring is subject to certain kinds of stresses or contortions, it will be damaged or broken. Similarly, the *li* determines that a father has certain roles to perform: protector,

nurturer, ethical guide, and so forth. If he fails to perform these roles, it introduces stresses into the family that will cause suffering, as well as making it more
difficult for others to perform their roles (mother, son, etc.).

We can, to some extent, usefully discuss the structure of the pattern.
The pattern manifests itself in sets of characteristics or processes that are isomor-
phic with certain paradigmatic sets of one, two, four, and five.[25] *Yin* and *yang*
are perhaps the best-known set of two. These terms are now so well known in
the West that they almost need no explanation. However, westerners sometimes
forget that *yin* and *yang* need to be present in the appropriate balance, and that
one thing may have both *yin* and *yang* aspects. For example, in a parental
relationship, a father should be *yang* and his child should be *yin*, but each of them
must learn to blend *yin* and *yang* appropriately in their own behavior. A father who
is excessively *yang* is too distant and severe; a daughter who is excessively *yin* lacks
the independence that would make her a person in her own right.

The virtues of benevolence, righteousness, wisdom, and propriety are one of
the most important sets of four. Adherence to these virtues contributes to a
flourishing life and successful relationships with others in a variety of contexts.
However, what it means to be benevolent, for example, will vary depending
upon the particularity of each relationship. For example, benevolence will
demand different things of a mother, teacher, and wife.

The "five phases," *wu xing*, are the most important quintet: earth, metal,
wood, fire, and water. The similarity to the "four elements" of the Aristotelian
tradition is specious. As the translation suggests, the Chinese phrase refers to
phases that something can be in. Those familiar with Chinese culture know that
the applications of the five phases are almost limitless. They can be brought into
correspondence with everything from bodily organs, to kinds of taste, to musical
notes, and more.

The notion of "unity" seems to lack much content. However, the concept is
important because the *Dao xue* philosophers are all, ultimately, monists. The
only real division is over how extreme a monism they embrace. Each thing must
be understood as, in some way, a part of a unified whole. Each part can only
properly function in some whole, and it can only be fully understood through
that whole.

As I observed earlier, there is no privileged ontology. All the preceding
patterns are only partially adequate abstractions from the totality of the *li*.
Furthermore, any of them could be applied to any possible object of discussion. Since there is no privileged ontology, there will be multiple, accurate
ways of describing reality. Which way to use language should be determined
by our purpose in speaking or writing.[26] For instance, since benevolence and
righteousness are aspects of the common pattern, they will in fact manifest
themselves, in some way, in each entity that exists.[27] It would not be inaccurate
to apply that particular description of the pattern to, say, a rock, but it would
almost certainly be unhelpful to do so. Furthermore, since the pattern only

exists in particular things, and since the particularity of each thing determines the manner in which the pattern manifests itself, any linguistic account of the pattern runs the risk of being an abstraction that falsifies by ignoring the genuine particularity of a thing, situation, or activity. There are, therefore, limitations on the adequacy of language. (We shall see that this fact is related to the major division within *Dao xue*.)

The preceding metaphysical view is clearly very different from any of the major metaphysical alternatives in the West. It also seems to me that there is nothing incoherent or obviously mistaken in the modified *Dao xue* view I sketched. Whether it is worth adopting can only be determined by the effort to elaborate its details and compare it with other metaphysical options.

Ethics

However, my own view is that *Dao xue* has more to offer as an ethical view. In particular, we find in *Dao xue* a very rich literature on ethical cultivation. The issue of how one becomes a better person is touched on by some Western philosophers,[28] but it has not received nearly the level of sustained attention in the West that it has in China. Furthermore, the debate between the two major wings of *Dao xue*—the School of *Li* and the School of Mind—is a fascinating debate over the proper methods of cultivation. This debate was reflected in subtle metaphysical disagreements between the two schools over the precise relationship between *li* and *qi*. However, I submit that it is not necessary to accept anything like the metaphysics of *Dao xue* in order to engage with and learn from their debates over ethical cultivation.

The School of *Li* (of the Cheng brothers and Zhu Xi) and the School of Mind (of Lu Xiangshan and Wang Yangming) agree about many things. Their conceptions of what a fully developed ethical individual would be like, and of how he would act, are almost identical. The two schools share an assumption that is uncommon in recent Western ethics, but is almost unchallenged in their own tradition: that practical reasoning about ethical matters is more like appreciating the taste of a fine wine, and less like being good at applied mathematics. Consequently, both schools agree that ethical cultivation is less like acquiring theoretical knowledge, and more like becoming an ethical connoisseur. Furthermore, both schools revere the same ancient sages: the sage kings, the Duke of Zhou, Confucius, and Mencius. The followers of each school were intimately conversant with the same classic texts. And both schools agree that each and every person is born with complete ethical knowledge within oneself.[29] The crucial ethical disagreement is over the possibility of accessing that innate ethical knowledge. According to Zhu Xi, most of us, in our untutored states, have ethical natures that are so obscured by selfish desires and errant passions that we cannot trust our own spontaneous ethical reactions. Consequently, it is necessary for us to submit ourselves to a long-term process of ethical cultivation, under the guidance of wise mentors, so that we can calm ourselves and be helped to gradually see the ethical truth within us more clearly. This process includes what Zhu Xi calls "the lesser learning" and "the greater learning":

> At the age of eight all the male children, from the sons of kings and dukes to the sons of commoners, entered the schools of lesser learning; there they were instructed in the chores of cleaning and sweeping, in the formalities of polite conversation and good manners, and in the refinements of ritual, music, archery, charioteering, calligraphy, and mathematics.[30] At the age of fifteen the Son of Heaven's eldest son and other imperial sons on down to the eldest legitimate sons of dukes, ministers, high officials, and officers of the chief grade, together with the gifted among the populace, all entered the school of greater learning; there they were instructed in the Way of probing principle *li*, setting the mind in the right, cultivating oneself, and governing others.[31]

The activities that were part of the "lesser learning" imparted basic skills that would be needed by a "gentleman," as well as inculcating good habits (e.g., defference).[32] The educational techniques used to impart the "greater learning" were all designed to help the student to come to see the truth for himself—*zi de zhi* (to get it oneself, as the *Dao xue* philosophers say). Seated meditation helps to calm the desires and passions. Studying the classic texts helps the student to recognize the truth, because the sages saw the truth themselves, and managed to express it in formulations that were as close to being timeless as any could be.[33] Reading commentaries and discussing the texts with fellow students and one's master helps avoid erroneous interpretations. (This was important since, after all, one's nature is so heavily obscured that, before undergoing cultivation, one cannot reliably interpret the classic texts without some assistance.)[34]

In contrast, Lu Xiangshan and Wang Yangming thought that the educational program Zhu Xi advocated could, and usually did, produce dry pedants rather than active men of virtue. As Lu wrote:

> Nowadays when people read, they pay no attention to what is simple and easy, but devote their vigorous efforts to study what can arouse people's admiration. When did ancient sages aim to arouse people's admiration? It is because the Way has not prevailed that when people see something unusual, their admiration is aroused. When I read, I merely look at ancient annotations, and the words of the sages are clear of themselves. Take the saying (from *Analects*, 1.6), "A student should be filial toward his parents when at home and respectful toward his elders when abroad." This clearly means that when at home you are to be filial and when away from home you are to be respectful. What is the need for commentaries?[35]

Perhaps Lu had Zhu Xi in mind specifically when he made this observation. Zhu Xi comments on *Analects*, 1.6 in his *Collected Commentaries on the Analects*, and we also know from the *Zhuzi yulei* that he discussed the passage with his students. In both cases, Zhu Xi's stresses the context of the line Lu cites. The entire passage from the *Analects* reads:

A student should be filial toward his parents when at home and respectful toward his elders when abroad. Careful in action and truthful in speech, he should display an expansive care for the multitude and seek to draw near to those who are *ren* [humane]. If in the course of his duties he finds himself with energy to spare, he should devote it to study of the *wen*, "cultural arts."[36]

Zhu Xi reads this passage in the light of some lines from the *Greater Learning*: "Things have their roots and their branches; affairs have their endings and their beginnings. If one appreciates what comes first and last, then one has come close to the Way."[37] Zhu Xi suggests that the virtues mentioned in *Analects,* 1.6— being filial, respectful, careful, truthful, caring, and humane—constitute "what comes first," the "root," while study is "what comes last," the "branches." In this way, Zhu Xi makes clear that he regards virtuous activity as more important than study. But he also stresses that study cannot be avoided: "If one energetically acts but does not study the cultural arts, then one will lack the where-with-all to investigate the established paradigms of the sages and worthies, and to under-stand how the principle of affairs ought to be. Thus, that which one does may come out of selfish intentions."[38] Academicians (like myself, or like most of my readers) will probably applaud Zhu Xi's sentiment here; we will also admire his ingenuity in finding so much internal structure in this brief *Analects* passage, and reading it in the light of another classic text. However, for Lu, this ingenuity is precisely the problem. It took me at least an hour to look up all the relevant passages from Zhu Xi, translate them, ponder them, and write the preceding paragraph. If Lu were alive today, he would probably ask: "Are you really a better person now after the scholarly spelunking you have engaged in? And couldn't you have spent that hour calling your aged father on the phone to brighten his day?" Lu has a point here.

According to Lu, "The *li* of the Way is right before our eyes."[39] Consequently, the arduous process of cultivation advocated by Zhu Xi is unnecessary: "Those who are 'misled by things' so as to pervert principle and deviate from righteous-ness 'simply do not concentrate upon them.' If they can sincerely examine themselves and concentrate upon it, their approval and disapproval, and their selecting and rejecting will all have subtle vigor, clear-cut intelligence, and decisive conviction."[40]

Several centuries later, after Zhu Xi's interpretations of the classics had be-come state orthodoxy, Wang Yangming took up the cause of Lu Xiangshan. Wang's distinctive teaching was "the unity of knowledge and action." For Wang, if one knows principle, one will act appropriately, and if one acts appropriately, one must know principle.[41] One of Wang's disciples is puzzled by this claim, observing, "there are people who know that parents should be served with filial piety and elder brothers with respect but cannot put these things into practice. This shows that knowledge and action are clearly two different things." Wang confidently responds:

The knowledge and action you refer to are already separated by selfish desires and are no longer knowledge and action in their original substance. There have never been people who know but do not act. Those who are supposed to know but do not act simply do not yet know. . . . Therefore the *Greater Learning* points to true knowledge and action for people to see, saying, they are "like loving lovely sights and hating hateful odors." Seeing lovely sights appertains to knowledge, while loving lovely sights appertains to action. However, as soon as one sees that lovely sight, one has already loved it. It is not that one sees it first and then makes up one's mind to love it. Smelling a hateful odor appertains to knowledge, while hating a hateful odor appertains to action. However, as soon as one smells a hateful odor, one has already hated it. It is not that one smells it first and then makes up one's mind to hate it. A person with a stuffed-up nose does not smell the hateful odor even if he sees a malodorous object before him, and so he does not hate it. This amounts to not knowing the bad odor. Or take one's knowledge of pain. Only after one has experienced pain can one know pain. The same is true of cold or hunger.[42]

Wang's argument, whether we agree with it or not, is lucid and challenging. Imagine smelling raw sewage. Revulsion seems to go automatically with the perception of the smell. If someone claimed to be smelling raw sewage but showed no aversion, we would typically suspect that, at the least, she had a very poor sense of smell. Similarly, imagine seeing a sight that you regard as sexually attractive.[43] Your motivations are engaged as soon as you realize what you are looking at. If your motivations are not engaged, then you are not perceiving it as a sexy sight.

Wang accuses scholars like Zhu Xi of failing to appreciate that knowledge and action go together, and of dividing ethical cultivation into a two-step process: coming to know principle, and then acting on that knowledge. The result, Wang thinks, will be disastrous:

> . . . people today distinguish knowledge and action and pursue them separately, believing that one must know before he can act. They will discuss and learn the business of knowledge first, they say, and wait till they truly know before they put their knowledge into practice. Consequently, to the last day of life, they will never act and also will never know. This doctrine of knowledge first and action later is not a minor disease and it did not come about only yesterday. My present advocacy of the unity of knowledge and action is precisely the medicine for that disease.[44]

And, indeed, Zhu Xi does say things that suggest the "two step" view:

> Knowledge and action are normally mutually dependent. It's like this: if a person has eyes but no legs, he cannot walk; if he has legs but no eyes, he cannot see. *As for their order, knowledge comes first.* As for their importance, action is more significant.[45] (Emphasis added)

The Intersection of Metaphysics and Ethics

One of the most intriguing aspects of the disagreement between the School of *Li* and the School of Mind is the manner in which their ethical disagreements are reflected in metaphysical disagreements. As with ethics, the two schools of *Dao xue* share many basic metaphysical views. However, Zhu Xi hints at an important disagreement in some puzzling comments he makes to some of his students:

> Someone asked whether *li* comes first and *qi* comes after. Zhu Xi responded, "Fundamentally, one cannot speak of *li* and *qi* coming first or coming after. But if you reason about it, it is like *li* comes first and *qi* comes after." He then asked, "How does *li* manifest itself in the *qi*?" Zhu Xi answered, "When it comes to *yin* and *yang* and the five phases mixing together yet not losing their sequence, that is due to *li*. But if the *qi* did not congeal, the *li* would have nothing to adhere to."[46]

It seems to be a basic consequence of the *Dao xue* view that one cannot have *qi* without *li* or *li* without *qi*. *Li* without *qi* would be structure without anything that it is the structure of, which seems incoherent. Equally incoherent seems to be the notion of *qi* without *li*, since that would be something like matter without any structure. So what does Zhu Xi mean when he suggests that there is some sense, albeit an abstract one, of talking about the *li* being prior to the *qi*? I believe that Zhu Xi's point is that one can, to a certain extent, conceptualize the *li* in itself, independently of its specific, concrete embodiments in the *qi*. This is an important point, because if it were not true, the educational program that Zhu Xi advocates would be unworkable. Zhu Xi wants us to learn to see the *li* in itself. The way to learn the *li* is through the guided study of the words of the sages: "Read books to observe the intentions of the sages and worthies. Follow the intentions of the sages and worthies to observe natural principle."[47] We are able to see the *li* in itself, and the words of the sages can give us an insight into the *li* in itself, only because the *li* can be, to some extent, abstracted from its particular embodiments in the *qi*. If the *li* could not be abstracted from its particular embodiments in the *qi*, then we could only see and respond to the *li* as it is embodied in particular concrete entities and situations. Furthermore, if the *li* could not be abstracted from its particular embodiments in the *qi*, then the words of the sages could only express what was appropriate in the particular contexts that the sages themselves were in; their words, in that case, would not be intrinsically applicable to our own situations.

Lu Xiangshan and Wang Yangming denied that the *li* were prior to the *qi* conceptually, and drew the specific consequences of that denial that I just sketched. This is part of what is at issue in Lu's criticisms of Zhu Xi's views on the Supreme Ultimate. Supreme Ultimate *tai ji*, is a phrase that occurs in the *Yi jing*, or *Classic of Changes*. The use of the phrase there is intriguing, but enigmatic. The later philosopher Zhou Dunyi, whom Zhu Xi credited with reviving the true philosophy of Confucianism, used the phrase in a famous work of his own,

"Explanation of the Diagram of the Supreme Ultimate," which begins, *Wuji er taiji*, "The ultimate of not-having and the Supreme Ultimate!" The Chinese text here is ambiguous. We could read it as expressing a temporal sequence between two distinct entities. However, Zhu Xi regarded it as a pair of expressions used to described two aspects of one thing. Specifically, Zhu Xi thought that Supreme Ultimate is a name for the *li* in itself. He also believed that Zhou Dunyi, by referring to it as "the ultimate of not-having," was making the same point that Zhu Xi had made by suggesting that *li* is prior to the *qi*. In other words, the Supreme Ultimate, the *li* in itself, may be described as the "ultimate of not-having" in the sense that it lacks any specific, concrete qualities.[48] Lu strenuously disagrees. In a letter he wrote to Zhu Xi, Lu suggests that the phrase "ultimate of not-having" may have been misattributed to Zhou Dunyi, and that (if he did use that phrase) it may have been a youthful error that he abandoned in his more sophisticated work. Lu also argues that the concept is essentially Daoist in its implications. This gives us insight into what bothers Lu about the notion, because his criticism of the Daoists and Buddhists is that they (allegedly) seek to escape from this world. We see, then, that Lu objects to Zhu Xi's interpretation of the Supreme Ultimate, because he regards it as leading people to focus their attention on an illusory "other-worldly" realm (i.e., the realm of *li* in itself). There is no such realm, Lu insists, not even conceptually: "*Li* exists in the universe from the very beginning. How can it be said to be not-having?"[49] It now becomes clear how deeply significant is a seemingly innocuous comment attributed to Lu Xiangshan: "Outside of the Way there are no events; outside of events there is no Way."[50] The Way is the *li*, and the *li* does not exist outside of its concrete embodiment in the things and affairs of this world. Thus, the *li* cannot be understood independently of those embodiments. Consequently, Zhu Xi's educational program, Lu thinks, is doomed from the start. The words of the sages cannot give us insight into the *li* outside of any particular context; their words are only expressions of what was appropriate for them in their own particular situations. Thus, "If in our study we know the fundamentals, then all the Six Classics are our footnotes."[51]

An Evaluation in Lieu of an Argument

Who is right in this debate? This is a controversy that began hundreds of years ago and continues to rage among Confucians today. Obviously, I cannot hope to say anything substantive about it in these brief comments. But allow me to express, as Zhu Xi would put it, the opinion of "ignorant me." It seems to me that Lu and Wang offer penetrating and insightful correctives to the sort of pedantic over intellectualization that some of us are prone to. Think of the academic philosophers whom you know. How many of them do you regard as highly virtuous? If you are like me, your experience will be that most academics are bright intellectually, and some are genuinely brilliant. However, most are fairly middling as ethical agents, and some are genuinely heinous. An intimate dinner at my home would allow plenty of room for all the academics whom I really admire as human beings. Lu and Wang give us a salutary warning that being a good person is not the same as being clever or learned, and that most of us make little if any effort at being more virtuous than we are.

Nonetheless, my own experience—as a teacher, friend, armchair psychologist, and highly fallible ethical agent myself—is that most of us cannot trust our ethical inclinations until these have been subject to extensive training and discipline. I think that Lu and Wang lived in cultures (or at least subcultures) in which most people whom they encountered as adults had already been subjected to intense (perhaps even excessive) socialization and literary education. Their views on ethical cultivation might have been different had they met many people who (like me) grew up with little respect for authority of any kind, and were fed a steady diet of escapist consumerism and mind-numbing television (Anyone's *qi* would be turbid after that!). Consequently, I think Zhu Xi is right about the need for an initial process of cultivation, beginning in youth with habituation in good habits and learning basic skills, followed by exposure to great works of literature, history, and philosophy, under the guidance of teachers who see these texts as sources of wisdom, rather than mere opportunities for theatrical "deconstruction." Of course, there are many aspects of Zhu Xi's thought that I think need to be modified. Like Saint Thomas Aquinas, Zhu Xi was a radical innovator and canon-transformer whose work became ossified in the hands of his epigones. We should be true to the spirit, rather than the letter, of Zhu Xi's thought, and open up the list of texts recognized as potentially ethically transformative. As different as they are in so many ways, Thucydides should be side by side with the *Documents*, the *Odyssey* should be read as well as the *Odes*, and even other genres ignored by Zhu Xi should be added. It is a platitude to point out that the plays of Shakespeare have much to teach those who will listen, as do great novels—*The Scholars*, *Invisible Man*, take your pick.[52] The list should be open-ended: a university may settle on a particular list of texts for its own internal curricular purposes, but different great works, even within the same genre, each teach in their own inimitable way. And the canon will be "essentially disputed." Aquinas had to fight to get Aristotle re-admitted to the Western canon. Cicero's writings were prized for centuries after his death, but I think it would be difficult to make the case now that one misses anything important by not reading them. And Mencius was for centuries a much less important figure in Confucianism; it was the *Dao xue* philosophers who dubbed him "the second sage," behind only Confucius himself.

We owe a great debt to scholars like Chen Lai who are reviving knowledge of Zhu Xi and other *Dao xue* philosophers in China, and passing that knowledge on to future generations. Having been a recipient of his kindness during a visit to China, I can also vouch for his commitment to Confucian generosity and propriety. I hope that there will be more philosophers like Chen Lai in the West too. Our own society is hungry for knowledge of Chinese culture and also—I think—for new ethical insights. *Dao xue* is a rich, and still largely untapped, source of wisdom.

NOTES

1. The distinction between the *li* in itself and the *li* as manifested helps to explain an otherwise puzzling aspect of *Dao xue* philosophy. Zhu Xi and others will sometimes speak as if there were particular, individuated *li*: the *li* of a cart, a boat, or a pen, for example. (See, e.g., Daniel K. Gardner, trans., *Learning to Be a Sage* [Berkeley: University of California Press, 1990], pp. 90–91.) This has led some interpreters to assume that *li* was something like Aristotelian "substantial form." However, when Zhu Xi speaks of "the *li* of a boat" and how it differs from "the *li* of a cart," he has in mind *li* as manifested in a particular sort of *qi*.

2. The Five Classics were the *Classic of Documents* (sometimes translated as the *History*), the *Classic of Odes* (also translated as the *Songs*), the *Record of Rites*, the *Classic of Changes* (sometimes just called the *Yijing* or *I Ching* in English), and the *Spring and Autumn Annals*. One sometimes sees a list of the Six Classics, which includes the *Book of Music* (which had been lost for centuries by the time of Zhu Xi) or the *Rites of the Zhou*.

3. Angus Graham, *Two Chinese Philosophers* (reprint; Chicago: Open Court Press, 1992), p. xxi. Graham's book is a milestone among Western works on Chinese philosophy, but see also the review by Mark Berkson, *Philosophy East and West* 45.2 (February 1995): 292–97.

4. Translation slightly modified from Chan, *A Source Book in Chinese Philosophy* (Princeton: Princeton University Press, 1963), p. 536. Citing *Er Cheng quanshu* (*Sibu beiyao ed.*), 6:2a.

5. Translation slightly modified from Chan, *Source Book*, p. 536. Citing 6:2a.

6. Chan, *Source Book*, p. 563. Citing 18: 8b–9a.

7. Translation heavily modfied from Chan, *Source Book*, p. 622. Citing *Zhuzi daquan* (1714 ed.), 42:27b–29a.

8. Chan, *Source Book*, p. 620. Citing 42:26b–27a.

9. Thomas Kuhn, *The Copernican Revolution* (Cambridge, MA: Harvard University Press, 1957), p. 214.

10. Kuhn, *Copernican*, pp. 247, 256. Cf. Kuhn's comments on the relationship between the physics of Newton and that of Galileo (Thomas Kuhn, *The Structure of Scientific Revolutions*, 3rd. ed. [Chicago: University of Chicago Press, 1996], p. 139).

11. Philip J. Ivanhoe and Bryan W. Van Norden, eds., *Readings in Classical Chinese Philosophy* (Indianapolis: Hackett Publishing, 2003), p. 145.

12. *Zhuangzi*, trans. by Paul Kjellberg. In *Readings in Classical Chinese Philosophy* (New York: Seven Bridges Press, 2001), p. 220.

13. I learned of this line of criticism through the work of my teachers, David S. Nivison and Philip J. Ivanhoe. See, for example, David S. Nivison, "Two Roots or One?" and "The Philosophy of Wang Yangming," in *The Ways of Confucianism* (Chicago: Open Court Press, 1996), and Philip J. Ivanhoe, *Confucian Moral Self Cultivation*, 2d ed. (Indianapolis, IN: Hackett Publishing, 2000). I owe them both a great debt. Of course, they are not responsible for any errors or misunderstandings evident in this essay.

14. John Ewell, trans., "Re-Inventing the Way: Dai Zhen's 'Evidential Commentary on the Meanings of Terms in Mencius' (1777)," (Ph.D. diss., University of California at Berkeley, 1990), p. 120 (gloss in Ewell's translation). Citing *Mengzi ziyi shuzheng*, I.5.

15. Ewell, trans., "Re-Inventing the Way," p. 150. Citing I.10. Dai Zhen cites biographical evidence regarding some of the major figures in *Dao xue* in support of this claim.

16. This phrase is found in the "Essay on the Golden Lion," by Fa Zang. I have not found a translation of this work that seems to me to be fully adequate. For translations that are somewhat successful, see Chan, *Source Book*, pp. 409–14, and Fung Yu-lan, *A History of Chinese Philosophy*, trans. Derk Bodde (Princeton: Princeton University Press, 1983), pp. 341–58. For a good secondary study of Hua-yen Buddhism, see Francis Cook, *Hua-yen Buddhism: The Jewel Net of Indra* (University Park, PA: Pennsylvania State University Press, 1977).

17. The underlying assumption seems to be that a "nature" would have to be unchanging and completely independent of everything else. I would reject this assumption, as would Mencius.

18. I am not assuming that there is a precise distinction between the empirical and the nonempirical, nor do I think that "testability" means definitive "verifiability" or "falsifiability." If we learned anything from the philosophy of science in the previous century (i.e., the twentieth), it is that these claims are mistaken. However, it does seem to me that some claims have more empirical content than others, and that some theories can more easily be tested in ways that rationally give us increased (or decreased) confidence in their truth. A theory is *more* scientific the closer it gets to the empirical and testable end of the spectrum.

19. Peter Winch, "Understanding a Primitive Society," in Bryan R. Wilson, ed., *Rationality* (Oxford: Basil Blackwell, 1984), pp. 78–111. Winch and Charles Taylor (see later in this essay) are discussing the witchcraft practices of the African Azande tribe, but I take their comments to be obviously relevant to evaluating *Dao xue's* beliefs.

20. Charles Taylor, "Rationality," from *Philosophy and the Human Sciences: Philosophical Papers II* (New York: Cambridge University Press, 1985), pp. 134–151.

21. For example, "five phases" theory explains and makes predictions about a variety of medical, political, and historical phenomena.

22. For example, how would *Dao xue* doctrines account for the efficacy of antibiotics?

23. See, for instance, Alasdair MacIntyre, *After Virtue*, 2d ed. (IN: University of Notre Dame Press, 1984), and Martha Nussbaum, "Non-Relative Virtues: An Aristotelian

Approach," in *Ethical Theory: Character and Virtue*, Peter French, Theodore Uehling, Jr., and Howard Wettstein, eds., vol. 13 of *Midwest Studies in Philosophy* (IN: University of Notre Dame Press, 1988), pp. 32–53.

24. It is not obvious how to treat *Dao xue* as a pure metaphysics. Consequently, my comments will only be speculation about one possible reformulation of *Dao xue* metaphysics.

25. There are other paradigmatic sets as well, including the trigrams and hexagrams of the *Yi Jing*. I think these are actually less important for mature *Dao xue*, though.

26. It is perhaps worth pointing out that this is pluralistic and particularistic, not relativistic. On the distinction, see Isaiah Berlin, "Alleged Relativism in Eighteenth-Century Thought," in *The Crooked Timber of Humanity* (New York: Knopf: Random House, 1991). The distinction between relativism versus pluralism and particularism helps to understand many aspects of *Dao xue*.

27. Zhu Xi explicitly states that one can identify the Confucian virtues in an inkbrush, although he admits that it would be difficult to do so. See *Zhuzi yulei* (Zhonghua shuju ed.), 61:12–13. Forgive me for some wild speculation: benevolence is manifested in the traits that make the brush helpful to humans—easy to hold, useful for writing, and so forth. Righteousness is manifested in the traits that make the brush maintain its own integrity—its resistance to destruction and deformation by outside influences, and so forth. Wisdom is manifested in the brush's appropriate responsiveness to its environment—the way the bristles bend just enough in response to pressure, and so forth. Propriety is manifested in the ornamental aspects of the brush—coloring or inlay on the handle, and so forth.

28. I shall make passing reference to some of these Western discussions. Still, I submit that, at the least, discussions of ethical cultivation have become increasingly rare in recent Anglo-American philosophy.

29. This follows from their shared metaphysical assumptions. The *li* is what accounts for the normative structure of the universe, the *li* is completely present in each human, and the human mind either *is* the *li* (according to Wang) or is some sort of composite of *li* and *qi* (according to Zhu Xi).

30. These are sometimes referred to as "the six arts."

31. Daniel K. Gardner, trans., *Learning to Be a Sage* (Berkeley: University of California Press, 1990), pp. 88–89. Citing Zhu Xi's Preface to the *Greater Learning*.

32. I think there is a nontrivial similarity to Aristotle's view that we must be raised with the right habits in order to be able to benefit from ethical philosophy. See Myles Burnyeat, "Aristotle on Learning to Be Good," in *Essays on Aristotle's Ethics*, A. O. Rorty, ed. (Berkeley: University of California Press, 1980), pp. 69–72. This is not to deny that there are also many, highly significant dissimilarities between the ethics of Aristotle and that of Zhu Xi.

33. Keep in mind, though, my earlier remarks on the limitations of language in expressing the *li*. Zhu Xi would agree that no verbal formulation could be *fully* adequate

to every context. Nonetheless, as we shall see, it distinguishes Zhu Xi from the School of Mind philosophers that he regards the texts of the classics as having significant applicability outside of their original contexts.

34. This is interestingly similar to what Alasdair MacIntyre describes as the Augustinean approach to education. See Alasdair MacIntyre, *Three Rival Versions of Moral Enquiry* (IN: University of Notre Dame Press, 1990), pp. 82–85.

35. Chan, *Source Book*, p. 584 (translation slightly modified, but ellipsis in Chan). Citing *Xiangshan quanji*, juan 35.

36. Translation by Edward Slingerland, *Readings*, p. 3 (gloss added). Slingerland's translation of *wen* as "cultural arts" is presumably influenced by Zhu Xi's commentary, where he says " '*Wen*' means the *Odes*, the *Documents*, and the six arts" (*Lunyu jizhu*). (See Zhu Xi's comments on the lesser learning, quoted above, for "the six arts.")

37. *Daxue, jing*. (Translation by Van Norden.)

38. *Lunyu jizhu*, commenting on *Analects*, 1.6. (Translation by Van Norden.)

39. *Xiangshan quanji, juan* 34. (Translation by Van Norden.) Cf. Chan, *Source Book*, p. 580.

40. *Xiangshan quanji, juan* 32. (Translation by Van Norden. Lu's quotations are from *Mengzi* 6A15 and 6A6.) Cf. Chan, *Source Book*, p. 580.

41. David S. Nivison has pointed out that Wang's position has certain affinities with the denial of *akrasia* found in some Western philosophers. See David S. Nivison, "Two Roots of One?" and "The Philosophy of Wang Yangming," in *The Ways of Confucianism* (Chicago: Open Court Press, 1996).

42. Translation modified from Chan, *Source Book*, p. 669. Citing *Chuan xi lu* (Sibu congkan ed.), 1:5b–8a.

43. My example is not gratuitous. The Chinese phrase Wang quotes from the *Greater Learning*, "lovely sight," *hao se* suggests something sexually attractive. Cf. the use of the expression *hao se* "fond of sex," in *Mencius* 1B5.

44. Chan, *Source Book*, p. 670. Citing 1:5b–8a.

45. Gardner, *Learning to Be a Sage*, p. 116. Citing *Zhuzi yulei* (Zhonghua shuju ed.), 148:4.

46. *Zhuzi yulei* 3:8–10. (Translation by Van Norden.)

47. Gardner, *Learning to Be a Sage*, p. 129. Citing 162:8.

48. This is generally the sense that *wu* has as a technical term in Chinese philosophy. Although "nonbeing" is often used as a translation of it, I think that this English phrase has very different connotations and philosophical resonances from "not-having" concrete qualities.

49. Translation significantly modified from Chan, *Source Book*, p. 578. Citing 2:9a–b.

50. Translation significantly modified from Chan, *Source Book*, p. 580. Citing 34:1a.

51. Translation modified from Chan, *Source Book*, p. 580. Citing 34:1b.

52. Martha Nussbaum has recently argued in great detail for the capacity of novels to be ethically transformative. See, for example, Martha Nussbaum, *Love's Knowledge: Essays on Philosophy and Literature* (New York: Oxford University Press, 1990).

PART TWO

BRINGING CHINESE PHILOSOPHY INTO THE GLOBAL DISCOURSE

CONTRASTING CONFUCIAN VIRTUE ETHICS AND MACINTYRE'S ARISTOTELIAN VIRTUE THEORY

Wan Junren

Translated by Edward Slingerland

In an interview with the British magazine *Cogito*, Professor Alasdair MacIntyre posed three thought-provoking questions: "What is our common inheritance from our common past? What should we have learned from our shared experience to value in it? and What in it is open to criticism and requires remaking?"[1] Answering these questions happens to involve making reference to the three core concepts (in MacIntyre's philosophical theory) of "tradition," "practice," and "community," and this explanation also happens to be the key to comprehending MacIntyre's virtue theory. I would now like to try to analyze the inner workings of Confucian virtue ethics by relying upon this group of concepts. Here we must note that I am using the term "Confucian virtue ethics" rather than Professor MacIntyre's customary "virtue theory" because, as MacIntyre has repeatedly charged, Confucius—the founder of Confucianism—left little room for any form of theorization, and even in later Song-Ming neo-Confucianism, this relative lack of theoretical orientation remained fundamentally unchanged.[2] I think that this assertion of MacIntyre's is based upon the standard of Western logical epistemology, such as Aristotle's *Posterior Analytics*. Although I myself have raised similar criticisms of traditional Confucian ethics over the past decade,[3] I no longer maintain that this criticism is valid. This is because this issue involves fundamental contextual differences between the thought and culture of the West and of China, which means that it is very difficult to use the epistemological standards of one side to call into question the rationality of the other side's ethical model. (This seems to accord with MacIntyre's idea of "incommensurability").

123

This being said, for the sake of argumentation, I am willing to continue to assume the validity of MacIntyre's charge for the purposes of this discussion.

THE INDIVIDUAL AND HUMAN RELATIONSHIPS: A DIFFERENT VIEW OF THE CONCEPT OF VIRTUE

According to the classic definition of the Aristotelian conception of *arete* or "virtue," virtue involves "a character (*pinzhi*) that causes a person to become good while also achieving excellent results."[4] Without understanding the context and practice background of the specific sense of this term of Aristotle's, it would be very easy for Chinese readers to form the following impression: Aristotle's *arete* seems very similar to the "morality" (*daode*) spoken of by such pre-Qin Confucians as Mencius and Xunzi, to the "virtue" (*de*) of the Confucian "gentleman" (*junzi*) (as in "the virtue of the gentleman is like the wind"—*Analects*, 12.19), or to the character of a sage or worthy. However, it is precisely here that a problem is introduced. In the works of Aristotle—or even the earlier products of the "Heroic Age" (such as the epic poems of Homer or the works of Pericles and Solon) or the later works of Socrates and Plato—a bearer of *arete* is already clearly an individual with a concrete, defined social role, which is to say a particularized or individualized civil individual. Therefore, virtue is always concrete and related to the function of the particular role of the individual or to the realization or perfection of the goals appropriate to that role. In this sense, virtue represents either the full consummation of a particular behavioral practice, or the outstanding excellence of the particular character manifested in action that leads to such consummation. The virtue of wisdom belongs to the person with "rational virtue" (*he arete dianoetike*), whereas the virtue of courage belongs to the type of heroic person who is not only naturally gifted with great physical strength, but who also is able to manifest courage in battle, while at the same time using his splendid martial achievements or heroic exploits to display this great state of character. The key to the concept of *arete* lies in the consummation of individual social practice or the realization of an end. It is for this reason that Socrates stands firm in the face of the temptation to escape from legal punishment and accepts with equanimity a sentence that he himself viewed as unjust. This may seem to be a sort of paradox—a type of tragic situation involving a tension or conflict between just beliefs and an unjust fate—but in fact what is embodied in this story is precisely the virtue of holding to justice displayed in Socrates' practical action of personally accepting a tragic fate. Socrates' entire life thus bears witness to his personal commitment to civil justice.

In traditional Confucian ethics, however, a different understanding of the virtuous person and the practice of virtue leads to fundamental differences in the conception of virtue. In other words, different definitions of the conception of the virtuous person (the bearer of virtue) create a difference in explanatory context.

While we cannot say that Confucian ethics lacks a clear conception of the "person" (*geren*), a survey of the relevant texts and secondary literature does show that Confucian ethics clearly lacks the sort of independent, substantial entity called the "individual" (*geti*) that we find in Aristotle or in Western ethics as a whole. More specifically, the concept of the "person" in traditional Confucian ethics has two aspects, depending upon whether we look at it from the angle of "absence" (*xu*) or "presence" (*shi*).[5] As for its absence, the concept of "person" does not and has never involved the explicit and clear demarcation of an independently existing entity. Therefore, when Confucianism discusses such concepts as "I" (*wo*), "self" (*ziwo*), or "myself" (*benren*), the context is always relative and nonsubstantial. This is rather similar to the concept that MacIntyre has introduced in a recent publication of human beings as "dependent rational animals."[6] However, looked at from another angle, the concept of the "person" in Confucian ethics does possess a certain degree of substantiality and reality. This element of presence lies in the fact that people themselves almost inevitably find themselves involved in a relationship of "inner" and "outer." With regard to the inner, a person's virtuousness can only be manifested through internal transformation of his conscious moral character and the soul-based pursuit of spiritual "cultivation" or the transformation of the soul. With regard to the outer, a person's virtuousness can only be developed through multiple layers and dimensions of human relations or ethics. Without the medium of ethics or human relations, we cannot speak of a person being virtuous. Therefore, Confucian virtue ethics is first and foremost a matter of the practice of coordination of obligatory norms within the realm of social relationships, as well as the internalization of these norms, rather than the perfection of the inherent value of an independent individual's ends or the realization of such an end.

Let us now discuss more concretely these two aspects of the Confucian conception of the person within the context of traditional Confucian ethics. It is a generally accepted view in the Chinese scholarly world that traditional Confucian ethics has its start in Confucius' "doctrine of humanity (*ren*)."[7] With his doctrine of humanity, Confucius continued an inheritance from the *Zhou Rites* while at the same time creating his own system of virtue ethics. Examining its historical content, the concept of virtue in the Western Zhou period was really expressed in terms of "filial piety" and "humanity," both of which served as the basic standards for evaluating the degree of virtuousness displayed in any given human action. While both of these concepts were of course directly tied to the establishment and central significance of contemporary patriarchal kinship and patriarchal clan institutions, they nonetheless constitute a type of virtue or social ethic, or a requirement for political order. In this respect, filial piety and humanity must both be put in the context of actual human relations if they are to be spoken of or given expression to. It is for this reason that Hou Wailu notes that, "'filial piety and virtue' served as the 'moral guidelines' for the Western Zhou period."[8] Although neither of these concepts—tied up as they were with contemporary

understandings of religious and political orders—possessed a purely moral character at this point in history, they must nevertheless undoubtedly be ranked in
value above such externally institutionalized ethical norms as "ritual propriety"
and "rightness" (*yi*).

The two characteristics mentioned above are fully manifested in the virtue
ethics of Confucius. In his thought, the ethics of "filial piety" have already been
included within the general concept of "humanity," and the normative prece-
dence of humanity over rituals is displayed even more clearly and prominently.
Although compared to the slightly later thinker Mencius, Confucius still preserves a sort of harmony and balance between humanity and ritual—and does
not, like Mencius, clearly elevate humanity over ritual[9]—we nonetheless find in
the *Analects* as many as one hundred and nine mentions of humanity, compared
to only a few mentions of ritual. This clearly illustrates where the central focus
of Confucius' entire ethics is to be found.

In this respect, Confucian virtue ethics actually seems to be expressing a kind
of humanity-virtue ethics, in that the core category of "humanity" has the function of governing the other varieties of virtue. In analyzing the meaning of the
text of the *Analects*, we can see that "humanity," as Confucius uses it has at least
three distinct senses: (1) representing the highest moral value or state of virtue
[as in *Analects*, 4.2, "the humane person is at ease in humanity, while the wise
person sees the benefit of humanity"]; (2) representing a moral evaluation of
someone [as in *Analects*, 18.1, "There were three humane people during the Yin
Dynasty"]; and (3) as a synonym for "human being" [as in *Analects*, 4.7, "by
observing where someone goes astray, you can thereby know their character
(*ren*)"[10]]. However, the fact that Confucius' concept of "humanity" can encompass several different meanings does not interfere with its ability to serve as a
general term for virtue.

To begin with, humanity, or the virtue of humanity represents the cumulative
embodiment of ethical morality in all human relationships. Confucius' humanity is not abstract, but is rather concretely embodied in various forms of interpersonal ethical relationships. In the thought of Confucius as well as the entire
Confucian ethical tradition, the patriarchal kinship relationships are the most
basic and important of ethical relationships. The virtue of humanity is concretely
manifested as the "kindness of a father," "filial piety of a son," "friendship of an
older brother," or "obedience of a younger brother." These represent Confucius'
humanity in the sense of "loving one's family," and are seen as the moral root
or "origin" (*arche*) of the "humane person"—that is, the person possessing the
virtue of humanity. As Youzi, a disciple of Confucius, explains: "The gentleman
applies himself to the roots. Once the roots are firmly planted, the Way will
grow. Might we thus say that filiality and brotherly respect represent the root of
ren?" (*Analects*, 1.2). In the words of Confucius himself: "If the gentleman is
kind to his relatives, the common people will be inspired toward humanity"
(*Analects*, 8.2). Later, Mencius will define it more explicitly: "loving one's parents

is humanity" (*Mencius*, 7A15), or "the substance of humanity is serving one's parents" (*Mencius*, 4A27). The basic meaning of "loving one's parents" or "serving one's parents" is "loving one's family." Because in Confucius' view these types of blood relations are affinity relations that still possess a strong degree of "superior-inferior" social hierarchy (*shangxia zunbei*),, "filial piety" is seen as the most basic and important ethical virtue.

Nonetheless, Confucius' virtue of humanity by no means represents a virtue of parochial relationships. It is an open virtue that can be broadened to include an "expansive care for the multitude," which involves an extension from loving one's family to loving other people. Responding to his disciple Fan Chi's question, "What is humanity?" Confucius declares, "loving others" (*Analects*, 12.22). In Confucius' view, "loving others" can be expressed in two basic ways. In its negative sense, "loving others" refers to the way of treating others with liberalness. In *Analects*, 12.2 we read:

> Zhong Gong asked about humanity. The Master said, "When in public, comport yourself as if you were receiving an important guest; in your management of the common people, behave as if you were overseeing a great sacrifice. Do not impose upon others what you yourself do not desire. In this way, you will encounter no resentment in your state or in your family."

In its positive sense, "loving others" refers to the way of loyalty and devotion: "Desiring to take his stand, one who is humane helps others to take their stand; wanting to realize himself, he helps others to realize themselves" (*Analects*, 6.30). Later Song dynasty Confucians explained it as "extending oneself to reach others" (*tuiji jiren*), and believed that, since all people shared this heart and that all hearts contained this principle, all people could therefore achieve humanity. The two aspects of the "love of humanity" together represent what Confucius called the "method of humanity" (6.30) or the "one thread" of "the Way of loyalty and sympathetic understanding (*zhongshu*)" (*Analects*, 4.15) that he continually emphasized.

Worth considering here is whether or not Confucius, in taking humanity or the love of humanity as his basic virtue ("the Way of the gentleman"), has taken his doctrine of humanity outside of the scope of virtue ethics. Is it perhaps simply a type of patriarchal kinship-oriented normative ethics? The process of answering this question brings to light another question, one that has not been carefully considered for a long time. How does the virtue ethics of Confucius or even the entire Confucian tradition—assuming, of course, that we can even speak of the existence of such a virtue ethic—understand the virtue of humanity? Are we to see its explanatory context as the practical action of the moral person or the normative significance of ethical relationships?

In contrast to Aristotle (or even the Western ethical traditional as a whole), the focus of the virtue ethics of Confucius or traditional Confucianism is the relational context of personal virtue practice. The primary reason for this is that Confucius and the Confucian tradition lack the kind of concept of the "person" or "individual" as an entity or bearer of rights (as an end) that we find in Western moral culture, and have instead only the concept of a "person" in the context of a certain relationship, as the bearer of particular duty, or as a "moral personality" serving as an ideal type for moral character. In the early stages of Chinese civilization, it is very rare to find reference to a decontextualized single person or single man. A person could be talked about through the invocation of their family or personal name, but it is very rare to find discussion of a "single man" divorced from family or personal name. In the "Duke Ai, Year 16" chapter of the *Zuo Zhuan*, we read that when Confucius passed away, Duke Ai of Lu referred to himself as "I, the single man" in his eulogy. For this he was re-proached by Zigong, disciple of Confucius, who reminded him that he was merely a feudal lord, and therefore had no right to usurp the appellation of "single man," which is properly the prerogative of the Son of Heaven. The later [*White Tiger Tong (haopian)*] explains: "When a king refers to himself as a single man, it is an expression of humility . . . what right does a vassal have to call himself a single man? This term is also a means by which the king is honored." Thus, we can see that referring to oneself as a "single man" in ancient China represented not only a serious moral issue, but also an extremely serious political issue. This degree of moral and political seriousness is consistent with the im-portance the ancient Chinese put upon recognition of the strictly hierarchical order of human and interpersonal relationships. To speak of oneself as an iso-lated, single person represents a potential violation of governmental regulations as well as egregiously unethical behavior.[11]

This gives rise to an interesting contrast. In the virtue ethics of Confucius and the Confucian tradition, the understanding of human or interpersonal relation-ships often reveals a form of paradox or contradiction: on the one hand, Confucius and the Confucian tradition emphasize the hierarchical nature of human rela-tionships and the absolute legitimacy of this hierarchy ("Only the most wise and the most stupid do not change"—*Analects,* 17.3)—a fact that does not sit well with the ideas and values of modern egalitarianism. On the other hand, however, within this hierarchical order, the structure of interpersonal relationships is marked by the sort of relational character found in the "intersubjectivity" of Martin Buber's "I-Thou" relationship.[12] Because the moral relationship in the "I-Thou" structure is one of reciprocity—the so-called Way of loyalty and sympathetic understanding (*Analects,* 4.15), or the meeting of minds and sharing of spirits (as it is said, "all people have this heart, and all hearts have this principle")—the virtue of humanity in the virtue ethics of Confucius and the Confucian tradition is a relational virtue that always possesses an interactive quality. The action or attitude of either given party involved in a relationship may become the reason for the action or attitude of the other party. In other words, the conditions for the realization of humanity are interactive and not a matter of purely individual practice. Moreover, the moral significance found in virtue itself is primarily ethical and deontic, and not related to normative ends.

Therefore, one must note that the central specific virtues (such as benevolence, righteousness, loyalty, filial piety, ritual propriety, etc.) of Confucius and the Confucian tradition can be classified as coordinated, human-relational virtues, whereas other virtues such as wisdom, courage, and the qualities especially pointed out by Confucius of "respectfulness, broad-mindedness, trustworthiness, diligence and generosity"[13] are all relegated to a secondary or subordinate status. From this we can see that Confucius emphasized more the interdependent virtues of human relationships, such as the righteousness of the ruler and loyalty of the minister, kindness of the father and filial piety of the son, fraternity of the elder brother and respect of the younger brother, and "the Way of loyalty and sympathetic understanding." We can thus say that, for Confucius and the Confucian tradition, it is not possible to speak of virtue outside of the context of human relationships and the ritual order of the patriarchal clan.

It is in this respect that Confucian ethics seems to contrast most strikingly with Aristotle's eudaemonism. Of course, the latter also emphasizes the significance of historic tradition and community (the city-state) as a prerequisite and precondition for the practice of individual virtue. Just as Professor MacIntyre has perceived, the practice of virtue is unthinkable apart from or outside of the individual's particular community and the traditional sources that he or she has inherited.[14] Nonetheless, these indispensable factors possess only *theoretical significance as part of the necessary explanatory context* for a given virtue ethic— they do not themselves *constitute the practice of virtue itself.* To put this more concretely, although both Confucius and the Confucian tradition and Aristotle and MacIntyre's Aristotelianism are of the opinion that the practice conditions, background, and evaluation of virtue is social in nature, it is nonetheless the case that, in the ethical conception of the former, the subject's practice of virtue can only be realized in the context of interactive human relations that are expressed in the sort of particular, interactive actions that constitute a "person to person" or (as Martin Buber puts it) "I and Thou" relationship. On the contrary, in the ethical conception of the latter, the virtue practice of the subject can only be personal or individual, unless what we are talking about is a kind of universal "social virtue." For instance, the virtue of wisdom belongs to *anyone* who possesses "rational virtue," the virtue of courage belongs to *anyone* who is a valorous and skillful *warrior*, and the virtue of temperateness or restraint belongs to *anyone* who is a law-abiding and obedient citizen. It is precisely for this reason that, for Confucius and the Confucian tradition, although the motivation for achieving virtuous action comes from oneself ("humanity comes from oneself"— *Analects,* 12.1), the actual successful practice or realization of virtue itself is related to other people. For this reason the deontological dimension of virtue is the most important and fundamental. In the opinion of Aristotle, on the other hand, not only does the motivation for achieving virtue comes from oneself, but also the actual practice of virtue is an individual, spontaneous undertaking, and thus is distinctly focused upon achieving the ends of an individual human life (happiness or goodness). For this reason, it is the teleological dimension of virtue that is most fundamental and ultimate for Aristotle.

There are many potential explanations for the differences and contrasts between the conceptions of the virtuous person in the Confucian and Aristotelian traditions, but in my view the crucial factor is the difference between the two traditions with regard to basic social structure (including politics, economics, and culture). In recognizing this point, it might seem that both Professor MacIntyre and myself have accepted the basic viewpoint of Marxism, and that MacIntyre has simply not been consistent or firm enough in applying Marxism to the comparison of Confucian virtue ethics and Aristotelianism. In fact, the extremely significant differences in the societies and cultures in which Confucius and Aristotle lived, along with the accompanying differences with regard to cultural resources and prestige, understanding of moral values, and linguistic structures and forms of discourse—including the variations in modes of moral reasoning and moral argumentation that such cultural factors engendered—are so internally consistent within each tradition as to suggest that they each arose sui generis. The age in which Confucius lived and the cultural resources upon which he depended—and we can extend this really to include all of traditional Chinese society—were from the beginning characterized by a lack of distinction between human relations (the ethical order) and heavenly relations (the natural order) and an identity between the ethical and political. As a consequence, kinship relations or spontaneous affinity were both seen as natural (heavenly) (*tianran*),[15] endowed with a kind of innate, immutable, and inviolable sanctity. This quality of naturalness in turn served as the most important and decisive premise for understanding all human events, behavior and interpersonal relationships.

One often hears complaints that such traditional Chinese conceptions as the identical structures of the family and state, the synonymous meanings of political loyalty and filial piety, and the unity of the natural (heavenly) and the human are overly ambiguous or unclear. In fact, it is precisely these conceptions that are as the natural expressions of the distinctive, native features of this type of culture. Therefore, considering this lack of clear distinction between the natural (heavenly) and human,[16] or the state and the family, we should see the naturalization of human relations and the impersonalization of the conception of the virtuous person as inevitable cultural products. The naturalization of human relations gives prominence to the status of kinship, which then serves as the *arche* or archetype of all interpersonal and social relationships. In this type of ethicized social and political structure,[17] it is not only impossible to form the kind of conception of "citizen" found in ancient Greek political theory, but even impossible to conceive of a Western-style "individual" bearing rights and constituting its own *telos*. Consequently, it is only with the general concept of "human relations" or the "single man" as the ruler of the myriad people—and never with an independent person or individual citizen—that we find a sense of an actual entity or substance being implied. This is perhaps the fundamental reason that "individualism is completely alien to traditional Chinese culture (including Confucian moral culture)."[18] Is this fortunate or unfortunate? In the end, this really depends upon one's perspective.

"ACHIEVEMENT" AND BECOMING A "PERFECTED PERSON" (CHENGREN)

Different Perspectives on Standards for Evaluating Virtue

Differences of understanding concerning the concept of the virtuous person directly give rise to dissimilar views of concerning the normative value and ends of virtue practice in Confucian and Aristotelian virtue ethics. Of course, such differences do not imply a complete divergence of opinion on these subjects, but, in this section, we are going to focus upon discussing the points of disagreement.

The virtue ethics of Confucius and the Confucian tradition can be classified as a type of coordinated virtue ethics located in human relationships. This is not only because most of its categories of virtue refer to role-specific virtues understood in terms of human relationships rather than typical individual virtues, but also—and more importantly—because this type of virtue ethic has its own distinctive standard for the evaluation of virtue. That is to say, virtue is neither viewed as a type of purely individual moral event, nor is the standards for virtue evaluation limited to considerations of the teleological value of virtuous action. On the contrary, the belief is that it is the deontological dimension of virtue that is the most fundamental and important, and that this deontological dimension serves as the ultimate evaluative standard for judging whether or not a person possesses virtue.

As a consequence, the first and most crucial task for this type of virtue ethic is to clarify the structural priority of various human relationships, to determine the location of the person within this relational structural order, and to identify the status conferred upon the person by virtue of their location within the order. This type of "relational structural order" is not only social in nature (the family and clan serving as its basic unit), but also has an inborn (heavenly), immutable and natural (ziran) quality (patriarchal kinship serving as its primordial relational archetype). In such a "relational structural order," the particular status conferred upon an individual is simultaneously inborn (heavenly) and social, which means that it is both natural and ethical. Regardless of their moral status, no person is able to change or overturn the hierarchical structural order that separates superior from inferior. To put this more concretely, the moral position and ethical dignity of the father is inborn/natural (heavenly) and a priori, and it cannot be altered due to a deficiency in morals or as a result of the moral nobility of his sons or daughters. Of course, *in practice* a completely dissolute or shameless gentleman or a malicious and base father could in the end conceivably forfeit his advantageous moral position and ethical dignity, but, as long as events have not degenerated to an intolerable extent, the preestablished order of human relations and the father's ethical position cannot be altered. Hence, Confucius' injunction, "Let the lord be a [true] lord, the ministers be [true] ministers, the fathers be [true] fathers, and the sons be [true] sons" (*Analects*, 12.11).

Clearly, the "virtue" of traditional Confucianism is a far cry from the standard of virtue in Aristotelianism. Aristotelian virtue has to be put into effect by an individual, for the following reasons:

1. The individual or the self is viewed as the subject in all relationships, which means that the other can be viewed only as an object.

2. As the end in itself of the realization of normative virtue, the individual or self enjoys a predetermined advantage. The end is always discussed as being relative to oneself. Therefore, the relationship between oneself and other or oneself and society is that of ends to means. As for the relationship between human beings and the world: "Man is the measure of all things; of what is, that it is; of what is not, that it is not" (Protagoras). As for the relationship between persons, the "I" or "self" is always prior, serving as the subject in all relationships. To invoke the terminology of Martin Buber, this type of relationship is an "I and Other" (subject-object) relationship, not an "I and Thou" (subject-subject) relationship.

3. Regardless of whether we are talking about a relationship between person and person or an individual and the social group, the person or individual both possess the status of an existing entity or noumenon of value—something that will not be substantially altered as a result of any form of relational restriction.

4. As a result of this consciousness of the distinction of human beings and social relationships, virtue is separately categorized as belonging to either the civil person as member of society or social community or the social community itself, which results in the formation of a sharp distinction between personal virtue and social virtue. This is to say that virtue in this understanding is for the most part seen as a social role-based, particularized and disassociated attribute, rather than a role-specific or relational virtue situated in a network of human relations.

In contrast to what we have just described, in traditional Confucian virtue ethics:

1. The person is, from beginning to end, seen as a mutually dependent subject located in human relations. In other words, both parties in the relationship enjoy the characteristics or status of being a subject.

2. Therefore, with regard to both parties in the relationship, the most important significance of virtue is not be found in the independent, autonomous ends of either party, but rather in reciprocal deontic norms.

3. As a consequence of this, the manifestation of normative virtue is primarily realized through the evaluation of one's relational partner or others. The manner in which one's relational partner or others evaluate oneself is thus an extremely important and essential consideration. To express this is in a common Chinese idiom, this is referred to as "caring about the opinion of others" (*zaihu bieren*).

4. Finally, because "relation" is elevated above "existence," a person located in human relations does not enjoy the status of an independent entity or a noumenon of value, but rather possesses only deontic significance in a relative or mutually reciprocal manner.

   This type of ethical consciousness that celebrates the priority of "relationship" represents a kind of consciousness of interrelation rather than differentiation, and has had a direct influence on the incomplete level of social differentiation or socialization in traditional China and the weakness of personal civil consciousness. This consciousness of interrelatedness or dependence has from the very beginning occupied a dominant place in the conceptual life of the Chinese people.

Nonetheless, the above discussion of contrasts between the two traditions is not meant to imply that traditional Confucianism lacks a sufficiently rigorous conception of personal virtue ethics. On the contrary, these contrasts show that the Confucian conception of virtue ethics possesses its own unique characteristic. Namely, in contrast to the differentiating consciousness of the ancient Greeks (or even Westerners in general), who classified virtue into the separate categories of individual and social virtue, the emphasis of Confucian virtue ethics is upon autonomous internalization and heteronomous externalization. This means that effort needs to be exerted upon both extremes—internal and external—of the human being. With regard to the inner realm of oneself, the emphasis is upon cultivation and reformation of one's heart/mind (*xin*)[19] in pursuit of the moral goal of "gentleman" (*junzi*) status. This represents a type of inner virtue of the heart/mind. With regard to the external realm of other people, the emphasis is upon the performance of actions for the sake of others and the realization of external values in pursuit of the moral eminence of the "worthy" (*xian*) or "sage" (*sheng*) status. This dual nature of the Confucian project is the reference of the saying, "internally get it within yourself, externally get it from others," and achieving a consistency between the internal and external realms is what it means to become a "perfected person" (*chengren*) or to "perfect humanity."

In the virtue ethics of Confucius and the Confucian tradition, "perfected virtue" is identified with the "perfected person," while at the same time serving as the fundamental precondition for someone becoming a perfected person. In his response to a question from his disciple Zilu, Confucius attempted to convey the essence of being a perfected person through a series of examples, and concluded by saying: "When seeing a chance for profit he thinks of what is right (*yi*); when confronting danger he is ready to take his life into his own hands; when enduring an extended period of hardship, he does not forget what he had professed in more fortunate times—such a man might also be called a complete person" (*Analects*, 14.12). The later Confucian thinker Xunzi elaborated on this sentiment, explaining: "After making your virtue constant you can be firm of purpose, and after becoming firm of purpose, you are able to be responsive to things . . . this is what is called being the 'perfected person'" (*Xunzi*, "Encouraging Learning"). This once again bears testament to the identity of "human beings" and "humanity" or "perfected virtue" and "perfected humanity" / "perfected person" in the Confucian moral perspective. Mencius saw morality as that which distinguishes human beings from the beasts and as the fundamental standard for what it means to be human, which in fact simply represents pushing this Confucian moral perspective to its logical conclusion.

Thus, we can see that, from the perspective of traditional Confucian virtue ethics, perfecting virtue and perfecting humanity are fundamentally related to becoming a perfected person, which means that the pursuit of virtue is nothing other than the effort to become a true person. In the words of Confucius, such a "true person" is referred to as the "person of humanity" or "gentleman," whereas Mencius refers to him as the "great man." The aim of such a person's life does not lay in pursuing the sort of specialized craft or skill that would result in material achievement or "happiness." The possession of skills such as eloquence, martial courage, and craftsmanship is thus not a necessary prerequisite to becoming a perfected person or for perfecting humanity,[20] but on the contrary simply represents an inevitable result of having achieved the status of a perfected person. Therefore, the first and primary task for a person hoping to possess virtue is to forge his or her moral character and cultivate a personal, internal virtuous nature, rather than to externally pursue any kind of technical perfection or realization of material end. The character of Confucius' "gentleman" demands that one abandon profit and instead seek after rightness and reject considerations of material benefit in order to preserve one's humanity. As we read in the *Analects*, "the gentleman admires rightness most of all" (17.23), "the gentleman takes rightness as his substance" (15.18), and "the gentleman understands what is right, while the petty man understands what is profitable" (4.16). Later, Mencius explains this idea more concretely in a description of his exemplar of moral character, the "great man": "wealth and honor cannot corrupt him, poverty and disgrace do not move him, and he remains uncowed by displays of social or military force" (*Mencius*, 3B2).

The emphasis with this idea of the perfected person or perfected virtue is upon the internal "substance" of virtue and not upon its external "form," which also means that the acquisition of virtue is a matter of subjective initiative and represents a spiritual process. From this, it is not difficult to see that, from the Confucian perspective, the practice and acquisition of virtue is first and foremost a matter of "exerting effort internally"—that is, searching for it in one's heart/ mind. All that is necessary is for one to first internally "go after the lost heart/ mind" (*Mencius*, 6A11), and only after this has been accomplished can one expand this heart/mind into the external realm. This is the point of the saying: "Simply make yourself good, and in this way you may save the entire world." Professor Tu Wei-ming has summarized the Confucian practice of self-cultivation in a diagram involving concentric circles, portraying it as a continuous process of extension from the inside to the outside: the self (mind) —> family —> community —> state —> world —> beyond. This portrayal thoroughly illustrates the moral-spiritual initiative involved in "selfhood as creative transformation."[21] The diagram itself portrays part of the scheme of self-cultivation presented in the *Great Learning*.[22] According to *The Great Learning*:

> In ancient times, those who wished to manifest their bright virtue in the world first brought order to their states. Those who wished to bring order to their states first regulated their families. Those who wished to regulate their families first cultivated themselves. Those who wished to cultivate themselves first rectified their heart/minds. Those who wished to rectify their heart/minds first made their intentions sincere. Those who wished to make their intentions sincere first extended their knowledge. Extending one's knowledge requires the investigation of things (*gewu*).[23] Investigate things, and then your knowledge will be extended. Once your knowledge is extended your intention will be sincere. Once your intention is sincere your heart/mind will be rectified. Once your heart/mind is rectified your self will be cultivated. Once your self is cultivated, your family will be regulated. Once your family is regulated, your state will be ordered. Once your state is ordered, the whole world will be at peace.

This schematic portrayal of Confucian virtue practice still manages to convey the Confucian ethical spirit: the unity of wisdom and virtue, the blending of substance and function, and the mutual communication of inner and outer. In this way it preserves the dimension of personal inner teleology in Confucian virtue ethics, while at the same time restricting this teleological dimension to the realm of ethical deontology, since it views the results of virtuous practical action as merely the externalized manifestation of personal, internal, mental virtue in different moral environments (family, state, the world) and as representing the ethical realization process of a person becoming a "perfected person," rather than the realization of some merely personal end. Therefore, the key to self-cultivation is to be found in the molding of innate moral character in accordance with ethical requirements (loyalty, filiality, humanity, rightness, etc.) rather than in the realization of some individual's personal end. "Success in affairs," or the realization of substantial value, is certainly necessary for the perfection of personal virtue, but such success has the normative value of a mere side effect. It is only internal, purely mental perfection that is absolutely necessary. In this way, the end of virtue is understood in terms of the spiritual state of one's own mind rather than the external completion of any type of particular practice. The moral end of ethical-spiritual pursuit can thus from the very beginning only be displayed within the context of a complex and ordered system of human relations. Therefore, internal virtue teleology and externalized ethical deontology are so tightly interwoven that they can never be understood separately, and the appropriateness and degree of perfection of moral ends is ultimately judged by the normative standard of ethical deontology.

In the Aristotelian ethical tradition—or even the Western ethical tradition as a whole—*telos* or "end" has the sense of "end state" or "finality." To put this more simply, to "end" means to finish, complete or perfect. For this reason, moral teleology is always linked to normative consequences or consequentialism. In contrast, within the explanatory framework of Confucian virtue ethics, moral teleology and normative consequentialism can be rationally separated. The basic approach is to understand the moral end itself in terms of pure moral internalism or nonmaterialistic ethical deontology. In the Confucian viewpoint, the fact that "human being" is equivalent to the virtue of "humanity" means that the fundamental nature of human beings is a type of ethical nature, and moral ethics is thus based upon making a person into a true person or "person of humanity." This conception differs significantly from Aristotle's explanation of human basic substance in terms of "practice" or "social practice" in two primary ways. To begin with, the Confucian conception of human nature is ethical, and can only be clarified in terms of an explanatory context of particular human relations. This point has already been explained many times above. Second, the Confucian conception of human nature is dynamic, and can only be explained by means of the concrete process of becoming a "perfected person." Human nature is thus something that is gradually nurtured during the process of becoming a perfected person. This means that any explanation of human nature based upon a form of substantialism will prove inappropriate when applied to the Confucian conception of human nature.

Because Confucian virtue ethics is focused upon the practical step of "self-cultivation," one's personal, interior self-cultivation is the key to virtue practice and the essential precondition for one becoming a "perfected person." When Confucius says that "humanity comes from oneself" (*Analects*, 12.1) or "if I merely desire humanity, I will find that humanity is already here" (*Analects*, 7.30), he is clearly viewing the personal self as the subject initiating the process of perfecting humanity or becoming a perfected person. The *Great Learning*, a later Confucian classic, also highlights the function of internal moral cultivation performed by "being watchful even when alone" (*shenqidu*). At this point, it is not difficult to see that the basic normative goal of Confucian virtue ethics lies in the overall establishment of morality in one's life—in the fundamental perfection of the ethical person or "person of humanity"—rather than in any kind of concrete achievement of practical success. This goal is moral in nature because its ultimate realization is necessarily and solely dependent upon personal moral consciousness and the practice of moral cultivation. It is at the same time ethical, because the end of personal moral practice and the objective confirmation of its normative realization are necessarily and solely attainable only in the context of particular human relationships. The goal of becoming a perfected person is not to obtain worldly success, status or renown, nor to confirm one's social standing or role through excellence in worldly affairs. Rather, the goal is to cultivate one's moral character and confirm one's status in the context of human relationships through the performance of deontic duties. The standard for determining whether or not one is a "perfected person" is not based upon external effects brought about by one's actions, but is instead based upon the possession of an internal character capable of governing ethical actions. To put this in another way, the realization of personal moral ends can only be accomplished through the cultivation of personal moral character and the assumption of deontic responsibilities. Therefore, becoming a "perfected person" means becoming a "sage" or "worthy," or realizing the virtue of humanity.

In response to our above discussion, Aristotelians might raise two sorts of objections. To begin with, the doctrine of moral character involved in becoming a "sage" is very likely to cause virtue ethics to float in the vacuum of moral idealism, failing as it does to value realistic moral practice. The virtue practice of Aristotle is always grounded in the concrete context of social, communal role-specific practice, and the player of this practice-role is always a substantial individual possessing or endowed with a particular social role or even unusual ability. The "wise person" describes someone with the virtue of wisdom, not a person with courage. Similarly, the maker of a musical instrument or weapon is not required to pursue any excellence or virtue beyond the technical skill required to produce the instrument or weapon (not even a further specified instrument or weapon). Moreover, the standard of whether or not the particular virtue characteristic of a given role has been realized cannot depend upon the self-proclaimed character of the person who fills that role. Whether or not this person truly possesses virtue must be proven by the concrete achievement of his specific obligations. As Aristotle says:

> Just as with other crafts, we can only acquire virtue after first undertaking activating activities. We must first produce the things we wish to learn, for only in the process of producing these things do we learn how to do them. For example, only by building a house do we become builders, and only by playing the harp do we become harpists. . . . Further, just as is the case with crafts, the means by which we produce any virtue is also the means by which we can ruin it.[24]

Aristotle in the same way emphasizes the practical character of virtue. However, he ties the practice of virtue to the action of a person within a particular social role, and makes particular or specialized behavioral ability the basis of virtue practice. For this reason, his standard for the normative evaluation of virtuous behavior possesses both concrete social reality and normative justifiability.

In contrast, Confucianism locates virtue practice in the cultivation of the inner, personal mind. It does not require any type of particular craft activities or other specialized ability, only demanding that one devote oneself body and mind to the task and focus one's entire spirit on the development of the ideal inner character—even to the point of sacrificing one's own bodily life for a deontic principle or moral ideal (as in Confucius' ideal of "sacrificing the self to realize humanity," or Mencius' "giving up one's life for rightness.") Naturally, the normative evaluations of the virtue practice associated with this type of internal transcendent orientation represent first and foremost an ethical deontology rather than a moral teleology. Moreover, because this sort of internally transcendent behavior lacks or consciously rejects the value of practical achievements or success, it is very difficult to objectively and fairly evaluate it. To put this in another way, it lacks an objective moral normative standard that is both outside of the individual and higher than the level of the individual's mind. If we cannot look to a person's achievements or results, how are we to determine whether or not this person has "perfected humanity" or become a "perfected person?" In this respect, it is difficult to avoid the specter of some sort of Eastern moral subjectivism or relativism. More importantly, because the ideal of the "perfected sage" or humane gentleman is so abstruse and far from reality, it is likely to cause a person to be hesitant to undertake it, which makes it something unlikely to be consciously adopted as an ideal in the average person's daily moral life. This is indeed a problem for Confucian virtue ethics. If we are not able to explain it away, the type of Aristotelian objection about Confucian virtue ethics described above might well prove to be justified.

Aristotelianism might also make a second complaint against Confucian virtue ethics, related to the first objection. On the one hand, Confucian virtue ethics advocates the need for the cultivation of inner virtue; while on the other hand it also emphasizes that such virtue practice can be pursued only in the context of human relationships. Is it possible to reconcile this internalist, subjective teleology and externalist, relational deontology? Or does this in fact represent an internal paradox characteristic of Confucian virtue ethics? My answer would be that, if we consider the first complaint by Aristotelianism against Confucianism to be justifiable, then differences in cultural traditions between the plaintiff and the defendant make it difficult to sustain this second charge. The most crucial point to understand is that—as a result of the unique Confucian understanding of the concept of virtue and the bearer of virtue as discussed above—the understanding of the human being and of human nature is always in terms of human relationships. This not only makes it difficult for traditional Confucianism to form a conception of the "individual" as an independent, substantial entity (which makes the normative conceptions of Western individualism that arose from this concept equally alien), but also determines the fact that the Confucian virtue ethical ideal of becoming a "perfected person" is basically nothing other than the ethical, deontological ideal of realizing the virtue of humanity or realizing rightness. For precisely this reason, the aim of Confucian virtue practice is not based upon the achievements of particular personal virtue practice, but rather lies in ethical principles (loyalty, filial piety, humanity, rightness, or humanity, rightness, ritual propriety, wisdom, trustworthiness) and is based upon human relationships. This divergence in the understanding of virtue and its types has its origin in the diversity of cultural traditions. Therefore, something that is considered an internal paradox in one cultural tradition might, from the perspective of another cultural tradition, be viewed instead as a Kuhnian "necessary tension."

"INTELLECTUAL VIRTUE" VERSUS "HUMANITY AND (MOREOVER) WISDOM"

Differences in Methods of Virtue Practice

The inherent relationship between virtue and education is something that, with almost no exceptions, has been viewed as highly important by classical ethical traditions. Whether in traditional Chinese Confucian ethics or ancient Greek virtue theory, education has been seen as the basic model for nourishing virtue and passing it down to the next generation. In his conflation of virtuousness and knowledge, Socrates saw "discourse" as the method for pursuing knowledge and wisdom as well as the educational practice designed to inculcate excellence and virtue. Moreover, the practice of free discourse itself was seen as the basic model of virtue education. Although Socrates' disciple Plato and next-generation disciple Aristotle revised the content of this type of virtue education to varying degrees, this practice of virtue education had nonetheless already become a consistent, unbroken educational tradition. If we see the academies of Plato and Aristotle as the earliest institutionalized forms of this educational tradition, then we can also see Socrates' "discourse" as its origin or source. Aristotle, however, went a step farther by adopting a kind of technologized intellectualism or moral rationalism, moving the practice of virtue-knowledge education from the kingdom of the form of the ultimate good (Plato and Socrates) to the concrete realm of the end (happiness), practice, and realization (achievement) of virtue. In this way, the question of how to realize the end of virtue was also brought to the level of technical rationality (understood as intellectual virtue's "doctrine of the mean"). With the theoretical attitude that "I love my teacher, but I love the truth more," Aristotle criticized Socrates' theoretical tendency to conflate knowledge and virtue. As he put it:

> He (referring to Socrates) makes virtue a kind of knowledge, which is in fact impossible. This is because all knowledge involves reason, and reason is found only

in the intellectual part of the soul. According to his perspective, all of the virtues are to be found in the rational part of the soul. In this way, we can conclude: because he makes virtue a kind of knowledge, he discards the irrational part of the soul, and thereby also discards passions and morals. For this reason, it seems that this way of understanding virtue is incorrect.[25]

This criticism of Aristotle's is based upon his dualistic conceptual presuppositions concerning virtue. In contrast to Socrates' conflation of knowledge and virtue, Aristotle drew a sharp distinction between knowledge and ethics, which is the reason for his declaration that ethical virtue contains within it an irrational component. In Aristotle's view:

> Virtue can be classified into two different types: intellectual virtue (*he arete dianoetike*) and ethical virtue (*he arete ethike*). Intellectual virtue is mostly produced and is nurtured through education, which means that it requires both experience and time. Ethical virtue arises through habituation into cultural norms, which is why the term "ethics" (*ethike*) is derived from an alternate spelling of the word *ethos*. From this it can be seen that there is no ethical virtue that is produced in us naturally. This is because there is no naturally existing thing that can be changed through habituation.[26]

The characteristics of "experience and time" indicate the need for concrete verification and the protracted nature of knowledge acquisition, both of which determine that education intended to produce the intellectual virtues will possess all of the characteristics and demands of the scientific spirit. These demands in turn cause virtue practice to tend toward technical verifiability and normative universality. The characteristic of unnatural "habituation" indicates a type of virtue practice that is "tradition-based," and determines that the education designed to produce intellectual virtue will demand and be characterized by cultural normative continuity produced through habit transmission or inheritance. This demand will in turn cause virtue practice to tend toward traditionalism and cultural particularity. This is just to say that intellectual virtue relies primarily upon intellectual and technical instruction, and that this type of education will thus be based upon generalizable experience and knowledge, whereas ethical virtue relies primarily upon tradition and the continuous transmission of culture, and that this type of education will thus be based upon particularized cultural transformation or transmission brought about through habituation or acculturation.

The "achievement" of virtue practice entirely relies upon whether or not the virtuous person is able to understand, master and appropriately apply the technical and behavioral conditions for intelligent, rational action. In the Western cultural context, a person's "achievements" might be seen as a manifestation of character, and thereby serve as proof that he or she has realized the ends of his or her particularized character. By means of his success in battle (military achievements), the brave soldier demonstrates that he has played his martial role or manifested his particularized character. In the same way, by means of his wisdom or ability, the wise person expresses his excellent character in the role of the wise person. We could cite many similar examples. In the traditional Chinese cultural context, however, "achievement" is always particularized and substantial, and therefore would seem an insufficient representation of a person's overall character. Therefore, although the normative standards of virtue represented by "achievement" (*chengjiu*) and "becoming a perfected person" (*chengren*) may look similar, a careful examination will reveal that they are in fact quite different, the primary difference being that "achievement" refers to the particularized role-character of the person and its end-realization, whereas "becoming a perfected person" refers to the end of an entire human life—especially to the moral ideal.

At first glance, it might seem that this type of difference would not result in widely varying conceptions of virtue, and that we could simply say that both the Confucians and Aristotelians basically understand virtue as "causing people to become good and to acquire a character representing the achievement of excellence" (see section one above). In fact, however, the Confucian conception of virtue emphasizes the first half of this definition; the second half (acquiring the achievement of excellence) represents an unspoken, related side effect, and is by no means to be understood as a necessary component of the conception of virtue itself. The most important point to note here is that the focus of Confucianism is on the problem of acquiring a virtuous character, as opposed to the Aristotelian focus on the question of excellent results or outstanding achievements. The link between technology-craft and virtuous action is thus not nearly as strong in Confucianism as in Aristotelianism. For the latter, the normative end is fundamental, practical, and even the sole concern; for the former, on the other hand, the normative end is mental, ideal, and subsumed under even higher deontic demands.

As described above, Confucian virtue ethics establishes a bi-polar "internally get it in oneself, externally get it from others" moral practice orientation, at the same time laying out a virtue practice strategy of both "moral self-cultivation" and transformation through social ethical education. This has been referred to as the "simultaneous cultivation of inner and outer" (*neiwai shuangxiu*). This "simultaneous cultivation of inner and outer" represents the basic model for Confucian moral education, and has as its content the "simultaneous cultivation of wisdom and virtue" (*zhide shuangxiu*). In Confucian thought, and even traditional Chinese culture as a whole, the general sense of "education" can be summed up by the two basic aspects of transformation by means of culture and education by means of the influence of virtue.[27] Moreover, because traditional Confucians held to a sort of "virtue leads to knowledge" pan-moralist, intellectual normative viewpoint similar to that of Socrates, "cultural" transformation (*wenhua*) and virtue-education (*dejiao*)[28] are in fact simply two sides of the same coin, or even identical and fundamentally inseparable.

Within the system of Confucian thought, a pedagogical strategy that takes the virtue of humanity as its basis perfectly harmonizes with a morality that celebrates the "perfected person," because the distinguishing mark of the Confucian perfected person is "perfected humanity" (*chengren*) rather than "perfected achievement" (*chengjiu*). How, though, does one actually go about perfecting humanity? The basic Confucian strategy is to do so through moral education—under which rubric we can include both self-education (cultivating the self) and social, ethical pedagogical transformation—with the aim of enabling the person to become the "humane and wise" person of humanity, or gentleman. Humanity and wisdom—and sometimes even courage—are cited together by Confucius, and seem to enjoy equal normative ranking. Hence, the passage from the later *Doctrine of the Mean* where the three are referred to as the "three perfected virtues." After Confucius, however, humanity and wisdom are singled out as the paradigmatic Confucian virtues. Mencius, citing a disciple of Confucius named Zigong, writes: "Learning without growing tired—this is wisdom; teaching without growing weary—this is humanity. Humane and wise, the Master was certainly a worthy" (*Mencius,* 2A2).[29] This explanation of humanity and wisdom is couched narrowly in terms of education (teaching and learning).

In the Confucian view, humanity is the foundation and root of virtue-education, while wisdom is the basic condition that allows one to become humane or to "see the benefits of humanity" (*liren*). The virtue of humanity involves "getting it internally from the self"—hence, the claims that "humanity comes from oneself" (*Analects,* 12.1), or "if I merely desire humanity, I will find that humanity is already here" (*Analects,* 7.30). It also involves "externally getting it from others"—that is, undergoing social ethical education, receiving the instruction of one's parents and elders, and being subtlety transformed through habituated into traditional mores until one is able to both comprehend and put into practice the ethical virtues of loyalty, filial piety, humanity, rightness, and so forth. However, it is important to keep in mind that the virtue of humanity is not abstract, but is rather by necessity intimately related to the concrete details of everyday human interactions in the world, and—most of all—requires appropriate normative means or models for realization, in the same way that realization of any type of normative end requires appropriate normative means.

Within the framework of Confucian thought, wisdom serves as precisely this basic condition and method for the realization of the normative end of humanity. The fundamental meaning of the phrase, "humane and (moreover) wise" is that in order to perfect humanity it is necessary to be wise. Confucius says that "The humane person is at home in humanity; the wise person understands its benefits" (*Analects,* 4.2). The metaphor of "feeling at home" in humanity expresses the attitude of the already humane person, who is content with morality. "Understanding humanity," the wise person clearly grasps the principle of humanity or the benefits of perfecting it, and is thereby better able to spur himself on in pursuit of it. This is the main principle behind the process of educating someone to become humane.

The best method for forging the virtue of humanity remains moral practice itself—the Confucian "Way of holding to the mean (*zhongyongzhidao*)." Here again, we see a point of commonality with regard to the Confucian and Aristotelian definitions of virtue. The former sees the "Way of holding to the mean"— the way of making the optimum choice that will result in one's "hitting the intermediate mark" of various type of normative possibilities—as the optimum choice for acquiring virtue, or even as virtue itself. Aristotle says: "Virtue is simply holding to the mean (*zhongyong*)—hitting the intermediate mark."[30] Similarly, Confucius declares, "acquiring virtue through holding to the mean— is this not best?" (*Analects*, 6.23). What Confucius means by "acquiring virtue through holding to the mean" is the way of acting in a mean-like fashion (*zhongxing*) or being centered/correct (*zhongzheng*). He himself explains this in another passage where he notes that it is as bad to "overstep" (*guo*) as to "fall short of" (*buji*) virtue (*Analects*, 11.16). Thus, the term *zhongyong* means something like "taking the 'mean' as one's constant Way."

According to this interpretation, the Confucian "Way of holding to the mean" in fact has two senses. The first refers to an appropriate way of acting that accords with the standards of ritual. According to the "Confucius Dwelling in Yan" chapter of the *Book of Rites*, "The Master said, 'The rites, oh, the rites! They are the means by which one restricts oneself to the mean." The second sense refers to virtuous action itself—"acquiring virtue through holding to the mean." Holding to the mean of virtue involves the rationality of a given mode of moral action: if one is able to hold to the mean, one's behavior itself will accord with morality, and will therefore possess inherent moral value. Thus, Confucius demands of the gentleman that he be "conscious of his own superiority without being contentious, and sociable without getting involved in cliques" (*Analects*, 15.22), as well as "generous but not extravagant, hard-working without overdoing it, aware of his desires without being greedy, casual without being arrogant, and stern without being fierce" (*Analects*, 20.2). From this we can see that there is a high degree of similarity with regard to how "the way of holding to the mean" is understood from the perspective of both Confucian and Aristotelian virtue ethics. Both see holding to the mean as representing virtue itself or as according to the way of virtuous practice.

However, we are still able to uncover cognitive differences between Confucius and Aristotle even within these sorts of similarities. Even though Aristotle clearly includes holding to the mean under the rubric of "ethical virtue,"[31] he nonetheless continues to emphasize that the way of holding to the mean represents a normative state concerned with choice, and is therefore governed by human reason. As he says: "Virtue is a way that represents holding to a mean relative to us, and is a state concerned with our capacity for choice, determined by reason and resembling the sorts of demands that would be made by a wise person."[32] This is because both reason and wisdom are required if one is to recognize the difference between "overstepping" and "falling short" and find the "mean state" between these two extremes. The question that this raises is how Aristotle, understanding the way of holding to the mean in this fashion, can nonetheless continue to classify it as an "ethical virtue." In the virtue theory of Aristotle, is not "ethical virtue" something that—like "nature" and "habituation"—cannot be altered?[33] If it is to be understood as an inalterable ethical virtue, how can the way of holding to the mean possibly be reconciled with the capacity for free choice? Looking at it this way, from the perspective of Confucian virtue ethics, this problem represents an internal paradox within Aristotelian virtue theory.

However, this problem dissolves if one looks at it from within the perspective of Aristotelian virtue theory itself. This is because the Aristotelian distinction between the "intellectual virtues" and "ethical virtues" is merely a heuristic device, and does not imply any sort of actual normative differentiation. In other words, from the perspective of Aristotelianism, both intellectual and ethical virtues serve a common end—the highest good of "happiness." Thus, both natural "ethical virtue" and the sort of "rational virtue" created through education exist merely as necessary conditions or basic methods for realizing the noble, normative end of happiness. When Aristotle refers to the "way of holding to the mean" as "the highest good and extreme excellence,"[34] his basic intention is to refer to the method of choosing action that "hits the intermediate mark," and which can be expected to bring to the chooser of action the most suitable normative outcome (happiness or a sense of happiness). Nevertheless, in Aristotle's virtue theory, "intellectual virtue" is a kind of technical virtue—cognitive virtue. "Ethical virtue," on the other hand, is something to be discussed from the perspective of virtue production and tradition. What the latter expresses is the type of traditional continuity or consistency characteristic of already-produced virtuous habits. Therefore, ethical virtue and intellectual virtue possess different conceptual characteristics.

If this analysis is reliable, then we might say that, from the perspective of Confucian virtue ethics, the "problem" with Aristotelian virtue theory described above is perfectly suited to serve as a starting point for the development of a conversation between Aristotelian virtue theory and Confucian virtue ethics. This is because it is precisely here that Confucianism and Aristotelianism can find a topic for mutual "collaboration," and where each tradition can perhaps learn from the other's differences of opinion. In the past, both Confucians and Aristotelians had faith in and strove to establish a type of ethical virtue tradition, and moreover sought to express the internal consistency and enduring comprehensiveness inherent to this sort of ethical virtue. This sort of traditionalist stance not only endows the tradition of virtue ethics with the prestige of historical legitimacy (presenting them as preestablished "customs" or "practices"), but also makes moral education possible. Of course, the sort of "moral education" we are talking about here is not the type of Enlightenment education held dear by modern liberalism—for instance, the "blank slate" method of education described by eighteenth-century French Enlightenment thinkers, or the "learn by doing" method of education championed by John Dewey. On the contrary, the moral education envisioned by traditionalism accepts the student's capacity for free choice; while at the same time shows faith in the intellectual legitimacy and authority of the tradition itself. This is the type of standard for the development of virtue that Aristotle sought to convey with his model of the continuous development of virtue that is characteristic of the transmission between teacher and apprentice within a craft tradition.

Education is fundamentally a linguistic exchange and intellectual communication between the two aspects of teaching and learning. Learning cannot consist of simply passive absorption with no room for choice, but at the same time education cannot arise in a vacuum—it must have something upon which it can be based and upon which it can rely. This basis for education is precisely the sort of cultural knowledge that is produced and preserved by traditional forms. The concepts of "intellectual virtue" and "ethical virtue" discussed by Aristotle correspond quite nicely to the two dimensions of "learning" and "teaching" that we have just now described as part of the practice of virtue education, and in the same way, the educational goals of "inner cultivation" and "external education" ("the simultaneous cultivation of virtue and wisdom") found in Confucian virtue ethics can also be understood as encompassing both of these dimensions.

However, with regard to the practice of virtue education, Confucian virtue ethics does not make a clear distinction between the two aspects of "inner" and "outer" or "virtue" and "wisdom," and even less does it understand virtue in terms of the practice of craft technology. On the contrary, Confucian virtue ethics believes that inner and outer are mutually inclusive and that virtue and wisdom are one, and in most cases goes so far as to conflate virtue and wisdom, to see virtue as a representation of wisdom. Therefore, within the ethical framework of this sort of moral supremicism, virtue of course becomes a question of practice—not only with regard to behavioral techniques, but even more importantly with regard to the fundamentals of one's life. It thus becomes a question related to the realm of self-cultivation or to one's normative ideals. It is precisely for this reason that the Confucians saw perfecting virtue as being more important than life itself; hence, the possibility that one might be called upon to "allow the self to perish in order to perfect humanity" or "give up life in order to realize rightness." Compared to the virtue theory of Aristotelianism, the type of strict moralism found in Confucianism—along with the educational scheme that equates virtue and wisdom—is perhaps even farther removed from modern moral sensibilities, and is certainly more lacking when it comes to the sort of practicality or general applicability characteristic of technical reason. However, if Professor MacIntyre's judgment that the "moral scheme"[35] of the Enlightenment movement has already failed is a valid one, then we might be able to say that the way

of practice and route of education offered by Confucian virtue ethics—and
perhaps Aristotelian virtue theory as well—could, as an antidote to modern
moral theory, provide us with a unique moral-cultural resource. In this way, the
cultural conversation desired by Professor MacIntyre could not only serve as a
sort of intercultural mirroring, but also holds out the prospect of allowing each
tradition to theoretically complement the other. Is such a conversation in fact
possible? We will just have to wait and see.

NOTES

1. "An Interview with Alasdair MacIntyre," *Cogito,* (Summer 1991): (Bristol,
England), 69.

2. Alasdair MacIntyre, "Incommensurability, Truth and the Conversation Between
Confucians and Aristotelians About the Virtues," in *Culture and Modernity,* E. Deutsch
ed. (Honolulu: The University of Hawaii Press, 1991).

3. Junren Wan, "On the Destiny of Chinese Ethics," in *Journal of Peking University*
1 (1990). (edition of philosophy and social sciences)

4. *Nichomachean Ethics,* 1106a 20–25. [Translator's note: all quotations from Aristotle
will be translated literally from the Chinese; the author is relying upon the standard
Chinese translation of *The Complete Works of Aristotle* (Beijing: Miao, 1992). For reference, I will also provide the standard English translation from the *Complete Works* (Barnes,
1984). This line is rendered in *Complete Works,* Barnes 1984 (Princeton: Princeton
University Press, p. 1747): "the excellence of man . . . will be the state which makes a man
good and which makes him do his own work well."]

5. [Translator's note: that is to say, whether we view the concept in terms of what
it denies existence to or in terms of what it affirms the existence of.]

6. Alasdair MacIntyre, *Dependent Rational Animal—Why Human Beings Need the
Virtues,* (Chicago: Open Court Publishing Company, 1999).

7. The "No Divided Attention" chapter of the *Lushi Chunqiu* says: "Confucius
honored humanity." [Translator's note: In its earliest usages, *ren* means something like
"handsome" or "nobly formed," and refers to the appearance of the aristocratic gentleman. In other early usages, it referred to the kindness shown by a superior to an inferior.
Confucius moralized the term, and in the *Analects,* it refers to the supreme Confucian
virtue characteristic of the moral gentleman. Because it is cognate with the word for
person (*ren*), it is often rendered as "humanity," or the virtue of being "truly human."

8. See Wailu Ho, ed., *The General History of Chinese Thoughts* (Beijing: the People's
Publishing House, 1957), 1:92–95.

9. In the *Mencius,* humanity is elevated to the status of a concept related to the
loftiest end-nature and possessing a high degree of ontological value, with ritual being
viewed as merely a condition or means for realizing humanity. Consider *Mencius,* 4A:27:
"The substance of humanity is serving one's parents. The substance of rightness is obey-

ing one's older brother. The substance of knowledge is knowing these two things and not letting them go, while the substance of ritual is to restrain and adorn them." Please note: my reference to "end-nature" (*mudi xing*) is restricted to the context of contrasting humanity and ritual, and is not intended as an expression of ethical teleology.

10. [Translator's note: Professor Wan is here following the suggestions of some commentators that *ren* "humanity" be read as its cognate *ren* "human being" (by extension: how one is as a human being; i.e., one's character). The example cited, though, would seem to represent a case of the borrowing of a cognate character rather than a distinct meaning of the word *ren* itself.]

11. For more on this point, the reader can refer to Jiao Guocheng, *On the Relation between I and the Other in the Ancient Times of China* (Beijing: China Renmin University Press, 1991), intro. and chap. 1.

12. Within the framework of his religious ethics, Martin Buber (1878–1965) proclaims the relationship of "man to man," which in turn reveals two structures with different characters: (1) the "intersubjectivity" of the "I and Thou" relationship (a structure within which both "I" and "Thou" are simultaneously subjects), and (2) the "subjectivity-objectivity" of the "I and Other" relationship. The former involves equality, whereas the latter involves inequality. See Martin Buber, *Ich und Du*, translated into Chinese by Chen Weiwang 1986, as well as R. G. Smith 1961 (Heidelberg: verlag Lambert Schneider, 1983).

13. In *Analects*, 17.6, the disciple Zizhang asks Confucius about humanity. Confucius replies: "The person who is able to put into practice five qualities wherever he may be in the world is a person of humanity." The "five qualities" he lists are "respectfulness, broad-mindedness, trustworthiness, diligence and generosity."

14. See especially Alasdair MacIntyre's *After Virtue* (IN: University of Notre Dame Press, 1981), *Whose Justice? Which Rationality?* (IN: Notre Dame University Press, 1988), *Three Rival Versions of Moral Enquiry* (IN: Notre Dame University Press, 1990), and so forth.

15. [Translator's note: literally, "so because of Heaven"; conventionally translated as "natural," but (especially in the context of traditional Confucian thought) possessing more of a religious and normative thrust than the English word "natural." The Chinese word *tian* retains both the earliest sense of an anthropomorphic supreme Being (Heaven) and the later, more impersonal (but still normative) sense of "natural order" or that which is inborn, and will thus, as appropriate, be translated as "natural (heavenly)" or "inborn (heavenly)."]

16. In the entire Confucian tradition or even traditional Chinese culture as a whole, Xunzi's proposal to "clarify the distinction between the heavenly (natural) and human" stands as a unique exception, and is quite out of the mainstream.

17. About the enquiry on "politicized ethics" or "ethicized politics," see Jiantao Ren, *Enquiry on Ethical Politics—from the Perspective of Early Confucianism* (Guangzhou: Zhongshan University Press, 1999).

18. Qian Mansuo, *Emerson and China—Reflection on Individualism* (Beijing: Shanlian Books, 1996), p. 211. (SDX and Harvard—Yenching Academic Library, 1996).

19. [Translator's note: the word *xin* refers to the physical organ of the heart, which in the traditional Chinese view is the seat of cognition as well as certain types of "intelligent" emotions (such as compassion, moral indignation, etc.) and the virtuous dispositions to which these emotions are related. Although by late Warring States times it had come to refer primarily to the seat of cognition and linguistic ability (and thus in thinkers such as Zhuangzi or Xunzi is perhaps better rendered simply as the "mind"), in early Confucianism (the *Analects* and the *Mencius*), it still retains its link to our affective nature, and might thus be better rendered as "heart/mind." The modern Chinese understanding of *xin* is, however, focused more exclusively upon the cognitive, which is why the author in his discussion of Confucian self-cultivation at times substitutes the modern compound *xinling* (mind, spirit) for the classical *xin*. The lone classical term *xin* will be rendered as "heart/mind" throughout, and "mind" resorted to only when the author switches to the modern compound.]

20. As Confucius says: "One who possesses virtue will inevitably be able to speak well, but one who speaks well does not necessarily possess virtue. One who possesses humanity will inevitably possess courage, but one who is courageous will not necessarily possess humanity" (*Analects,* 14.4).

21. Tu Wei-ming, "Confucianism," *Our Religions,* Arvind Shaarma, ed., (San Francisco: Harper Collins Publishers, 1993), pp. 142–46. And also Wei-ming Tu, *Confucian Thought— Selfhood as Creative Transformation* (Albany: State University of New York Press, 1985).

22. [Translator's note: the *Great Learning,* along with the *Doctrine of the Mean,* was originally a rather obscure chapter in the *Book of Rites,* a late Han dynasty collection of ritual and miscellaneous texts. It and the *Doctrine of the Mean* were later singled out by neo-Confucians as significant writings, attributed to Confucius' grandson Zisi (also the supposed teacher of Mencius), and made part of the orthodox neo-Confucian canon. Together with the *Analects* and the *Mencius,* they make up the so-called Four Books put together by Zhu Xi that later became the basis of the civil service examination from 1313–1905.]

23. [Translator's note: there is a fair amount of commentarial controversy over how to render the term *gewu;* our rendering here follows the orthodox interpretation of Zhu Xi.]

24. *Nichomachean Ethics,* 1103a31, 1103b5. [Translator's note: cf. Barnes: ". . . excellences we get by first exercising them, as also happens in the case of arts as well. For the things we have to learn before we can do, we learn by doing, for example, men become builders by building and lyre-players by playing the lyre. . . . Again, it is from the same causes and by the same means that every excellence is both produced and destroyed, and similarly every art."]

25. *Magna Moralia,* 1182a15–15. [Translator's note: cf. Barnes (*Complete Works of Aristotle:* The Revised Oxford Translation, Princeton, NJ: Princeton University Press) 1984: 1868: "He used to make the excellences sciences, and this is impossible. For the sciences all involve reason, and reason is to found in the intellectual part of the soul. So that all the excellences, according to him, are to be found in the rational part of the soul. The result is that in making the excellences sciences he is doing away with the irrational part of the soul, and is thereby doing away also both with passion and character; so that he has not been successful in this respect in his treatment of the excellences."]

26. *Nichomachean Ethics,* 1103a14–20. [Translator's note: cf. Barnes (*Complete Works of Aristotle:* The Revised Oxford Translation, Princeton, NJ: Princeton University Press) 1984: 1742: "Excellence, then, being of two kinds, intellectual and moral, intellectual excellence in the main owes both its birth and growth to teaching (for which reason it requires both experience and time), while moral excellence comes about as a result of habit, whence also its name is one that is formed by a slight variation from the word for 'habit'. From this it is also plain that none of the moral excellences arises in us by nature; for nothing that exists by nature can form a habit contrary to its nature."]

27. [Translator's note: as noted above, virtue (*de*) was seen by the Chinese tradition as having a transformative power.]

28. [Translator's note: "moral education" might be a more felicitous rendering, but this would require translating *de* differently than we have been doing up to now. I have decided to go with the admittedly awkward "virtue-education" to maintain consistency, and also to indicate the special nature of this idea of education through the almost magical power of virtue, which is a slightly different idea than what would be conveyed by "moral education."]

29. [Translator's note: in this passage, Zigong is making reference to *Analects,* 7.33: The Master said: "How could I dare to lay claim to either sageliness or humanity? What can be said about me is no more than this: I learn without growing tired and teach without growing weary."]

30. [Translator's note: cf. Barnes (*Complete Works of Aristotle:* The Revised Oxford Translation, Princeton, NJ: Princeton University Press) 1748: "Excellence is a kind of mean, since it aims at what is intermediate."]

31. He says ". . . ethical virtue is a mean state . . ." (*Nichomachean Ethics,* 1109a19). [Translator's note: cf. Barnes 1984: 1751: ". . . moral excellence is a mean . . . "]

32. *Nichomachean Ethics,* 1106b32–1107a1. [Translator's note: cf. Barnes 1984: 1748: "Excellence, then, is a state concerned with choice, lying in a mean relative to us, this being determined by reason and in the way in which the man of practical wisdom would determine it."]

33. See *Nichomachean Ethics,* 1103a14–25.

34. *Nichomachean Ethics,* 1107a1. [Translator's note: cf. Barnes (*Complete Works of Aristotle:* The Revised Oxford Translation, Princeton, NJ: Princeton University Press) 1984: 1748: "with regard to what is best and right it is an extreme."]

35. Alasdair MacIntre, *After Virtue* (IN: University of Notre Dame Press, 1981).

ONCE MORE ON CONFUCIAN AND ARISTOTELIAN CONCEPTIONS OF THE VIRTUES

A RESPONSE TO PROFESSOR WAN

Alasdair MacIntyre

Professor Wan Junren has once again given me reason for gratitude both by his discussion of my own work and by extending the inquiry to issues that go far beyond that work. He has indeed raised so many questions that I cannot hope to comment on more than a few. So my response will be highly selective. It is also worth noting at the outset that both Professor Wan and I are contributing to a much larger set of ongoing discussions between adherents of and scholars at work on Confucianism, on the one hand, and representatives of a variety of Western philosophical traditions, on the other. And we should also note that the former group includes a continually increasing number of Europeans and North Americans, while the latter group includes a smaller but significant number of Chinese and Japanese thinkers.

The greatest of my own debts are to Angus Graham, David Nivison, Henry Rosemont, and David Wong, but I have also learned from others, although as yet not nearly enough. And I do not read Chinese, so what I write about Confucianism must necessarily be to some large degree tentative and exploratory. It is my task to ask questions rather than to supply answers. Yet the importance of opening up even a little further the possibilities of dialogue and debate, even of shared inquiry, between Confucians and Aristotelians encourages me to respond to Professor Wan's essay by raising provocative questions, some about how the differences between Confucius and Aristotle should be characterized and some concerning how it may be possible to adjudicate between them. But the full significance of these questions will only emerge if I begin by considering briefly the nature of our common enterprise.

All reflective ethics needs to develop, whether explicitly or implicitly, a comparative dimension. For, insofar as I employ one particular evaluative and normative vocabulary rather than another, implicitly or explicitly I judge it to be superior to other rival vocabularies. And, insofar as I justify my evaluative and normative judgments in this way rather than in that, I likewise judge this particular mode of justification rationally superior to other rival modes of justification. The vocabulary that I use will always be that of some particular community and tradition with which I identify myself. And the mode of justification will appeal to those standards that happen to govern practical judgment and argument in that particular community. But the claims made on behalf of that vocabulary and mode of justification will be at least implicitly universal claims, claims to truth and claims to rational justification.

Truth is claimed for the particular account of agency and of social relationships that are presupposed by the evaluative and normative principles of my own particular standpoint. And rational justification is claimed not only for my particular moral and political judgments and principles, but also for that presupposed account. Of course these claims do often remain implicit. And for long periods there may be no need to spell them out. But when the adherents of some particular standpoint became aware of the claims that are made on behalf of other rival and incompatible standpoints, and this not in an abstract and general way, but in some way that puts them to the question at the level of practice, then issues of truth and justification become difficult to avoid.

So there will emerge a set of claims that some particular, culturally specific and local set of practices and beliefs, embodying values and norms of universal import, are values and norms that every human being has good reason to acknowledge. The evaluation of such claims necessarily involves an attempt to distinguish what it is that is *merely* local from what it is that may justifiably be taken to possess universal import and to require universal allegiance. The histories of both Confucianism and Aristotelian provide examples of just such attempts. Thus, it is a central Confucian claim that we can distinguish between compliance with the particular ritual requirements of the patriarchal, kinship, and inheritance systems transmitted from the Zhou dynasty, which are a local phenomenon, and the practice of the virtue of *li,* the virtue of ritual propriety, which is, so it is claimed, an excellence of human beings as such, anywhere and everywhere. And, it is likewise an Aristotelian claim that we can distinguish between those aspects of Aristotle's characterizations of the virtues that are inseparable from the particular local institutional arrangements of the fourth and fifth century Greek *polis* and those that can be justified as parts of an account of the virtues of human beings as such. And at once it is evident that these Confucian and Aristotelian claims by themselves provide matter for contention.

In no Aristotelian catalogue of the virtues, for example, indeed in no Western catalogue of the virtues, do we find any mention of *li,* the Chinese name of the virtue of ritual propriety. Two things about this virtue are particularly noteworthy: first that its exercise is not limited to ceremonial occasions, but extends to the circumstances of daily life, how one lies in bed and sits at home, how one responds to a gift or to the presence of someone in mourning, what foods are to be eaten, and how and what clothes are to be worn;[1] and, second, the close relationship between *li* and *ren*, the virtue of humaneness. To Yan Hui, Confucius said: "The practice of humaneness comes down to this: tame the self and restore the rites" (*Analects,* 12.1). This and other passages make evident the Confucian view that the practice of the virtue of ritual propriety is an essential constituent of the exercise of *ren*, the virtue of humanity, which is the supreme virtue of human beings as such. To be humane is to have succeeded at being a human being; to be defective in the practice of *ren* is to have failed as a human being. It is because of this that the different uses of *ren* noted by Professor Wan are not perhaps, as he suggests "three distinct senses" of the expression, but should rather be understood as three uses of a single concept.

Ren as Professor Wan says, names the highest state of virtue (*Analects,* 4.2), is used to evaluate individuals (18.1), and can be translated by "character" (4.7), although I do not think that Professor Wan is correct in suggesting that, in *Analects,* 4.7, it is used "as a synonym for human being." But even if it were so used, this would not require us to posit an additional sense of "*ren*." For it is the nature of human beings to excel or to fail to excel in the practice of *ren*. And whether they so excel or not determines how they are to be evaluated and is the salient feature of their character. So, there is a core unity of meaning throughout the variety of uses of *ren*, and the central moral importance of *ren* is, in a Confucian view, undeniable. Therefore, if Confucians are right in supposing that one cannot achieve excellence of character without the exercise of ritual propriety, then Aristotelians, so it seems, must be precluded from achieving excellence of character. And, if Aristotelians are right in supposing that excellence of character does not require ritual propriety, then the Confucian conception of the humane is gravely flawed. One question with which I shall be concerned in this essay is whether this opposition between the two standpoints is as sharp and as serious as it at first appears. But to answer this question, I must first consider some other issues raised by Professor Wan.

There is a tension between the thesis advanced by Professor Wan in the second part of his paper concerning the absence of any substantial conception of the individual in Confucianism and his account in the third part of his paper of what it is to become a perfected person. Professor Wan asserts that "Confucius and the Confucian tradition lack the kind of concept of the 'person' or 'individual' as an entity or bearer of rights (as an end) that we find in Western moral culture" and that they "never developed the concept of an independent, distinct person." He also contrasts a conception of the bearers of virtue as "individualized or made more substantial" with one in which they are "conceived in terms of human relationships or sociopolitical ties," arguing that the focus of Confucianism on "the relational context of personal virtue practice" distinguishes it

sharply from Aristotelian ethics. Yet Professor Wan also insists upon the importance of becoming a perfected person, thus raising the question of how one can
become a perfected person without being an independent, distinct person.

In responding to this question, I shall suggest, first, that Aristotelianism and
Confucianism are on these matters somewhat closer than Professor Wan believes,
and that, when we have understood this, we are also able to understand how the
contrast in conceptions of the moral agent, as formulated by Professor Wan, is
misleading. Consider, therefore, Aristotle's view of the human individual as moral
agent in *Politics* I (1253a1–39). An individual whose nature was such that she
or he could dispense with participation in the relationships of political society
would not be a human being, but either a brute beast, or a god. To be a member
of a political society is to share with others a concept of the just and the unjust,
the good and the bad, while to be outside political community is to be deprived
of the possibility of developing the excellence specific to human beings. Only in
and through the relationships of the household and the political community are
human beings able to develop as human beings. Our social relationships are
constitutive of our individual humanity and of our capacities as moral agents.
So where Professor Wan suggests that *either* we must conceive of the individual
qua moral agent as one who is an independent and distinct person *or* we must
conceive of that individual in relational terms, taking the former to be the
Western view and the latter to be the Confucian alternative, Aristotle argues that
the individual as independent and distinct person is constituted by her or his
social relationship and ties.

Moreover, just as the Aristotelian view of the individual is more relational
than Professor Wan allows, so too the Confucian view seems to be more deeply
committed to an account of individuals as having a substantial reality than
Professor Wan always recognizes, although he does concede that, on the Confucian view, individuals have at least "a certain degree of substantiality and
reality." For it is individuals who are evaluated as more or less perfect in the
virtues that they exhibit in their relationships to others. So in *Analects*, 18.1, a
passage that Professor Wan cites, Confucius remarks of three individuals that the
Yin dynasty had "three models of humanity" (Simon Leys' translation).

Of course, Professor Wan is right in emphasizing that the Confucian moral
agent is not to be understood as the kind of individual who is a "bearer of rights"
or "an end." However, Aristotle's conception of the moral agent is similarly at
odds with such distinctively modern Western conceptions of the individual.
And, perhaps, as Confucianism developed, its understanding of the individual
moral agent became very close to that of the Aristotelian. It may be the case that
in early Confucian texts, only relational aspects of the self receive attention,
although I am not sure even of this. As the Confucian view of the moral
development of individuals was spelled out further, it became clear to Confucians, as it did to Aristotelians in a very different social context, that individuals

can only act as they are required to in their relationships because of features of the self that belong to them as individuals. How so?

The grounds for saying this are to be found in Professor Wan's discussions of the Confucian conception of moral achievement and of becoming a perfected person, in the third part of his paper. For in order to become a perfected person, individuals, as understood in the Confucian tradition, have to reflect on themselves and on how on occasion they may have failed to act as they should have in their relationships. Confucian teaching is always a summons to such self-corrective inner reflection and the individuals who reflects upon their relationships in this way exhibit in so doing what it is in themselves that is more, and other than their participation in those relationships, namely, their capacity for and their practice of independent reflection.

This conception of a self that is, in important respects, genuinely independent, is not, so I have been suggesting, incompatible with at least some relational conceptions of the self and it is, I think, presupposed by much that Professor Wan says. Consider, for example, his remark that "the emphasis of Confucianism virtue ethics is upon autonomous internalization and heteronomous externalization." Yet, of course, insofar as the self is autonomous, it is independent of external pressures. In what way then is the self, as conceived by Confucians, autonomous? Professor Wan seems to suggest that it is possible for it to be autonomous in some respects (internalization) and heteronomous in others (externalization). But this surely cannot be right. What Professor Wan says about the movement of the self toward a perfected performance of its duties suggests that we should rather think of autonomy as an achievement of the self, and of the agent's progress in the exercise of the virtues as a movement away from heteronomy and towards autonomy.

The initial stages of Confucian moral education are ones in which students not only conform increasingly to norms that are imposed by others, but do so by reason of their wish to secure approval from others and to avoid disapproval. But, as students mature, they find their own good reasons for acting as the norms require, and they seek not just to be approved by those others to whom they owe respect, but to deserve to be so approved. Initially they may be exclusively motivated by external pressures. Later, they are still motivated by a regard for others, but only insofar as they have found their own good reasons for having and exhibiting that regard. They have thus moved from heteronomy to autonomy and that autonomy is exhibited as much in their external conformity to the norms as in their internal reflections, feelings, and attitudes.

So far, I have followed Professor Wan in my use of such expressions as "internal" and "external." And, in some contexts, those expressions can be used without obscuring what it is philosophically important not to obscure. But in other contexts we need to question their use. For what is commonly taken to be "inner"—thoughts, feelings, and attitudes, decisions—may stand in a variety of relationships to what is commonly taken to be "outer"—such as bodily movements and speech. And while to some large degree and in some complex ways what is outer is always an expression of, an embodiment of what is inner, there can also be a range of differences and discrepancies between the two, so that what is outwardly expressed is at variance with and even in conflict with our thoughts and feelings.

So it often is with individuals who are not yet autonomous, but are already dissatisfied with the condition of heteronomy. In such individuals there is a division within the self, such that what is embodied in their actions is not yet an adequate expression of what they wish for themselves. There is a gap to be closed, and progress in the moral life partly consists in the closing of that gap. Why does this matter? It does so because it throws additional light on the importance of *li*, the virtue of ritual propriety. *Li* has at least two dimensions. On the one hand, commentators have rightly stressed the ways in which ritual perceptions provide a shared code which enables those whose activities are governed by it to interpret and to respond to one another. As David Nivison has written: "*Li* involves countless gestures and acts that, whether required or simply available to me, serve as signals to you and invite response from you in such a way as to reassure both of us that you and I are 'we' . . ."[2] In saying this, Nivison was following the lead of Herbert Fingarette who argued that we need to recognize, and that Confucianism invites us to recognize, the extent to which the transactions of our everyday life have a generally unacknowledged ceremonial character: "Promises, commitments, excuses, pleas, compliments, pacts—these and so much more are ceremonies or they are nothing."[3]

Yet these aspects of ritual do not by themselves explain why the exercise of ritual propriety is a virtue, a human excellence, rather than merely an approved form of social practice. To understand that, we have to look at a second dimension of *li*. It matters for the exercise of *li* that you not only conform to the requirements of ritual, but that it is indeed you who give expression to yourself in so conforming, so that the ritual is not an imposition upon you, but that which you have made fully your own. Xunzi said that "If you do as ritual prescribes, it means that your emotions have found rest in ritual."[4] And to say that the emotions are at rest is to say both that they are harmonious and that they have found adequate outward expression. The gap between inner and outer has been abolished. Autonomy has been achieved and externalization is no longer heteronomous. Or rather, and more radically, the distinction between inner and outer no longer has application. In saying this, I am indebted to David L. Hall and Roger T. Ames who stress both the connection between the notion of ritual propriety and the notion of appropriation and also a conception of ritualized bodily movements as a medium through which individuals express themselves, just as a calligrapher expresses meaning in the strokes of the pen and the shapes of the characters.[5]

If this is how *li* is to be understood, then the indispensability of *li* to *ren*, the virtue of humaneness, is no longer puzzling. *Ren*, humaneness, comprehends what non-Confucians might think of as a family of virtues. Confucians speak of it as consisting in five practices: courtesy, tolerance, good faith, diligence, generosity (*Analects*, 17.6). What each of these practices requires, like the practice of other virtues, is ritual: "Without ritual, courtesy is tiresome; without ritual, prudence is timid; without ritual, bravery is quarrelsome; without ritual, frankness is hurtful" (*Analects*, 8.2). What is missing, when ritual is absent, is the unity of inner thought and feeling with outward bodily expression that constitutes integrity. Without that unity, there will either be outward performances without conviction and settled emotion, so that, for example, courtesy becomes a burdensome set of formalities, or there will be an inner wish and will to do what is right and prudent, but the agent's behavior will fail to express that wish and will, so that prudence becomes the victim of timidity. It is in and through ritual, thus understood, that our dispositions to respond adequately and relevantly to particular social situations and to communicate to others the character of our responses are exhibited. Hence, it is not just that without the exercise of *li* we cannot possess *ren*. It is that without the exercise of *li*, we cannot genuinely possess *any* virtue.[6]

This is not only a striking, but also a compelling claim. For on any plausible view of the virtues, it would seem impossible to ascribe perfected virtue to someone whose inner thoughts, feelings, and desires were not adequately integrated with their outward bodily expression. Aristotle and Aquinas both recognize the possibility of such a discrepancy and of its incompatibility with virtue in their accounts of the continent human being and of the difference between continence and virtue. Both, therefore, appear open to the charge that they need to include in their catalogue of the virtues what is notably absent from those catalogues, the virtue of *li*.

To this, someone might reply that it is, in both Aristotle's and Aquinas's views, through habituation that one acquires the virtues (*Nicomachean Ethics*, 1103a31–b25 and see also Aquinas's *Commentary*), and that the merely continent agent has not yet been sufficiently habituated. Habituation of judgment and feeling, as well as of action, is what closes the gap between the inner and the outer, so that actions become judgment-informed and feeling-informed. But to this, the Confucian may respond by arguing that, at best, the Aristotelian account habituation is misleading. For in saying that we become just by performing just actions and courageous by performing courageous actions, Aristotle omitted to point out that the just actions of those who are not yet just and the courageous actions of those who are not yet courageous are precisely actions in which the outward behavior is one thing and the inner motivation quite another. The young novice does not act as justice requires *because* justices requires it, but to avoid the approval or disapproval of parents and teachers. So the outward appearance of justice does not express the agent's inner attitude. And it is not only that the agent's inner attitude has to be transformed, but also that it has to be transformed in such a way as to close the gap between inner and outer. Habituation that issues in *li* is required for habituation in justice, courage, and the other virtues.

How then should a Thomistic Aristotelian respond to these claims? A three-fold response is perhaps required. First, it can immediately be acknowledged that the integration of the inner and the outer is central to the moral life and to the acquisition of all virtues. This is not only not inconsistent with an Aristotelian account of the moral virtues, but is already recognized in that account. Second, there must therefore be a corresponding recognition of the need either for *li* or for some form of habituation that will function to the same effect as *li*. One mark of a moral education that is well-designed to function in this way would be that it inculcates a deep respect for standards of civility in all social relationships, a regard for which would be expressed in bodily comportment and in formalities of behavior, so that good manners would be treated as a sign of good character.

Third, the Thomistic Aristotelian should again readily acknowledge the importance for all social life of ceremonial forms, forms as various as those taken by the meals that the members of a family in good order eat together and by those occasions that mark the formal opening of a deliberative assembly or the installation of a public official. About this importance and about the relationship between respect for ceremonial forms and the practice of the virtues in general, we Aristotelians do have a good deal to learn from Confucians, and I hope that we are duly grateful.

What I am suggesting, then, is that a scrutiny of Confucian claims about *li* leads to the conclusion that those claims embody truths that *any* virtue ethics needs to acknowledge. The attentiveness to and respect for ritual of the Western Zhou period was a local cultural phenomenon, bearing the marks of time, place, and the history of class-structure. It was the genius of Confucius and of his immediate followers to develop out of that attentiveness and respect a virtue ethics that, although generally presented in hierarchical terms that remain culturally and socially specific, bears within it a recognition of aspects of the virtues that deserve universal allegiance. And it seems to me to have been one of the achievements of modern Confucians to have disentangled that recognition from its association with those imperial and patriarchal family structures in terms of which it had for so long been presented.

I am not clear what Professor Wan's judgment is on this matter. He speaks of "a form of paradox or contradiction," arising from the conjunction of a traditional emphasis upon the importance of the hierarchical nature of human relationships and the treatment of the virtue of humaneness in terms of a recip-rocal "meeting of minds and sharing of spirits." But he does not say whether or not he believes that Confucianism can be reformulated in such a way as to rid itself of this contradiction. If it could not, it would indeed have proved unable to move adequately from the culturally local and specific to the universal. Yet I believe that modern Confucianism has, in some key respects, at least achieved just this.

Professor Wan chides me with not being "consistent or firm enough in applying Marxism to the comparison of Confucian virtue ethics and Aristotelianism." Wan insists that the crucial differences between them arise from the differences in the structure of the societies from which they emerged. Let me in turn chide Professor Wan for allowing Marxism to blur the distinction between that which, in both Confucianism and Aristotelianism, is susceptible to explanation in Marxist terms—construing the notion of a Marxist explanation somewhat liberally—and that which is not. It has been a consistent weakness in Marxism and a source of Marxism's own recurrent moral corruption, that it has lacked the resources to distinguish that in morality which is merely local from that which not only claims, but deserves the universal allegiance of rational agents.

Consider now a second area of apparent disagreement between Confucians and Aristotelians, that of teleology. Professor Wan contrasts Aristotle's eudaimonism, "focused," in Professor Wan's formulation, "upon achieving the ends of an individual human life (happiness or goodness)" with a Confucian moral teleology which excludes "the realm of practical consequences of life achievements or personal happiness." Here it is important, first of all, to remember that *eudaimonia* is the name given to a kind of life that would be regarded as happy only by those who had themselves achieved the moral virtues. This is not the notion of "happiness" invoked by many consequentialists, a notion of happiness as consisting in a balance of pleasure over pain or in the maximization of preference satisfaction that can be defined independently of, and prior to, any conception of the virtues. Someone who acts for the sake of *eudaimonia* may be required by the virtue of courage to give up his life in defense of his political community against unjust aggression (*Nicomachean Ethics,* 1115a29–35). So, "personal happiness" is a bad translation of *"eudaimonia."*

Yet, even if we revise Professor Wan's statement of the contrast to accommodate these points, he is clearly in the right in identifying at least a contrast and perhaps a conflict between the teleologies of Confucius and of Aristotle, and even more between the teleologies of Confucius and of Saint Thomas Aquinas. Consider two aspects of this contrast. Professor Wan says that Confucianism "always elevates ethical deontic requirements above merely personal ends." What gives a Confucian virtue ethics its own teleological character is that each individual does indeed have a goal and that "goal is to cultivate one's moral character and confirm one's status in the context of human relationships through the performance of deontic duties." It is by reference to the deontological standards that must be achieved, if one is to become perfect, that the teleological aspects of the moral life are defined. For Aquinas, by contrast, the deontic requirements of the natural law are what they are because the ends, the goods to be pursued by a rational human being, are what they are. It is from the teleology of the moral life that those deontic requirements derive their character.

Second, those deontic requirements are, in Aquinas's view, not only precepts conforming to which is necessary if we are to achieve our common good, but they are precepts of reason (Aquinas, *Summa Theologiae,* Ia–IIae 90, 1 and 2). And it is as animals who are reasoners that we are directed by our nature towards the common good and towards our individual goods. This conception of human beings as, by their nature, practical reasoners is largely absent from the classical Confucian texts. It is not that those texts do not represent agents as having and giving reasons for what they do, and virtuous agents as knowing how to distinguish between good and bad reasons for acting in this or that way. Mencius after all ranks *chih*, intelligent practical discrimination, as one of the four principal virtues. But the insights of the wise, those insights that justify the ascription of *chih*, are generally not represented as, nor justified as, conclusions of arguments, let alone as conclusions of arguments whose first premise is of the form "Since the end and the best is such–and–such . . ." (*Nicomachean Ethics,* 1144a 32–3).

Both Aristotle and Aquinas recognized, of course, that agents generally and characteristically do not need to reflect upon their immediate choice of action by constructing arguments that justify that choice by deriving it from considerations concerning the ultimate end of human beings. The premises of practical reasoning will in the vast majority of cases concern only those goods that are immediately at stake and, often enough, virtuous agents will be disposed to judge, to feel and to act rightly in response to the alternatives that confront them, without any need to argue at all. Nonetheless, in an Aristotelian or Thomistic view, it will always be possible to justify such responses, or to show that they are unjustified, by making explicit the argument that was presupposed by that particular response. And to make such an argument explicit is also to make explicit the way in which that particular response was directed towards that agent's ultimate end.

It matters, therefore, that agents should on occasion reflect upon their immediate ends in the light of their ultimate end and reflect also upon the nature of that ultimate end, in order to avoid misconceiving it. Such practically directed reflection is an important constituent of the moral life and one required of us by our nature as rational animals.[7] This, then, sharply differentiates the Aristotelian, and especially the Thomistic, understanding of the moral life from the Confucian understanding.

I noticed earlier that the deontic requirements of the natural law, as formulated by Aquinas, are justified teleologically. But it is important also to notice that this justification is taken to be available to plain persons, to agents engaged in the everyday tasks of the moral life, and not just to philosophers commenting upon those tasks. So, ordinary agents in their everyday lives possess resources that enable them to interrogate themselves and others concerning the rational justification or lack of justification for their actions. And such interrogation is integral to, for example, the relationship between rulers and the ruled. The precepts of the natural law are, as I also noted earlier, precepts of reason directed towards the common good. They are, in fact, those concepts conforming to which is required, if we are to deliberate with the other members of our households and political communities about what, in our particular situation, our common good is and about how each of us must act if that common good is to be achieved. And, as such, they provide us with a standard by which we can evaluate the positive laws enacted and promulgated by those who rule over us. What does not conform to the standards of the natural law is not merely unjust, but, in Aquinas's view, not law at all. It has, therefore, no authority over rational agents. Enactments that violate the natural law are "acts of violence rather than laws" (Aquinas, *Summa Theologiae*, Ia—IIae 96, 4), and rulers who impose them are tyrants who no longer have any right to our political allegiance.

What Aquinas establishes is thus simultaneously a standard by which in their everyday lives individuals may evaluate both their own actions and those of others with whom they interact, and a standard by which the ruled may stand in judgment on those who rule them.[8] And this suggests that in classical Confucianism, the notable failure to provide systematic grounds for the withdrawal of political allegiance and even for justified rebellion is not unconnected with the absence of standards of practical reasoning, ordered teleologically.

How then is a Confucian to justify particular precepts? In the *Analects* and in many other Confucian texts, the terminus of justification is generally the simple assertion of some particular value. So, for example, the love of learning is justified because without learning, benevolence is apt to lead to foolishness, cleverness to issue in wrong action, trustworthiness to produce harmful consequences, forthrightness to intolerance and so on (*Analects*, 17.8). Commenting on another passage in the *Analects*, Angus Graham wrote: "Confucius does not argue, simply offers his own preference for consideration. Argument would be pointless, since the issue is which course you find yourself preferring in the light of your whole knowledge of the world and of yourself . . . the crux of the matter is which way you spontaneously tend in full knowledge."[9] Yet this doctrine itself seems to require rational justification, a justification that would consist in showing first what kind of character it is that issues in spontaneous preferences for right action; second, how human flourishing depends upon the development of just that kind of character; and third that there are sufficient reasons for holding that this Confucian conception of human flourishing is superior to other rival and alterative conceptions, including that advanced by Thomistic Aristotelians.

I am not here arguing for the superiority of the Thomistic Aristotelian account of the rational teleology that characterizes human beings as moral agents. I am suggesting that, once the contrast between that account and a Confucian view has been adequately characterized, Confucians confront questions concerning the rational justification of their standpoint which go unanswered in the classical texts. It may perhaps be appropriate to argue that they should go unanswered. But this itself should not go unargued.

My suggestion is then that the differences between a Confucian account of the virtues and that advanced by Thomistic Aristotelians raises questions for both. The Confucian emphasis upon the place of *li* among the virtues requires a response from Thomistic Aristotelians. And the Thomistic Aristotelian thesis about the kind of justification that an ethics of the virtues needs to supply requires a response from Confucians. It is one of the great merits of Professor Wan's paper that the differences between Confucians and Aristotelians which he helps us to identify have this kind of significance.

NOTES

1. *Analects,* 10.24, 10.23, 10.25, 10.7, 10.8, and 10.6 tr., in Simon Leys, *The Analects of Confucius* (New York: Norton, 1999).

2. Bryan W. Van Norden, ed., *The Ways of Confucianism: Investigations in Chinese Philosophy* (Chicago: Open Court, 1996), p. 76.

3. *Confucius—The Secular as Sacred* (New York: Harper and Row, 1972), p. 14.

4. As translated by David Nivison in *The Ways of Confucianism,* (Chicago: Open Court, 1996), p. 49.

5. David L. Hall and Roger T. Ames, *Thinking from the Han: Self, Truth, and Transcendence in Chinese and Western Culture* (Albany: State University of New York Press, 1998), pp. 33–35.

6. For a more critical discussion of *li* see A. S. Cua, "*Li* and Moral Justification," *Philosophy East and West* 33, 1 (1982).

7. Not all Aristotelian commentators agree in understanding Aristotle in this way; for different views see Sarah Broadie, *Ethics with Aristotle* (New York: Oxford University Press, 1991); and John McDowell "Deliberation and Moral Development in Aristotle's Ethics," in *Aristotle, Kant and the Stoics: Rethinking Happiness and Duty,* eds., S. Engstrom and J. Whiting (Cambridge: Cambridge University Press, 1996). For a defense of the view that I have taken here, see Alasdair MacIntyre, *Rival Aristotles* (Albuquerque: department of Philosophy, University of New Mexico, 2000). It is in my view, one of the many merits of Aquinas's commentaries on Aristotle that they enable us to understand Aristotle in this way.

8. See on this Alasdair MacIntyre, "Natural Law as Subversive: The Case of Aquinas," in *Journal of Medieval and Early Modern Studies* 26, no. 1 (1995).

9. Angus Graham, *Disputers of the Tao,* (LaSalle, Il: Open Court, 1989), p. 28.

The Polished Mirror: Reflections on Natural Knowledge of the Way in Zhuangzi and Alvin Plantinga

Kelly James Clark and Liu Zongkun

INTRODUCTION

While many topics in comparative philosophy are widely discussed from the East to the West today, it is difficult to imagine any similarities between Alvin Plantinga, a contemporary American Christian philosopher, and Zhuangzi, an ancient Chinese Daoist philosopher. These two philosophers differ in time, methodology, vocabulary, viewpoint and even character. Plantinga is a Protestant Christian teaching at a Roman Catholic university in the latter half of the twentieth and first part of the twenty-first centuries. He earned his reputation using precise and austere analytic philosophy to defend religious belief against the deafening tide of secularism and positivism in the West. Although his work is filled with humor, rigorous argument, and keen philosophical insight, there is little of Zhuangzi's rich but enigmatic narrative style. Plantinga's precise analytic approach and Christian world view seem separated by more than centuries from Zhuangzi's existential storytelling approach and naturalistic world view.[1] Zhuangzi, born Zhuang Zhou, lived in the midst of China's fourth century B.C. golden age of philosophy. In Confucius, Mengzi, Laozi, and Zhuangzi, China had her own Socrates, Plato, and Aristotle. This fertile period was an age of freedom, wisdom, and creativity. Zhuangzi's unique contribution to Chinese thought and culture was his sustained, literary reflection on spiritual freedom.

In spite of the myriad differences which separate these great thinkers, Plantinga and Zhuangzi share a concern for the same fundamental questions about reality and how it can be known. A Chinese idiom says we can reach the same destination by different paths. Although their paths differ, they embark on their respective paths for the similar reasons: both are responding to restrictive philosophical systems that elevate philosophical method above natural human capacities and dispositions. Zhuangzi is responding to the excessive and restrictive moralism of Confucius and the relentless rationalism of Hui Shi. Plantinga is responding to the incessant demand for evidence of Enlightenment thinkers such as Descartes, Locke, and Hume (and their contemporary counterparts) with its concomitant commitment to the remarkably restrictive classical foundationalism. Both thinkers believe that rigorous adherence to these methods is unnatural and cuts people off from the most important truths and ways of living. Liberating people from their hubristic bondage to rationalistic method with all of its promise of certainty requires a fundamental inquiry into the nature of knowing.

The question as formulated in Plantinga's contemporary idiom is "What warrants belief?" A warranted belief has whatever property is necessary to turn true belief into knowledge. Under what conditions does one know something? In Zhuangzi's narrative style, the question is: "Am I a man dreaming that I'm a butterfly or am I a butterfly dreaming that I'm a man?" Although they develop different ways to answer these questions, they come to remarkably similar answers. The issues which imbed these questions involve many contemporary philosophical disputes: the limits of reason (i.e., rationalism) and argument (evidentialism), the myth of certainty, the effects of world view on beliefs and their justification, internalism versus externalism, and realism versus antirealism. In this essay, we will examine the views of these two thinkers especially as they relate to natural knowledge of ultimate reality (of the Dao in Zhuangzi's case and of God in Plantinga's case).

Before proceeding, the difficulty of interpreting Zhuangzi needs to be conceded. The comeliness of Zhuangzi's peculiar narrative style is bought with a price: it is difficult to determine Zhuangzi's actual views on many important matters. Historically the common opinion is that Zhuangzi is a radical skeptic and a relativist. In spite of the appeal of this view on a superficial reading of the *Zhuangzi*, there are many passages which cut against this skeptical and relativist interpretation.[2] Even if we grant that Zhuangzi is not a thoroughgoing skeptic and a radical relativist, it is difficult to discern his precise claims and world view. So, in this paper, we shall offer a plausible and defensible interpretation of Zhuangzi that has substantial support in the text.[3]

DAO VERSUS GOD

Before we go further in exploring the epistemologies of Plantinga and Zhuangzi, we should clarify the philosophical differences between God and the Dao. For westerners, understanding the nature of God is not so difficult, for God stands in the center of Christian belief, which played a foundational role in the development of Western culture. According to Plantinga, Christian belief includes the following components: "God is a person: that is, a being with intellect and will. A person has (or can have) knowledge and belief, but also affections, loves, and hates; a person, furthermore, also has or can have intentions, and can act so as to fulfill them. God has all of these qualities and has some (knowledge, power, and love, for example) to the maximal degree. God is thus all-knowing and all-powerful; he is also perfectly good and wholly loving. Still further, he has created the universe and constantly upholds and providentially guides it."[4] Christian theism is, like its Jewish forebear, monotheistic. God is a person with qualities that are maximally exemplified. God as Creator is entirely distinct from but deeply involved in the world. God is the source of the Good and of goodness and exercises providential control over the world and human history.

Could Zhuangzi find something here familiar with the Dao? Certainly, because, as we shall see, everything is similar (and different) from every other thing in this or that respect! Are there any deep similarities between God and the Dao? The Dao is Creator: the One from which the universe was begotten:

> In the Great Beginning, there was nonbeing; there was no being, no name. Out of it arose One; there was one, but it had no form. Things got hold of it and came to life, and it was called Virtue. Before things had forms, they had their allotments; these were of many kinds, but not cut off from one another, and they were called fates. Out of the flow and flux, things were born, and as they grew they developed distinctive shapes; these were called forms. The forms and bodies held within them spirits, each with its own characteristics and limitations, and this was called the inborn nature.[5]

The Dao is One and is the "creator" and "designer" of the world. The Dao is the source of virtue (*de*); but *de* means something like the characteristic power or powers of a thing than anything distinctly moral. Beyond these points of similarity, Zhuangzi would likely disagree with any attempts to equate God to the Dao. For example, the Dao is not a person and did not create the universe intentionally. It has no form, but exists at all times, everywhere in the universe. And, although Dao is the primary principle that pervades Heaven (i.e., the sky) and Earth, it is more like nature unpersonafied than a divine person.[6] Dao generates and regenerates spontaneously in a natural way and does not rely on motives and sources. Think of the ultimate, multifarious powers of nature, join those contradictory or complementary powers (*yin/yang*) into One, and you are close to thinking of the Dao.

ZHUANGZI ON NATURAL KNOWLEDGE OF THE DAO

In the most famous passage of the *Zhuangzi*, Zhuangzi reflects on how dreams entangle our knowledge of reality:

> Once Chuang Chou dreamed he was a butterfly, a butterfly flitting and fluttering around, happy with himself and doing as he pleased. He didn't know he was Chuang Chou. Suddenly he woke up and there he was, solid and unmistakable Chuang Chou. But he didn't know if he was Chuang Chou who had dreamt he was a butterfly, or a butterfly dreaming he was Chuang Chou. (*Zhuangzi*, 2.45).

One account of this beautiful but murky story is that Zhuangzi is negating the objectivity of knowledge and, thereby, endorsing radical skepticism. Since it is impossible to determine if one is awake or dreaming, one cannot tell if one's beliefs capture the real world instead of one's dream world. But Zhuangzi offers many examples of skillful persons, including Cook Ting whom we shall discuss later, who clearly know things; this militates against the claim that Zhuangzi is a radical skeptic. These craftspersons don't simply know how to do well whatever it is that they do. They also know the Dao, the Way, and they align their lives with the Dao.

One point clearly follows from the butterfly story. Zhuangzi does not take for granted the common sense conviction that the beliefs a person gains by perception are objective or reliable. Perceptual beliefs are not indefeasible or self-presentingly warranted due to the possibility that one might be dreaming. This may seem the philosopher's ploy, indeed the peculiar ploy of the analytic philosopher who often revels in the nonstandard counterexample. Zhuangzi has more than the possibility of dreaming in his repertoire of arguments against the common conviction of the indubitability of sense perception. Illusion, diversity of beliefs, the difficulty of grasping things as they are (instead of things as they appear), and the effects of one's world view and affections on one's beliefs all serve to diminish the conviction of perceptual certainty. Zhuangzi is profoundly aware of the difficulties facing the objectivity and reliability of our perceptual beliefs.

The butterfly story concludes with two lines that highlight the effects of world view on beliefs: "Between Chuang Chou and a butterfly there must be *some* distinction! This is called the Transformation of Things" (*Zhuangzi*, 2.45). This passage might be taken as follows: there is a distinction between Chuang Chou and the butterfly, but they are able to transform into one another. But such an outrageous view is nowhere else defended in the *Zhuangzi*. So the things in "the Transformation of Things" does not refer to Chuang Chou and the butterfly. What is transformed in the story is the world of the butterfly into the world of Chuang Chou. This may be too strong: the butterfly and Chuang Chou inhabit the same world but their different cognitive equipment ensures that their beliefs will countenance different things. Change the butterfly's cognitive equipment to that of a person and "the things" of butterflies will transform into "the things" of persons. According to this view "a thing" is not belief-neutral; *what there is* depends upon what one already believes. Seeing is believing, or is at least deeply influenced by our believings. Zhuangzi is defending a kind of perspectivism: one's perspective determines what one believes to exist. What one takes to constitute the world is a function both of one's experience and one's prior commitments. Experience is not sufficiently powerful to create identical beliefs in the minds of believers with radically differing fundamental commitments. Experience is this, that or nothing, depending on the perceiver's commitments and expectations. The butterfly story makes this point with a narrative argument about dreaming. Dreaming makes us aware of the transformation of things between "the world" of Zhuangzi and "the world" of the butterfly, but dreaming is not the only way to support perspectivism.

In the chapter of the *Zhuangzi* that contains the butterfly story, Zhuangzi offers many different arguments against the claim that whatever seems to us to exist or be true, right, or beautiful, exists or is true, right, or beautiful. What most decisively counts in favor of a thing's existence, truth, goodness, or beauty is one's perspective not the experience of that thing. Consider the following passage concerning an argument between two interlocutors:

> Suppose you and I have had an argument. If you have beaten me instead of my beating you, then are you necessarily right and am I necessarily wrong? If I have beaten you instead of your beating me, then am I right and the other wrong? Are both of us right or are both of us wrong? If you and I don't know the answer, then other people are bound to be even more in the dark. Whom shall we get to decide what is right? Shall we get someone who agrees with you to decide? But if he already agrees with you, how can he decide fairly? Shall we get someone who agrees with me? But if he already agrees with me, how can he decide? Shall we get someone who disagrees with both of us? But if he already disagrees with both of us, how can he decide? (*Zhuangzi*, 2.43–44)

This is often considered an argument from disagreement. It should, of course, give one pause when a sincere person of apparently equal cognitive capabilities and information disagrees with one. But the sheer fact of disagreement is insufficient to generate perspectivism or skepticism. The interlocutor, one may judge, is only *apparently* sincere, equally cognitively capable or informed. If the interlocutor had seen what I've seen, one might reason, she'd believe what I believe; but she hasn't so she doesn't. So disagreement can often be easily handled by diminishing the interlocutor's character, intellect, or data. More significant is the fact that, at least on matters of fundamental human concern, there is no neutral standard (in Zhuangzi's example no neutral judge) by which to judge the competing hypotheses. The debate may be settled by one interlocutor's possession of several nonalethic characteristics: cleverness, sophistry, loudness, wittiness, and intellectual quickness and power. But winning the debate is not equivalent to settling the truth of the matter. Is there some common standards which the interlocutors share (or should share) which permits just the right experiential inputs and the corresponding belief outputs?

Zhuangzi considers several kinds of persons that might be called upon to settle the dispute: a person who agrees with just interlocutor *a*, a person who agrees with just interlocutor *b*, a person who agrees with interlocutor *a* and *b*, and a person who disagrees with interlocutor *a* and *b*. But, for obvious reasons, none of these sorts of persons will be able to settle the dispute. And, to help Zhuangzi along, no jury constituted by a set of judges could settle the matter either. The epistemological problem is not, according to Zhuangzi, disagreement. The problem is, rather, rational unsettle-ability. We live in a world where the truth of our most fundamental beliefs cannot be settled once and for all to everyone's satisfaction. While one may be comfortable within the circle of one's bequeathed and inculcated beliefs, one can have no belief-neutral assurance of their truth. Zhuangzi's conclusion is even stronger: "Obviously, then, neither you nor I nor anyone else can know the answer" (*Zhuangzi*, 2.44). This sort of excursus induces epistemic vertigo!

Although often interpreted as a skeptic and a relativist, Zhuangzi is a perspectivist. Skepticism, in its strongest form, is the claim that no human person knows or could know anything. As mentioned previously, Zhuangzi's heroes are people that not only know things, but they also know some of the most important things. So Zhuangzi is not a skeptic. Epistemological relativism, in its strongest form, is the claim that what is true depends on person and circumstance; what is true (or false) for one person may not be true (or false) for another person. If a person *a* reasonably believes that the Earth is flat, and a person *b* reasonably believes that the Earth is round, then the proposition *the Earth is flat* is true for *a* and false for *b*.[7] According to skepticism, no one knows anything and according to relativism virtually all of one's beliefs are true. Perspectivism often finds it place in the middle of this muddle. Perspectivism is the view that one's perspective (which is inculcated in a person by her needs, wants, desires, affections, intellectual proclivities and sociohistorical situation) affects what one believes. A perspectivist will not countenance the wildly implausible claim that both *a* and *b* are right. Nonetheless, the perspectivist will note how sociohistorical conditioning affects the justification of beliefs. So, noting that *a* lived in sixth century B.C.E. and *b* lives in twenty-first century America, the perspectivist might claim that *a* is justified in believing that the Earth is flat and *b* is justified in believing the denial. Unlike the relativist, the perspectivist can go on to claim that *a*'s belief is false; that is, *a* holds a justified but false belief. That Zhuangzi is defending perspectivism rather than relativism or skepticism is evident in the following passage which discusses claims to know the distinction between good and evil:

Nieh Ch'üe asked Wang Ni, "Do you know what all things agree in calling right?"

"How would I know that?" said Wang Ni.

"Do you know that you don't know it?"

"How would I know that?"

"Then do things know nothing?"

"How would I know that? However, suppose I try saying something. What way do I have of knowing that if I say I know something I don't really not know it? Or what way do I have of knowing that if I say I don't know something I don't really in fact know it? Now let me ask you some questions. If a man sleeps in a damp place, his back aches and he ends up half paralyzed, but is this true of a loach? If he lives in a tree, he is terrified and shakes with fright, but is this true of a monkey? Of these three creatures, then, which one knows the proper place to live? Men eat the flesh of grass-fed and grain-fed animals, deer eat grass, centipedes find snakes tasty, and hawks and falcons relish mice. Of these four, which knows how food ought to taste? Monkeys pair with monkeys, deer go out with deer, and fish play around with fish. Men claim that Mao-chang and Lady Li were beautiful, but if fish saw them they would fly away, and if deer saw them they would break into a run. Of these four, which knows how to fix the standard of beauty for the world? The way I see it, the rules of benevolence and righteousness and the paths of right and wrong are all hopelessly snarled and jumbled. How could I know anything about such discriminations?" (*Zhuangzi*, 2.40–41)

Far from establishing skepticism, this passage establishes the most benign form of relativism: there is disagreement. The passages questions whether there is or could be agreement among all things about what is good (and later adds, beautiful). One wonders who might have made such a claim and Zhuangzi does not put the question into the mouth of his standard adversaries. All things cannot agree upon what is good, because living in a tree is good for the monkey, but not for the loach or the human being. What is good for the goose may be good for the gander but not for the camel, mosquito, or fish. What is good depends upon the nature of the creature and the nature of the object for fulfilling the needs, wants, and desires of the creature. We might generalize:

Something *a* is good for creature *b* if and only if *b*'s needs, wants, and desires are satisfied by *a*.[8]

This understanding of "good" is kind-relative. And the sorts of goods involved permit making the absolute judgments that are made in the aforementioned passage:

1. If one is a human being, living in a tree is not good for one;

2. If one is a monkey, living in a tree is good for one;

3. If one is a human being, sleeping in the damp is not good for one;

4. If one is an eel, sleeping in the damp is good for one;

5. If one is a human being, eating the flesh of grass- and grain-fed beasts is good for one;

6. If one is a deer, eating the flesh of grass- and grain-fed beasts is not good for one;

7. If one is a human being, Lady Li is beautiful;

8. If one is a fish, Lady Li is not beautiful.

What is good or beautiful depends on, is relative to, the kind of creature one is. But this sort of relativism is not inconsistent with the absolute claim that sleeping in the damp is not good for human beings. That is, 1–8 could all be true in a nonrelative, absolute sense. What is more, surely the sage wishes to know the good *for human beings*, not the good *simpliciter*.

Less benign relativisms concern matters of truth and goodness that are specific to humans. For there is often disagreement among, for example, human beings about the good and the true. Nonetheless, we ought not exaggerate the disagreements as many seem wont to do. There is little disagreement about whether or not it is wrong to torture babies for fun, to kill anyone you please under any circumstances, or for a man to have sex with any women he pleases, or that sleeping in the damp is bad for humans. So disagreement is not typically total. The same could be said for the true. There is a great deal upon which nearly everyone agrees. But, agreement notwithstanding, there is widespread and troubling disagreement about the most fundamental of human concerns: the nature of human beings, for example, the good for humans, the goal of human existence, the nature of ultimate reality, and the proper ordering of human society. Concerning these one may wish to settle the matter but whatever answers one offers are faced with Wang Ni's question "How would I know that?" Here Zhuangzi's perspectivism bites us on the nose. Any answers to this sort of question, at least on matters of fundamental human concern, will involve world view assumptions (i.e., one's perspective) that shape, even determine, the answer.

Perspectivism of the sort described above does not entail strong skepticism because the perspectivist may claim that, in spite of the effect of perspective on beliefs, some propositions may still be known. The denial of certainty does not entail the denial of knowledge. Nonetheless, perspectivism lends some credence to more modest forms of skepticism which claim that nothing can be known with certainty. Indeed, the inability to answer the question, "How would I know that?," seems to entail the denial of certainty. What is involved in answering this question? The right answer to "How could I know?" questions will likely involve reference to things humans could not know. That is the conditions that warrant our beliefs may not be within human purview; such conditions may exceed our cognitive capacities. So, we may know things without knowing how we know. Zhuangzi rejects the idea that in order to know things we have to know how we know them. In "Autumn Floods" (section 17), Zhuangzi discusses the vicissitudes of human knowing. In the midst of this excursus on knowledge, he inserts this fetching story:

> The K'uei [one-legged creature] said to the millipede, "I have this one leg that I hop along on, though I make little progress. Now how in the world do you manage to work all those ten thousand legs of yours?"
>
> The millepede said, "You don't understand. Haven't you ever watched a man spit? He just gives a hawk and out it comes, some drops as big as pearls, some as fine as mist, raining down in a jumble of countless particles. Now all I do is *put in motion the heavenly mechanism in me*—I'm not aware how the thing works." (*Zhuangzi*, 17.105; emphasis added)

People don't know how they expectorate, digest food, or gain restoration through sleep, they just do.[9] They just spit, eat, and sleep, all the while following "the heavenly mechanism within." Likewise people don't know how light rays that pass through their eyes stimulate the rods and cons, which send signals through the nerves to their brain, produce the sensation of and corresponding belief that there's a green tree before me. In addition, there may be (and likely are) countless other factors involved in warranting the belief that there's a green tree before me. We can't be inebriated, the light must be good; we need to be looking at a real tree (not one like the well-constructed fake plant I have in my office that routinely tricks people into thinking that it's real). Our visual and cognitive faculties must be adequate to the task (maybe ultimate reality is just waves of various kinds so that when light waves impinge upon us our cognitively faculties misleadingly convert them into perceptual beliefs which we in turn project onto the world). . . . And these are the warranting conditions for perceptual beliefs; what about warranting conditions for memory beliefs, beliefs about the past, inductive beliefs, belief in other minds, and so forth? Again, we are unlikely to know all of the conditions necessary for the warranting of such beliefs. Yet, Zhuangzi believes that in spite of our inability to access the conditions that are jointly necessary to warrant our beliefs, we may still know things. This means that we can know without being certain that we know.

Zhuangzi's concern seems not to be directed at knowing proper but at the deleterious effects that claims to certainty might have on a person. There are people of great understanding, people who know how to move successfully through life, people of wisdom. But there are also petty people of little understanding. Such people arrogantly and self-righteously exalt themselves based on their puny and partial grasp of "the truth." Believing that they are right and everyone else is wrong, they feel morally supreme while everyone else is morally defective. They know the truth so everyone else wallows in ignorance. Knowledge of the true and the good are used to diminish the other and puff up one's self. Zhuangzi is anguished at the moral viciousness of the use to which some people put knowledge. In discussing the difference between great understanding and small understanding, Zhuangzi writes:

> Great understanding is broad and unhurried; little understanding is cramped and busy. Great words are clear and limpid; little words are shrill and quarrelsome. In sleep, men's spirits go visiting; in waking hours, their bodies hustle. With everything they meet they become entangled. Day after day they use their minds in strife, sometimes grandiose, sometimes petty. Their little fears are mean and trembly; their great fears are stunned and overwhelming. They bound off like an arrow or crossbow pellet, certain that they are the arbiters of right and wrong. They cling to their position as though they had sworn before the gods, sure that they are holding on to victory. They fade like fall and winter—such is the way they dwindle day by day. They drown in what they do—you cannot make them turn back. They grow dark, as though sealed with seals—such are the excesses of their old age. And when their minds draw near to death, nothing can restore them to the light. (*Zhuangzi*, 2.32)

Claims to certainty, even on petty matters, do not entail arrogance but they do make arrogance harder to resist. Pride—"they cling to their position as though they had sworn before the gods"—exalts the self by denigrating the other who lacks our superior wisdom and virtue. There are, likewise, epistemic consequences to fixing oneself on one's petty certainties such as closing oneself off to discovering the truth. Making fine distinctions between the true and the not-true, fearing all the while the upset of one's comfortable and conventionally circumscribed world, hinders the unfettered pursuit of truth and virtue. One moves like an arrow or crossbow pellet in a single direction too rapidly to change course if circumstance or information warranted. In another section we read: "You can't discuss the Way with a cramped scholar—he's shackled by his doctrines." Zhuangzi goes on in that passage to commend the person who has come out beyond their banks and borders and has seen the great sea (*Zhuangzi*, 17.97). People who continue to reside comfortably behind their restrictive and distorting banks and borders are pursuing death not life and they grow dark, "as though sealed with seals." Zhuangzi is not an antimoralist but he is an anticonventionalist who is concerned that our comfortable "certainties" prevent us from fully knowing and living. To use Zhuangzi's terms: saying that something is a "this" may prevent us from seeing that it is also a "that." The goal then is not to deny that there is any truth or goodness, the goal is to deny one's self: "Therefore I say, the Perfect Man has no self; the Holy Man has no merit; the Sage has no fame" (*Zhuangzi*, 1.26)

Zhuangzi was not unaware of the hindrances to proper cognition. Realizing that our faculties may be preoccupied by passions and other things that keep it from functioning properly, he advocated the "fasting of the mind." The fasting of the mind empties the mind of the haughty self that is enthroned within by which one believes oneself to be the arbiter of the world. The self with its blinding "certainties" must die. In section 4, Zhuangzi describes the fasting of the mind: "Make your will one! Don't listen with your ears, listen with your mind. No, don't listen with your mind, but listen with your spirit. Listening stops with the ears, the mind stops with recognition, but spirit is empty and waits on all things. The Way gathers in emptiness alone. Emptiness is the fasting of the mind" (*Zhuangzi*, 4.54). The passage is immediately followed by a remarkable description and commendation of the loss of self: "When Hui has never succeeded in being the agent, a deed derives from Hui. When he does succeed in being its agent, there has never begun to be a Hui." Note that human agency is only fully realized when one is freed from the shackles of self. Of the emptiness of mind Zhuangzi writes: "Hold on to all that you have received from heaven but do not think you have gotten anything. Be empty, that is all. The Perfect Man uses his mind as a mirror—going after nothing, welcoming nothing, responding but not storing. Therefore he can win out over things and not hurt himself" (*Zhuangzi*, 7.94–95). Here to be empty means to make one's mind as clear as a mirror which perfectly reflects reality; a mind polished free from impurities is returned to its natural state. Thus, a prepared mind is keenly and finely aware. Emptiness and forgetfulness are sought: empty and forgetful of one's incessant self. The epistemic results of the fasting of the mind: we may break through the limits of sensual perception. By listening with the ear, we may have a sensual perception of a natural sound; by listening with mind, we may understand what makes this sound; by listening with spirit that is empty and as clear as a mirror, however, we may approach the Dao embodied in the natural sound.

The original state of nature and human mind is damaged and corrupted which causes the Dao to hide itself. Our corrupted cognitive capacities, which are misdirected by the self, are incapable of perceiving the Dao. However, if we prepare our minds properly, the Dao reveals itself to us. The mind, thus prepared, is restored to its natural state and is thus capable of mirroring the Dao. Consider the famous story of Cook Ting:

Cook Ting was cutting up an ox for Lord Wen-hui. At every touch of his hand, every heave of his shoulder, every move of his feet, every thrust of his knee—zip! zoop! He slithered the knife along with a zing, and all was in perfect rhythm, as though he were performing the dance of the Mulberry Grove or keeping time to the Ching-shou music.

"Ah, this is marvelous!" said Lord Wen-hui. "Imagine skill reaching such heights!"

Cook Ting laid down his knife and replied, "What I care about is the Way, which goes beyond skill. When I first began cutting up oxen, all I could see was the ox itself. After three years I no longer saw the whole ox. And now—now I go at it by spirit and don't look with my eyes. *Perception and understanding have come to a stop and spirit moves wherever it wants. I go along with the natural makeup,* strike in the big hollows, guide the knife through the big openings, *and follow things as they are.* So I never touch the smallest ligament or tendon, much less a main joint.

A good cook changes his knife once a year—because he cuts. A mediocre cook changes his knife once a month—because he hacks. I've had this knife of mine for nineteen years and I've cut up thousands of oxen with it, and yet the blade is as good as though it had just come from the grindstone. There are spaces between the joints, and the blade of the knife has really no thickness. If you insert what has no thickness into such spaces, then there's plenty of room—more than enough for the blade to play about in. That's why after nineteen years the blade of my knife is still as good as when it first came from the grindstone.

"However, whenever I come to a complicated place, I size up the difficulties, tell myself to watch out and be careful, keep my eyes on what I'm doing, work very slowly, and move the knife with the greatest subtlety, until—flop! The whole thing comes apart like a clod of earth crumbling to the ground. I stand there holding the knife and look all around me, completely satisfied and reluctant to move on, and then I wipe off the knife and put it away."

"Excellent!" said Lord Wen-Hui. "I have heard the words of Cook Ting and learned how to care for life." (*Zhuangzi,* 3.46–47; emphasis added)

There is much to be noted here:

1. The denial of strong skepticism: Cook Ting clearly knows his craft and, more importantly, the Dao;

2. The denial of moral relativism: Cook Ting's life is morally exemplary and preferable to the host of morally deficient lives that Zhuangzi recounts in other sections;

3. Knowledge of reality is not achieved by reason or through the senses, it is attained naturally, by intuition or mystical awareness. Zhuangzi writes: "Perception and understanding have come to a stop and spirit moves wherever it wants."

4. The proper way of knowing the Dao is the natural way, that is, when one's damaged heart/mind has been returned to its original, natural state through proper methods. Reorienting one's mind to accord with the Dao permits one "to follow things as they are" (that is, in accord with the Dao).

The universe and human beings were both born out of the Dao, and the generation and regeneration of the Dao is a natural process. Accordingly, the belief in the Dao is a kind of natural knowledge, based on the natural state of human mind under the restorative effects of the Dao. When *I go along with the natural makeup* I can *follow things as they are.* This natural state, wherein in one grasp reality, precinds from the state of cognition that is distorted by the merely human conventions and categories. When my heart/mind is returned to its natural state through the fasting of the mind, I can know (and live in accord with) the Dao.

PLANTINGA ON NATURAL KNOWLEDGE OF GOD

Just as Zhuangzi had his foils in Confucius and Hui Shi and their disciples, so Plantinga has his foils in René Descartes and David Hume and their disciples. Although Descartes was a Christian and Hume an atheist, they shared the Enlightenment desire to expose all of our beliefs to the searching criticism of reason. If a belief could not be supported by the evidence, it was considered irrational to believe it. W. K. Clifford sums up this attitude: "It is wrong, always and everywhere, to believe anything on insufficient evidence."[10] The Enlightenment demand for evidence is often used as the key premise in an argument against belief in God—the evidentialist objection to belief in God which is stated as follows:

1. It is irrational to believe in God without the support of sufficient evidence or argument;

2. There is insufficient evidence or argument for the existence of God;

3. Therefore, it is irrational to believe in God.

The evidentialist objection does not attempt to disprove God's existence; the conclusion of the argument is not "God does not exist." Rather the evidentialist objection claims that even if God were to exist, it would be irrational to believe in God. Plantinga's so-called "Reformed epistemology" is a sustained attack on premise (1); belief in God, Plantinga contends, does not require the support of evidence or argument in order for it to be rational.[11]

The first problem with the universal demand for evidence is that it cannot satisfy its own standard. This can be seen in the Enlightenment evidentialist's assumption of classical foundationalism.[12] Classical foundationalism is a view that knowledge must be structured properly, from the bottom up. Beliefs at the bottom, "the foundation," are used to evidentially support higher level beliefs. One might imagine a pyramid with its crucial bottom layer of stone that provides firm support for all of its higher levels. The bottom layer of beliefs, what Plantinga calls "basic beliefs," are beliefs that are justified without the support of other beliefs; in a sense, basic beliefs are self-justifying. All of one's higher-level beliefs—one's nonbasic beliefs—find their justification by being properly supported ultimately by one's basic beliefs. Rules of inference transfer the justification from the lower-level beliefs to the higher level beliefs. Classical foundationalism has very strict requirements on which sorts of beliefs are self-justifying and thus allowable as evidence for our other beliefs. According to the classical foundationalist, self-justified, basic beliefs are those that are acquired through *sensory experience* or are *self-evident* like logic and mathematics or are *incorrigible* (beliefs about which we could not be wrong: usually first-person psychological states like "I am being appeared to redly").[13] Suppose you were to make a list of all of your beliefs starting with your experiential beliefs: *The sky is blue, grass is green, men spit,* and *millipedes have lots-o-legs.* . . . Add to your list of beliefs your logical and mathematical beliefs: *2 + 2 = 4, every proposition is either true or false, all of the even numbers that I know of are the sum of two prime numbers,* and *in Euclidean geometry the interior angles of triangles equal 180°.* . . . And, finally, add all of your incorrible beliefs: *I am being appeared to redly* and *I seem to see something round.* From this list of beliefs (which is your set of evidence as allowed by classical foundationalism), try to deduce Clifford's maxim: that it is wrong, always and everywhere, for anyone to believe anything on insufficient evidence. None of the propositions that are allowed as evidence have anything at all to do with the conclusion. So Clifford's universal demand for evidence, in so far as it is rooted in classical foundationalism, cannot satisfy its own standard: it is self-referentially inconsistent. Therefore, by Clifford's own criterion, it must be irrational.[14]

The problems that classical foundationalism poses for Clifford's maxim and itself likewise afflict most of the beliefs that we hold. Very few of our beliefs could survive Clifford's test (given what classical foundationalism admits as evidence). As Plantinga writes: "One crucial lesson to be learned from the development of modern philosophy—Descartes through Hume, roughly—is just this: relative to propositions that are self-evident and incorrigible, most of the beliefs that form the stock in trade of ordinary life are not probable—at any rate there is no reason to think that they are probable."[15] Think of the relatively impoverished set of basic beliefs permitted by classical foundationalism. Now think of how many of your beliefs, even scientific ones, are acquired not because they are inferable from your classically foundationalist set of basic beliefs but are acquired *just because someone told you.* Not having been to Brazil, I only have Ray and Ann's testimonial evidence that Brazil is a country in South America. And, since I have been to relatively few countries around the world, I must believe in the existence of most countries without support of evidence. We believe that e=mc² and that matter is made up of tiny little particles not because of experiments in a chemistry or physics lab but more likely because our science teachers told us so. Most of the beliefs that we have acquired are based on our trust in our teachers and not on careful consideration of what Clifford would consider adequate evidence.

The demand for evidence simply cannot be met in a large number of cases with the cognitive equipment that we have. How do we know, for example, that other minds and, therefore, other people exist?[16] How do we know that people are not simply cleverly constructed robots? How do we know that behind the person-facade lies a person—someone with thoughts, desires, and feelings? We can't experience another person's feelings; we can't see another person's thoughts (even if you were to cut off the top of their head and peer into their brain); and we can't feel another person's pain. Yet thoughts, desires, feelings, and pains are all essential to being a person. So we can't tell from the outside or just by looking, so to speak, if someone is a person. I can know that *I* am a person because I experience my own thoughts, feelings, and desires. But I can't know, because I don't have any access to your inner-experience, if you, or anyone else, is a person. And no one has ever been able to construct a good argument that there are other persons. So, if we had to meet the demand for evidence, we could not believe that other persons exist. And one has ever been able to prove that we were not created five minutes ago with our memories intact. No one has been able to prove the reality of the past or that, in the future, the sun will rise. This list could go on and on. There is a limit to the things that human beings can prove.

But surely we know that there are other persons, that the Earth is more than five minutes old, that the sun will rise tomorrow and that Zhuangzi lived long before Alvin Plantinga, and so forth. In these cases, we know lots of things but we cannot prove them. We have to trust or rely on the cognitive faculties which produce these beliefs. We rely on our memory to produce memory beliefs (for example, I remember climbing the Grand Teton mountain with Alvin Plantinga). We rely on an inductive faculty to produce beliefs about the veracity of natural laws (should I spit, the spit will fall to the ground). We rely on our cognitive faculties when we believe that there are other persons, there is a past, there is a world independent of our mind, or what other people tell us. We can't help but trust our cognitive faculties.[17]

It is easy to see why. Reasoning must start somewhere. Consider the following regress argument in support of some sort of foundationalism. Suppose we were required to offer evidence or arguments for all of our beliefs. If we offer statements 1–4 as evidence for 5, we would have to offer arguments to support 1–4. And then we would have to offer arguments in support of the arguments that are used to support 1–4. And then we would need arguments . . . .You get the point. There have to be some truths that we can just accept and reason from.

Most classical foundationalist accepted or would accept this regress argument. Where they differ from Plantingas is how they sought to characterize basic beliefs. And their severe restrictions on basic beliefs seems to be a function of two fundamental commitments on their part: the quest for certainty and epistemological internalism.[18] Of the quest for certainty Descartes writes: " . . . I will follow the same path I took yesterday, putting aside everything which admits of the least doubt, as if I had discovered it to be absolutely false. I will go forward until I know something certain—or, if nothing else, until I at least know for certain that nothing is certain."[19] If the foundations are certain and the principles of inference are truth- (i.e., certainty-) preserving, then the resultant beliefs must also be certain. The central contention of internalism is that the justifying conditions of a belief are somehow internal to the believing agent;

whatever it is that justifies belief is something to which the believer has internal access. Justification is a property of beliefs which can be "seen" or understood simply by looking within, by carefully examining one's own beliefs. One looks at one's set of foundational beliefs to see if they are adequately self-justifying; next one carefully attends to one's higher level beliefs to see if they are properly related to the basic beliefs. If any of one's beliefs fail to have the right sort of justificationl lustre or aura, they ought to be discarded. Internalism is attractive because it places the justification of our beliefs without our own intellectual purview and powers. One simply needs to check one's foundational beliefs, the inferences that one has made, and the resultant beliefs to see if one's beliefs are justified.

Plantinga, however, argues that in most cases of knowledge, we don't have direct access to all of the conditions that must obtain for our beliefs to move from justified opinion to knowledge. Plantinga calls the special property that turns true belief into knowledge "warrant."

> A belief B has *warrant* for one if and only if B is *(a)* produced by one's properly functioning cognitive faculties, *(b)* in circumstances to which those faculties are designed to apply; in addition *(c)* those faculties must be designed for the purpose of producing true beliefs.[20]

So, for instance, my belief that *there is a butterfly in front of me* is warranted if *(a*)* it is produced by my properly functioning perceptual faculties (and not by weariness or dreaming), and if *(b*)* I am not dreaming of a butterfly when one happens to be in front of me (this cognitive environment is not one for which our perceptual faculties were designed), or no one is tricking me by dangling an exact painted replica of a butterfly in front of me[21] (they have messed up my cognitive environment); and, finally, Plantinga believes that *(c*)* our perceptual faculties have been designed (by God) for the purpose of producing true beliefs.

Note briefly the portions of Plantinga's definition that are not within one's immediate or direct purview—whether or not one's faculties are functioning properly, whether or not one's faculties are designed by God, whether or not one's faculties are designed for the production of true beliefs, whether or not one is using one's faculties in the environment intended for their use. We cannot determine if our beliefs are warranted simply by attending to our beliefs. According to Plantinga, warranted belief, that is, knowledge, is not entirely up to us. It depends crucially upon whether or not conditions obtain that are neither under our direct rational purview nor our conscious control.

We have been outfitted with cognitive faculties that produce beliefs that we can reason from. We must rely on our God-given intellectual equipment to produce beliefs, more often than not[22] without evidence or argument, in the appropriate circumstances. Is it reasonable to believe that God has created us with a cognitive faculty which produces belief in God without evidence or argument?

There are at least two reasons that Plantinga offers to believe that it is proper or rational for a person to accept belief in God without the support of an argument.[23] The first is an inductive argument. As argued, knowledge, if it is possible at all, begins with trust not with doubt. If we cannot trust that our hearing, sight, memory, inductive faculties, belief in other minds, and so forth are truth-conducive, we have nothing upon which to reason to build up our view of the world. Parity suggests that we should extend the trust in our other cognitive faculties to belief in God as well. According to Plantinga, we have a natural knowledge of God which is not arrived at by inference or argument but in a more immediate way. Upon the perception of the beauty of nature and harmony of the universe, certain beliefs arise within us. Such beliefs, however, are not the results of logical reasoning, rather, "they are occasioned by the circumstances; they are not conclusions from them. The heavens declare the glory of God and the skies proclaim the work of his hands: but not by way of serving as premises for an argument."[24] It is natural to suppose that if God created us with cognitive faculties which by and large reliably produce beliefs without the need for evidence, God would likewise provide us with a cognitive faculty which produces belief in God without the need for evidence. Plantinga contends that God has given us an awareness of himself that is not dependent on theistic arguments. Plantinga calls this tendency to believe in God "the *sensus divinitatis*." He makes explicit the parity argument: "The *sensus divinitatis* resembles perception, memory, and *a priori* belief."[25] He finds inspiration for his view in John Calvin, the progenitor of reformed theology. John Calvin believed that God had provided us with a sense of the divine:

> "There is within the human mind, and indeed by natural instinct, an awareness of divinity." . . . To prevent anyone from taking refuge in the pretense of ignorance, God himself has implanted in all men a certain understanding of his divine majesty. Ever renewing its memory, he repeatedly sheds fresh drops. . . . Indeed, the perversity of the impious, who though they struggle furiously are unable to extricate themselves from the fear of God, is abundant testimony that this conviction, namely, that there is some God, is naturally inborn in all, and is fixed deep within, as it were in the very marrow.[26]

This natural knowledge of God, we shall see shortly, is damaged due to what Plantinga calls "the noetic affects of sin."

Second, belief in God is more like belief in a person than belief in a scientific theory. Compare the scientific approach—doubt first, consider all of the available evidence, believe later—to one's approach to personal relations. What seems manifestly reasonable for physicists in their laboratory is desperately deficient in human relations. Human relations demand trust, commitment, and faith. If belief in God is more like belief in other persons than belief in atoms, then the trust that is appropriate to persons will be appropriate to God. We cannot and should not arbitrarily insist that the scientific method is appropriate to every kind of human practice. The fastidious scientist, who cannot leave the demand for evidence in her laboratory, will find herself cut off from relationships that she could otherwise reasonably maintain—with friends, family, and, even, God.[27]

Plantinga believes, like Calvin, that the natural knowledge of God has been overlaid by sin. Part of the redemptive process will require the removal of the effects of sin on our minds. The primary obstacles to belief in God seems to be more moral and affectional than intellectual. The noetic effects of sin must be removed or diminished so that one can experience God. One can see God only when the haughty self is dethroned. Humility, not proofs, seems more appropriate to the realization of belief in God.

CONCLUSION

We have just climbed two great mountains. The paths we traveled were as different as a fish is from a bird. One path was luxuriant, very gradual, but hard to follow. The other seemed more barren and steep but easier to follow. Did we travel different trails to the top of the same mountain? Zhuangzi's perplexing narratives and Plantinga's difficult arguments have been our two paths. Where have they led?

As we've laid out the epistemologies of these two great thinkers, some remarkable similarities have emerged. Perhaps most significant is the view that our knowledge of ultimate reality is produced by a natural impulse or disposition. Both thinkers contend that this natural disposition to believe is corrupted by the self replete with its desires and affections. The first steps to recover one's natural disposition requires the removal of the moral and affectional obstacles to the perception of the truth.

A second significant similarity is their rejection of stifling rationalistic methods which are so ill-suited to our nature. The excessive moralism of Confucius and rationalism of Hui Shi violate our moral and believing nature. For Plantinga, the structures Enlightenment evidentialism with its assumption of classical foundationalism are arbitrary and indefensible. More importantly, the Enligtenment demand for evidence cannot be satisfied given our cognitive makeup: we simply do not produce enough basic beliefs (as countenanced by classical foundationalism) to justify any of our significant nonbasic beliefs. Both Zhuangzi and Plantinga courageously oppose the dominant philosophical methods of their day all the while defending people's natural impulses to believe. Part of their rejection of rationalism is that its methodologies would hinder and even prevent the acquisition of our most important beliefs.

And, finally, both Plantinga and Zhuangzi mine the epistemic consequences of creatureliness. One might look at the various philosophical options that they oppose as manifestations of human pride. Strong relativism, for example, would turn all humans into noetic gods—since truth is relative to time, place, and circumstance, all of one's beliefs could easily turn out to be true (people would be infallible if not omniscient). Rationalism and Enlightenment evidentialism are means of attaining a "god's eye view" of one's beliefs and the world—to gain an atemporal perspective that ignores contingency. Plantinga and Zhuangzi are keenly aware of the creaturely limitations on our knowings. We have this cognitive equipment, for better or for worse, and we are thereby permitted (because obliged) to use it. We acquire beliefs without being capable of assessing whether or not the conditions necessary for warrant obtain. We are creatures, not gods, and have limited access to our cognitive equipment and environment. This carries with it a corresponding commitment to human fallibilism and a loss of epistemic certainty. Yet neither thinker makes the facile (yet in the case of many of Plantinga's more fashionable contemporaries, irresistible) inference that fallibilism and uncertainty entail relativism or antirealism. Our perspective- or world view-infected beliefs are true or false depending upon the way the world is. And the way the world is not up to us. Although we can't be certain, both authors maintain that we can grasp enough of the truth, through our natural dispositions, to properly order our lives in accord with the truth. With mirrors polished through the renunciation of self our natural heart/minds reflect the Way.

NOTES

1. Plantinga's approach is not only foreign to Zhuangzi's approach in particular, it seems totally alien to Chinese thought in general. Classical Chinese thought is more at home in the practical ethics of Confucius and Mencius than the possible worlds semantics of Leibniz and Plantinga.

2. For an excellent discussion of the various ways of interpreting the Zhuangzi, see Philip J. Ivanhoe and Paul Kjellberg, eds., *Essays on Skepticism, Relativism, and Ethics in the Zhuangzi* (Albany, NY: State University of New York Press, 1996). For a book-length defense of Zhuangzi as a nonrelativist/nonskeptic, see Robert A. Allinson, *Chuang-Tzu for Spiritual Transformation* (Albany, NY: State University of New York Press, 1989).

3. Plantinga's views, on the other hand, are generally fairly clear.

4. Alvin Plantinga, *Warranted Christian Belief* (New York: Oxford University Press, 2000), p. vii.

5. Burton Watson, trans. *The Complete Works of Chuang Tzu* (New York: Columbia University Press, 1968), sec. 12, p. 131. All Zhuangzi references indicated *within the text* are from *Chuang Tzu: Basic Writings*, trans., Burton Watson (New York: Columbia University Press, 1964). The references will be indicated by section and page. We will focus on the so-called inner chapters which are the sections most likely to have their source in Zhuangzi.

6. Watson, *The Complete Works*, p. 126.

7. Zhuangzi is also concerned with moral relativism. Moral relativism is the claim that what is good (or bad) for one person may not be good (or bad) for another person. If a person *a* reasonably believes that cannibalism is good and a person *b* reasonably believes that cannibalism is bad, then the proposition *cannibalism is good* is good for *a* and bad for *b*. That Zhuangzi is not a moral relativist is clear from his unwavering belief that people who do not live according to the Dao are, in spite of their perspectives, woefully misguided.

8. A similar but contrary definition of "bad for creatures" could be offered as well.

9. Hegel, in a rare fit of lucidity, makes a similar claim about knowledge of God: "The (now somewhat antiquated) metaphysical proofs of God's existence, for example, have been treated as if a knowledge of them and a conviction of their truth were the only and essential means of producing a belief and conviction that there is a God. Such a doctrine would find its parallel if we said that eating was impossible before we acquired a knowledge of the chemical, botanical, and zoological characters of our food; and we must delay digestion till we had finished the study of anatomy and physiology."

10. W. K. Clifford, *Lectures and Essays* (London: Macmillan and Co., 1886), p. 339–63.

11. For a thorough discussion of Plantinga's epistemology, see Kelly James Clark, *Return to Reason* (Grand Rapids, MI: Eerdmans Publishing Compnay, 1990).

12. See "Reason and Belief in God," in Alvin Plantinga and Nicholas Wolterstorff, eds., *Faith and Rationality* (IN: University of Notre Dame Press, 1983), pp. 16–93.

13. Note that belief in God is neither self-evident, incorrigible, nor acquired through our five senses. So, according to the classical foundationalist it cannot properly be a basic belief. Hence, the demand for evidence to support it.

14. Classical foundationalism, Plantinga well argues, is itself self-referentially inconsistent. We've used Clifford's maxim for ease of discussion. See Alvin Plantinga, "Reason and Belief in God," in *Faith and Rationality,* Alvin Plantinga and Nicholas Wolterstorff, eds. (IN: University of Notre Dame Press, 1983), pp. 59–63.

15. Plantinga, "Reason and Belief in God," p. 59.

16. Plantinga discusses this in his *God and Other Minds,* (Ithaca: Cornell University Press, 1972).

17. Plantinga discusses these issues in his trilogy on epistemology, especially in *Warrant: The Current Debate* and *Warrant and Proper Function* (New York: Oxford University Press, 1993)

18. Plantinga discusses internalism in *Warrant: the Current Debate,* ch. 1.

19. Descartes, *Medidations on First Philosophy*, trans., Donald A. Cress, (Indianapolis, IN: Hackett Publishing Company, 1979), med. 2.

20. I have stated this succinctly, roughly, partially and without nuance. For a full discussion, see Alvin Plantinga, *Warrant and Proper Function* (New York: Oxford University Press, 1993).

21. Conrad Q. Bakker, one of Clark's colleagues in the art department, held a "garage sale" that consisted entirely of his artistic renditions of garage sale stuff including, for example, typewriters, and tools. Many visitors were fooled, some, looking for a bargain on real hammers, unhappily.

22. "It is only in a smallish area of our cognitive life that the warrant of a belief has for us derives from the fact that it is accepted on the evidential basis of other beliefs." Alvin Plantinga, *Warrant and Proper Function* (New York: Oxford University Press, 1993), p. 178.

23. Plantinga does not contend that belief in God could not or, in some cases, should not be based on evidence or argument. Indeed, he argues that theistic arguments could provide some, noncoercive, evidence of God's existence. By noncoercive, he means that the theistic arguments aren't of such power and illumination that they should be expected to persuade all rational creatures. See "Arguing for God," in *Readings in the Philosophy of Religion,* by Kelly James Clark, (Peterborough, Ontario: Broadview Press, 2000), pp. 126–137. Disagreements about these arguments typically resolve into underlying world view, or metaphysical commitments.

24. Alvin Plantinga, *Warranted Christian Belief* (New York: Oxford University Press, 2000), p. 175.

25. Plantinga, *Christian Belief,* p. 175.

26. As found in Plantinga, "Reason and Belief in God," 65–66.

27. This sort of argument is implicit in most of Plantinga's writings on the rationality of religious belief. It is quite explicit in William James, "The Will to Believe," in *The Will to Believe and other essays* (New York: Dover, 1956), pp. 1–31.

Reflections On "The Polished Mirror"

Alvin Plantinga

First, I'd like to thank Kelly Clark and Zongkun Liu for their fascinating exercise in comparative philosophy. Initially their project has an unpromising look about it: the enormous differences in time and culture suggests that comparison here would be about as useful as (as they say) comparing apples and oranges. In fact it promises to be much less useful: apples and oranges, after all, are alike in very many salient and important ways and certainly worthy of comparison. Both are fruits, grow on trees, are sought after by human beings and other primates; they are about the same size, cost about the same per unit, are shipped all over the world, are good to take rock climbing, suffer upon being frozen, used to be great as Christmas stocking stuffers, and the like. Comparing apples and oranges makes eminently good sense; a more accurate complaint would be about comparing apples with, say, *E coli*, or jet airliners, or Brazil, or the number 27.

However that may be, Clark and Zongkun's project looks initially unpromising; a second look, however, reveals that there really could be a sensible basis of comparison here. For what is it, according to Clark and Zongkun, that is Zhuangzi's central concern? That concern, apparently, has to do with the fact that there are deep divisions among human beings, deep disagreements on matters of the greatest import, such as the good for human beings, what the world is really like, how human beings should live, what is right and wrong, and the like. Well, so there are deep disagreements among human beings: so what? What's the problem? One problem is that one might think such disagreements throw real doubt on the possibility of *knowledge* in this or other areas, or even of rational or justified belief. Suppose, for example, philosophical naturalism (contrary to fact) were the truth of the matter. Given that the vast bulk of humankind disagrees with them, could naturalists—Daniel Dennett or Richard Dawkins, for example—*know* that it's true? Suppose they realize that their views are not shared by everyone, and in fact are held by only a tiny minority of the world's population: could they be rational in continuing to hold them? Could they be *justified*?

Clark and Zongkun suggest that some of Zhuangzi's concerns lie in the neighborhood of these questions. They suggest that he doesn't take the facts of disagreement to imply that we human beings can't or don't have any knowledge at all, or even knowledge on the topics of the disagreements; they ascribe to him, not skepticism about these matters, but *perspectivism*:

> Although often interpreted as a skeptic and a relativist, Zhuangzi is a perspectivist. Skepticism, in its strongest form, is the claim that no human person knows or could know anything. As mentioned previously, Zhuangzi's heroes are people that not only know things, they know some of the most important things. So Zhuangzi is not a skeptic.
>
> What he is instead is a perspectivist, that is, he holds that one's perspective (which is inculcated in a person by her needs, wants, desires, affections, intellectual proclivities, and sociohistorical situation) affects what one believes. . . . [T]he perspectivist will note how sociohistorical conditioning affects the justification of beliefs. So, noting that *a* lived in sixth century B.C.E. China, and *b* lives in twenty-first century America, the perspectivist might claim that *a* is justified in believing that the Earth is flat, and *b* is justified in believing the denial.

A perspective, presumably, is a connected congeries of beliefs; no doubt a perspective will also have an effect on which other beliefs one holds. (Presumably a perspective will also involve a connected congeries of affections, likes and dislikes, loves and hates.) Further, the perspectivist thinks one's perspective bears on the *justification* of what one believes, on what is such that you are within your rights in believing it. Still further, she will also think, no doubt, that one's perspective bears on the *rationality* of what one believes, where rationality is a matter of proper function, so that a belief is rational, in given circumstances, if a human being whose cognitive capacities are not subject to dysfunction could hold that belief in those circumstances. Does one's perspective also bear on the *warrant* of one's beliefs? Say that warrant is the property that distinguishes knowledge from mere true belief. My earnest conviction that I will win the lottery, based, as it is, just on my inveterate optimism, doesn't constitute knowledge even if, as it happens, I do win the lottery. What *is* this property that a belief must have to constitute knowledge? According to me, it's the property a belief has when it is produced by cognitive faculties functioning properly in an appropriate cognitive environment according to a design plan successfully aimed at truth.[1] And now our questions: Does the fact that one's perspective influences one's beliefs imply that one doesn't have knowledge of those beliefs whose formation is at least partly due to one's perspective? Does it do so, according to Zhuangzi?

Clark and Zongkun suggest that, according to Zhuangzi, this perspectival influence doesn't imply *strong* skepticism, that is, the thought that no one really knows anything. That certainly seems to fit with the passages they cite. Zhuangzi's perspectivism might, however, imply more limited forms of skepticism. For example, it might imply that no one can be *certain* of anything, or anything about which there is perspectival dispute; or perhaps the idea is that beliefs influenced or arising out of perspectival differences can't constitute knowledge. Perhaps we could put it like this. First, people differ in their perspectives. We needn't tarry to try to say just what a perspective is, but ways of thinking and valuing like Christianity, Daoism, philosophical naturalism, empiricism, rationalism, and the like would be examples. Many of these perspectives are incompatible with each other, as, for example, Christian belief or theism, on the one hand, and philosophical naturalism on the other. Second, these perspectives themselves constitute disagreements, and, in a variety of ways, induce disagreement about other propositions. One way, of course, is that beliefs or propositions, constituting a perspective, will entail propositions incompatible with those entailed by other perspectives. There may also be differences of more subtle kinds. For example, perhaps there are some beliefs held in common by people who accept competing perspectives; perhaps one of the perspectives, conjoined with those commonly accepted beliefs, will entail the denial of some proposition in another perspective. Or perhaps certain propositions are much more likely with respect to one perspective together with commonly accepted beliefs than with respect to another perspective.

By way of example, consider philosophical naturalism and Christian or more broadly theistic belief. There are many propositions on which Christians and naturalists will agree: that there is an Earth, that it contains many living things, that at one time the Earth contained no living things, that (accordingly) therefore there must have been first living things, and the like. They will also agree on less general things: that the Miller-Urey experiment produced some amino acids, that scientists have not been able to create life in the laboratory, that in fact they are enormously far from doing so, and so on. (According to Francis Crick [himself no fan of theism] life must be regarded as the next thing to a miracle; says Harold P. Klein, "The simplest bacterium is so damn complicated from the point of view of a chemist that it is almost impossible to imagine how it happened.")[2] So consider the set of beliefs that includes what is common to reasonably well-educated contemporary Christians and naturalists and call it "*S.*" And consider the proposition that life on Earth arose "naturalistically," that is, by some combination of Jacques Monod's chance and necessity. Certain events happened just by chance; then, by virtue of the ordinary laws[3] of physics and chemistry living things came to be.

This is at least plausibly thought to be possible with respect to the Christian perspective. For first, if, in fact, (given God's necessary existence and essential omniscience and omnipotence) genuine chance events are impossible, we could think of Jacques Lucien Monod's combination of chance and necessity as a limiting case where chance plays no part and all is necessity. Alternatively, suppose the existence of genuine chance *is* compatible with God's existence and character. Then perhaps God could have brought it about that there should be

life of the sort he intends by employing knowledge of *counterfactuals of chance*
—counterfactuals that specify what would happen by chance under various
conditions God could cause to be actual.[4]

So life's arising naturalistically is possible with respect to the Christian perspective. It is also, of course, possible with respect to the naturalistic perspective.
But it is much more likely with respect to the latter, together with beliefs shared
by theist and naturalist, than it is with respect to the former together with those
shared beliefs. For the theist sees, of course, that God could have done it that
way; but he could also have done it in many other ways. For example, he could
have brought about the existence of the first living beings—or for that matter
full grown horses—by virtue of some kind of special creation. From the theistic
perspective, the enormous difficulties in seeing how life could have arisen the
naturalistic way make it relatively unlikely that God did it in that way. It is, of
course, *possible* that he did it in that way, and possible that further research or
discoveries will disclose just how it happened. But relative to theism and our
present evidence, it isn't likely that it happened that way. With respect to naturalism, however, it is very likely indeed that life on Earth arose in this fashion:
there is no remotely plausible alternative. For the naturalist, then, it is much
more likely that a naturalistic account of the origin of life is true than it is for
the Christian. The difference in perspective induces a difference with respect to
the probability of the proposition in question.

Accordingly, there are a variety of ways in which perspectival differences can
induce differences in belief. Now consider S and S*. S believes P and S* believes
Q, which is incompatible with P; and suppose this difference is attributable to
their difference of perspective. (In the trivial case, P is part of S's perspective and
Q is part of S*'s perspective.) Does it follow from this description of the case
that S does not know P and S* does not know Q? Well, why should we think
so? One possible reason for thinking so is mentioned by Clark and Zongkun and
perhaps alluded to by Zhuangzi: there is no neutral standpoint from which this
dispute can be adjudicated. As Clark and Zongkun put it:

> More significant is the fact that, at least on matters of fundamental human con-
> cerns, there is no neutral standard (in Zhuangzi's example, no neutral judge) by
> which to judge the competing hypotheses. . . . (Clark & Zongkun p. 167)

They go on:

> The epistemological problem is not, according to Zhuangzi, disagreement. The
> problem is, rather, rational unsettle-ability. We live in a world where the truth of
> our most fundamental beliefs cannot be settled once and for all to everyone's
> satisfaction. While one may be comfortable within the circle of one's bequeathed
> and inculcated beliefs, one can have no belief neutral assurance of their truth.
> Zhuangzi's conclusion is even stronger: "Obviously, then, neither you nor I nor
> anyone else can know the answer." (Clark & Zongkun p. 168)

So the problem, initially, is that there is no neutral standard from which this dispute can be adjudicated. But what would such a neutral standpoint be? And suppose S and S* disagree in such a way that the disagreement can't be settled from some neutral standpoint: does this fact imply that the beliefs they disagree about don't constitute knowledge on the part of either one? Again, what would a neutral standpoint be, and what would it be for a dispute to be settleable from it? A neutral standpoint, as between S and S*, would perhaps be a set NS of beliefs shared by S and S*. And perhaps a dispute is settleable, from NS, only if either NS implies, in some suitable strong sense, P or else it implies P*. This is a necessary condition of the disputes being settleable from NS; is it also sufficient? I don't think so. It is also required that S and S* be able to see the implication in question. Further, it is also required that each of them believes the conjunction of propositions in NS more firmly than they believe S and S*; otherwise one or both of them might just reason by *modus tollens* to the denial of the conjunction of NS. No doubt there are further necessary conditions as well; let's cheerfully (if falsely) assume that we have them firmly in hand. Whatever they are, they aren't going to change things much with respect to the matter in question.

Well, suppose S believes P and S* believes not-P, and there is no neutral standpoint from which the disagreement can be settled: does it follow that neither S nor S* knows the proposition she believes? I should think not. For perhaps one of them has a perspective that is really stupid, or really weird. Crazed by obsessive study of the ontological argument, S* has come to believe that he is the being than which none greater can be conceived (and in fact he isn't); he goes around forgiving sins and insisting on homage. In that case, any sensible S might disagree with S* about, say, whether S* really is a necessary being or has created the world. Now suppose still further that there is no neutral standpoint from which this dispute can be settled. For example, perhaps there is nothing S* believes more firmly than that he is the being than which it is not possible that there be a greater; and from that (he thinks) it immediately follows that he is a necessary being. (S, of course, doesn't believe anything from which it follows that S* is as impressive as all *that*.) So here is a dispute that can't be settled from a neutral standpoint: couldn't it be, nevertheless, that S knows perfectly well that S* is mistaken about being the greatest possible being? It certainly looks that way. So this argument—an argument for skepticism from the existence of disputes that can't be settled from neutral standpoints—isn't very strong. Is there a stronger argument lurking in the nearby bushes?

Perhaps. The salient thing about this fellow S* is that he appears to hold *insane* beliefs; he's deranged, suffering from delusions of grandeur; his rational faculties aren't functioning as they are supposed to. This is clearly relevant to our question, but exactly how? How can we take this into account? Something else Clark and Zongkun say, I think, provides a clue: these disagreements are characterized by "*rational* unsettle-ability." They can't be settled *rationally*. What does *that* mean? Well, perhaps what it means is that the dispute can't be settled on the basis of the *deliverances of reason*. Consider our "rational faculties": memory, perception, induction, rational intuition, introspection, maybe Thomas Reid's sympathy, perhaps John Calvin's *sensus divinitatis*, possibly others. We might use the term "reason" to denote the ensemble of these faculties. Now these faculties produce or deliver various beliefs in various situations. For example, given the sort of visual experience I have at the moment (and given my other beliefs) any human being whose cognitive faculties are functioning properly would form the belief that she's seeing trees and a very large lake. Any properly functioning adult human being will believe that $2 + 3 = 5$, that there are dogs, that people sleep, and so on. We might say that the deliverances of reason, with respect to a given situation, are the set of beliefs that a properly functioning adult human being would hold in that situation. I realize that's pretty rough, but perhaps it will do for present purposes. And now let's also say that a dispute (S believes P and S* believes not-P), can be rationally settled if and only if the deliverances of reason together imply P, in some suitably strong sense of "imply," or else, in that same sense, imply Q.[5]

That all disputes of this sort can be settled rationally was, of course, the dream of classical foundationalism. But classical foundationalism makes an even stronger claim. It adds (especially in its Cartesian, Humean version) that the deliverances of reason comprise only what's self-evident together with what is directly about one's own mental life, together with what can be properly inferred from these propositions. And I think it would indeed be a consequence of classical foundationalism that if S and S* are involved in a dispute that can't be settled rationally, in the above sense, then neither S nor S* knows what he believes.

Now perhaps Zhuangzi meant to agree (in anachronistically anticipatory fashion) with Descartes and Hume on this point: perhaps he, too, thinks that if a dispute can't be settled rationally, then neither of the disputants knows what he believes. As Clark and Zongkun say, it isn't easy to see just what Zhuangzi does mean to say; and as they point out, Zhuangzi doesn't seem to be committed to a *general* skepticism; but some of the quotations Clark and Zongkun produce seem to suggest that he embraces this more limited skeptical conclusion. ("Obviously, then, neither you nor I nor anyone else can know the answer.") If he does mean to hold this, is he right? If a dispute can't be settled rationally, does it follow that neither of the disputants has knowledge of the disputed proposition?

No, it doesn't follow. That is because it isn't necessarily true that the deliverances of reason are the only sources of knowledge. It is not a deliverance of reason that any item of knowledge, for a person S, is implied, in that suitably strong sense, by the conjunction of the deliverances of reason. This is true in particular because there may be *other* sources of knowledge, sources in addition to reason. For example, Christians typically think that *faith*, or divine *revelation* are sources of knowledge; but the deliverances of faith, or of divine revelation, are not (or are not all) among the deliverances of reason. Of course, it isn't just obvious that Christians are right on this point; it is equally unobvious, however, that they are wrong, and it is clearly at least *possible* that they are right. If that is clear, however, then it could be that a belief constitutes knowledge even if it is not among the deliverances of reason.

It's fascinating to note that Zhuangzi concerns himself, if only rather obscurely, with the same sorts of questions that agitated René Descartes and John Locke: What should we do in the face of profound and intractable disagreement? Does such disagreement preclude knowledge on the parts of the disputants? This problem, clearly enough, is very much still with us; one version of it is sometimes called "the Problem of Religious Pluralism." Ours, we like to say, is a pluralistic age; and, of course, we are right. With respect to religious belief there are all those competing systems and nonsystems clamoring for our allegiance: Christianity, of course, but also Islam, Judaism, Buddhism, Hinduism, and the like. There are also various Johnny-come-latelies such as New Age ways of thinking and other forms of syncretism. In addition, there are also, now, both in the Western world and in other parts of the world dominated or once dominated by Marxism, ways of thinking that eschew belief in any supernatural beings at all. Suppose one of these systems of belief is in fact true or close to the truth: can it be held in such a way as to constitute knowledge? Can it be held in such a way as to constitute knowledge even if the prospective knower is aware of all these other ways of believing, and perhaps also of the fact that some of those who accept them are at least as smart and upright as he is? Or must we say, with the sixteenth century writer Jean Bodin, "each is refuted by all?"[6]

But why should disagreement of this sort, preclude knowledge? For suppose that classical Christian belief is in fact true. It is part of such belief to affirm that God has specially inspired the Bible, and inspired it in such a way that he can properly be said to be its primary author. In the Bible, furthermore, it is said that Jesus Christ is the divine son of God the father, and that by way of his suffering, death and resurrection we human beings can be justified, made right with God. Still further, according to such belief, the third person of the Trinity, the Holy Spirit, influences us, persuades, invites us to believe these things, gives us the grace to see that the great things of the gospel are really true. This work of the Holy Spirit can be conceived variously;[7] whatever the details, however, it seems that beliefs formed in this fashion could easily meet the conditions of warrant. The beliefs in question could be formed by faculties or belief-producing processes in the right kind of cognitive environment according to a design plan successfully aimed at truth. So, if these beliefs are held with sufficient firmness, couldn't they constitute knowledge? And couldn't that be the case despite the fact that others don't hold these beliefs and indeed hold beliefs inconsistent with them?

Well, why not? That seems perfectly possible. If so, however, the disagreement about these issues doesn't preclude knowledge of the beliefs disagreed about—at any rate doesn't *logically* preclude such knowledge. But now let's take another step: suppose I believe the great things of the gospel, and it's not merely

the case that others disagree with me; in addition I *know* that they do. I am
aware of the facts of religious diversity; I realize that others, by all appearances
at least as intelligent and sensitive as I, hold beliefs inconsistent with mine.
Perhaps this realization is born out of personal discussions and conversation with
such people. I will therefore have to believe that I know something those who
disagree with me do not. Perhaps I think, with classical Christianity, that those
who have faith have been given grace not (or not yet) given to those who do not.
But suppose, still further, that I realize I don't have an argument from the
deliverances of reason, either for the proposition in dispute, or for the proposition that I have a source of knowledge these others don't have: *then* could it be
that my beliefs can still constitute knowledge? Under those conditions don't I
have a *defeater* for these beliefs, so that I can't rationally continue to hold them?[8]

Well, I can't see why. First, consider a philosophical analogy. I believe there
are necessary propositions that can be known a priori and that are genuinely
about the world. For example, I believe such propositions as that some objects
have nontrivial essential properties including essences. Serious empiricists—
W. V. Quine, Bas van Fraassen—disagree. I realize that they disagree, and I do
not know of any argument that could settle the matter. Can I continue rationally, in the face of this knowledge, to believe what seems to me true, that is,
that there are such necessary propositions? Can *they* rationally continue to believe that there *aren't* any such propositions? Again, I certainly can't see why not.
Quine and van Fraassen and others disagree with me; on the basis of experience
I doubt that I can convince them by philosophical argument that I'm right; but
why should that mean that I can't rationally continue to believe what I do
believe? And why should it mean that *they* can't rationally deny what I believe,
continuing to hold their conflicting beliefs?

Rationality, fundamentally, is a matter of cognitive proper function: what is
rationally believable, in given circumstances, is what can be believed by human
beings who aren't suffering from cognitive malfunction or dysfunction, human
beings whose cognitive faculties are working properly. But there is no reason to
think that in circumstances of this type, rationality permits only one cognitive
response. No doubt there are *some* circumstances in which rationality permits
only one response: if you come to entertain the proposition that $2 + 1 = 3$, you
can't sensibly, rationally refrain from believing that this proposition is in fact
true. The same goes for other self-evident propositions. But in other circumstances, rationality permits more than one cognitive response; there is more than
one proposition such that one can believe it without thereby displaying irratio-
nality. And among the sorts of propositions where rationality permits these
options, presumably, are philosophical propositions. Why think that either
empiricists must be irrational, or else rationalists must be—even if each agrees
that he can't rationally convince the other? Why think that either realists or
nominalists must be irrational, and either actualists or possibilists, and presentists
or four-dimensionalists? So, back to the dispute between empiricists and those

who think there are essences: it's merely arrogant for either to declare that the other's cognitive faculties are malfunctioning. Each, of course, thinks the other is mistaken; but neither properly thinks the other is irrational.

And isn't it the same with religious views, for example, the great things of the gospel? I realize that there are those who disagree with me here, and that I don't have an argument that would settle the matter. I don't have an argument from the deliverances of reason for these beliefs, an argument that would convince any intelligent, rational person of good will who was paying attention. But does rationality then demand that I give up these beliefs? If I don't or can't give them up, must I concede that I'm suffering from cognitive dysfunction of some kind? Surely not. Indeed, the proper response would be more like gratitude to God for the grace he's given me.

NOTES

1. This is the rough, zeroeth approximation; for fine tuning see Alvin Plantinga, *Warranted Christian Belief* (New York: Oxford University Press, 2000), pp. 153–161.

2. John Horgan, "In the Beginning" in *Scientific American* (Feb., 1991): 120.

3. Or regularities; we needn't commit ourselves here to the existence of physical laws. For a detailed argument against the existence of such laws, see Bas van Fraassen, *Laws and Symmetry* (Oxford: Clarendon Press, 1989), part I.

4. See Del Ratzsch, *Science and Its Limits: The Natural Sciences in Christian Perspective* (Downers Grove, IL: InterVarsity Press, 2000).

5. We should add here that the implication in question is discoverable by human beings; it is not so complex or difficult that reflective human beings can't grasp it. Or should we say that any properly functioning human being, with the right kind of training, could see the implication? And what is the relevant implication relation? Again, there are difficulties here in stating the matter exactly; I don't think our present project requires that we enter these difficulties.

6. Jean Bodin, *Colloquium Heptaplomeres de rerum sublimium arcanis abditis*, written by 1593 but not published until 1857. English translation by Marion Kuntz (Princeton: Princeton University Press, 1975). The quotation is from this translation, p. 256.

7. See Plantinga, *Warranted Christian Belief*, chap. 8.

8. See David Silver, "Religious Experience and the Facts of Religious Pluralism," *International Journal for the Philosophy of Religion* 49 (2001): 8 ff.

Heidegger's View of Language and the Lao-Zhuang View of *Dao*-Language

Zhang Xianglong

Translated by Stephen C. Angle

As far as we know, twice in works published during his lifetime Martin Heidegger discusses China's "*dao*,"[1] and in two other places quotes the *Laozi* and the *Zhuangzi* in order to clarify his own thought.[2] In the two places where he touches on "*dao*," as well as in the essay that quotes *Zhuangzi*, Heidegger uses various indirect but unmistakable means to point out the relationship between "*dao*" and language (*Sprache*). This should give us cause for contemplation. As we all know, no matter whether we look to the Eastern intellectual world or the Western worlds of sinology and Chinese philosophy, everyone emphasizes the relationship between *dao* and silence (*wuyan*), or else asserts that any language, no matter what its meaning (anything that "can be spoken") cannot attain the *dao* itself (the eternal *dao*). This tendency, as well as the translations of the Lao-Zhuang works themselves influenced by this tendency, cannot but have influenced Heidegger, a thinker who had a relationship with Daoism for several decades. However, it seems that Heidegger was not completely fettered by this kind of popular interpretation. During the short period (in the summer of 1946),[3] when he worked on translating the *Laozi* together with the Chinese scholar Xiao Shiyi, his tireless seeking after the meaning of each and every word in the Chinese version of the *Laozi* obviously led to a kind of direct understanding, which in turn led to his expressing the views alluded to above about *dao* and language in speeches and publications in the 1950s and 1960s. In this context, the thing on which we should focus is what intellectual background drove Heidegger to transcend the popular view and reach his interpretation of a certain kind of relationship between *dao* and language. In addition, we also want to know whether, in addition to expressing the direction of his own thought, Heidegger's interpretation in fact has any basis on the "Chinese side." In other words, is there anything in Chinese "*dao*" thought that can be brought out through a comparison with Heidegger's notion of "language?" The following discussion will explain these three counts. First, Heidegger's nonrepresentational and constitutive view of language is different from traditional views. Second, not only does the word "*dao*" have the meaning of "speech" as early as the Western Zhou, but Lao-Zhuang thought also does not completely cut off the fundamental relation between *dao* and language. Third, if we correctly understand Heidegger's view of language and the Lao-Zhuang view of *dao*-language (*daoyan*), then, although there are some differences, there are also possibilities for undertaking an intellectual dialogue.

HEIDEGGER'S VIEW OF LANGUAGE

The "view of language" that I speak of here should not be understood as follows: Heidegger has a fundamental viewpoint, from which can be derived a certain view of language. On the contrary, Heidegger's view of language is intimately and inextricably related to his most profound views. On this matter, therefore, the opinions of certain other Heidegger scholars are untenable. They believe that in his "early period" Heidegger was principally concerned with understanding the meaning of being (*cunzai*) through disclosing the modalities of *Dasein*'s being, and that he fundamentally overlooked the dimension of language. In his "later period," in contrast, he was principally concerned with understanding being and our technological age through discussing the nature of language, poetry, and appropriation (*Ereignis*). In fact, although there are differences in the ways Heidegger expressed himself and in the things he emphasized, the fundamental train of thought in both early and later periods is the same. Already in the 1920s, or even earlier, the existential significance of language was a major force driving his thought. This concern was blended into the central themes of *Being and Time* (1927)—namely, *Dasein* and the region of temporality—through the mediation of hermeneutics. In "Dialogs on Language" (1953–54), Heidegger mentions that an important force pushing him toward the philosophical path opened up by *Being and Time* was the hermeneutics with which he became familiar during his time studying theology in university (1909–10). Hermeneutics is a subject that examines the relation between the words in the Bible and theological speculative thought.[4] This relation is in fact a hidden form of the relation between language and being. When he was writing *Being and Time* (begun in 1923), Heidegger reached the fundamental ontology of *Dasein* by hermeneuticizing phenomenology.[5] Therefore, he wrote in *Being and Time* that: "The phenomenology of *Dasein* is the original meaning of hermeneutics. . . . This kind of hermeneutics is at the same time 'hermeneutics' in the sense of the working out of the conditions for the possibility of ontological investigation."[6]

Of course, when he did this, he also changed and deepened the meaning of "hermeneutics" from the "interpretation of art" to the "interpretation (*Auslegung*) of being" and the basic premises of understanding.[7] With this modality of *Dasein*, the relationship between language and being deeply penetrated the entire *Being and Time*, even though on the surface there were not many chapters which were concerned with language.

How, then, did Heidegger actually view the nature of language? Corresponding to his view of *Dasein*, he does not believe that primordial language is in any sense a ready-to-hand thing, no matter whether it is understood as "means of communication," "symbol system," or some kind of "human activity." Language is pure disclosing (*die Zeige*), namely "Let [it] disclose, be seen, and be heard."[8] Heidegger calls this "speech" (*die Sage*): "The essence of language (*Wesende*, which can also be translated as "Being") is this speech which discloses. Its disclosing (*Zeigen*) does not depend on any kind of symbol or sign (*Zeichen*); to the contrary, all symbols are born from various disclosures. Only in the region (*Bereich*) of these disclosings and from their intentions can symbols actually be symbols."[9] Therefore, the later Heidegger especially emphasized that true language is prior to our spoken language (*Spreches*); it is only through opening ourselves up to language, or entering the region of language's disclosing, that we can actually speak or think. Therefore, "language is more powerful than we are, and it is thereby more weighty."[10]

However, this does not mean that Heidegger's view of language in his later period was in any fundamental way different from the thought in *Being and Time*, since the concept of "*Dasein*" in that book already signified an ontology that went beyond traditional thinking on the "subject." His using *Dasein* to portray the nature of humans, like his use of the notion of disclosing to portray language, took traditional, ready-to-hand concepts—"person (or I) as subject"; "language as symbol system"—and turned them into constitutive regions that won their self-identities through being-toward (*Zusein*) and saying-toward (*Zusagen*). Therefore, to say that language is before speech is not to say that language is logically or temporally prior to speech and exists independently, but to say that that which makes us able to speak and allows us to speak has already been projected ahead of our speaking as a primordial horizon (*Horizont*); this gives us the ability to speak and a corresponding world about which to speak. Accordingly, we and this region always reflect one another like a self and its shadow: we mutually constitute one another. This is not just the marginal region spoken of in Edmund Husserl's phenomenology. According to Heidegger, it is the true "center" or "focus" of our being.[11] In the final analysis, in non-metaphysical terms, language and humans mutually create or constitute one another. No *Dasein* can be without such primordial language, and no language can exist in a non-*Dasein* way. This thought was of great concern to Heidegger starting in 1934, and indeed, runs through all his academic activities: self-appropriation (*Ereignis*), namely, all true beings become themselves and maintain themselves through mutual evocation. Language also acquires itself in this kind of appropriation. In the article "The Essence of Language," Heidegger used a pair of phrases to make clear the mutual constitution of appropriation: "the essence of language: the language of essence (*Das Wesen der Sprache: Die Sprache des Wesens*)." Therefore, to him, "the way to language is self-appropriation (*Die Weg ist ereignend*)."[12]

From what I have said above it can be seen that for Heidegger, language already had significance as a "horizon for understanding being" or "constituent region of ontology." [He wrote:] "Because language is the most exquisite, it is also most easily swayed by [various] influences. It preserves everything in the unresolved structure of self-appropriation. Insofar as our essence is created in the midst of this unresolved structure, we are always in the midst of self-appropriation."[13] Through such an "open region (*Offene*)" or "clearing (*Lichtung*)," we possess a world; all of it "is what it is" and "not what it is not." In the final analysis, the ideas centered around language play the same role in Heidegger's later thought that the "there (*Da*)" of *Dasein*, "care (*Sorge*)," and the region of "time" play in his earlier thought. This is a transformation (*Kehre*) of expressive form, but not of philosophical insight or fundamental orientation.

As this kind of ontologically significant constitutive region, language cannot be reduced to any particular being, whether it is a symbol system, the expression of ideas, or communicative activity. All we can say is that "language speaks (*Die Sprache spricht*)."[14] This is not a meaningless tautology, but shows language's capacity to hold sway in the midst of this region of appropriation, such that language speaks the pure meaning of its own constitution. At key points in expressing his ideas, Heidegger regularly uses this kind of "tautologous language" or "sticking language" to disclose self-disclosing meanings which cannot be conceptually defined. Some examples are: "the thing things (*Das Ding dingt*),"[15] "temporality temporalizes itself (*Zeitlichkeit zeitigt*)"[16] or "time exists originally as the timing of time (*Zeit ist ursprunglich als Zeitgung der Zeitlichkeit*),"[17] and "the regioning region (*die Gegend als das Gegnende*)."[18] Another technique is to make minor changes, as for instance in "*Dasein* is in the way that its "there (*Da*)" is (*Es [Dasein] ist in der Weise, sein Da zu sein*),"[19] "appropriation appropriates (*Das Ereignis eignet*),"[20] "appropriation is self-appropriation itself (*Das Ereignende ist das Eriegnis selbst*),"[21] and "path-making path (*be-weegende weg*)."[22] In addition, Heidegger takes advantage of every opportunity (usually by adding a prefix or suffix to the same root) to make clusters or groups of mutually related words. Some examples are: from "*sein*" to "*Da-sein*," "*Seinkoennen*," "*Zu-sein*," and "*In-der-welt-sein*"; from "*langen*" to "*gelangen*," and "*verlangen*"; from "*Riss*" to "*Aufriss*," and "*Grundriss*," and so on. These methods all aim at creating a mutually involving (*Zug, Bezug*) appropriating tension between words, and between earlier and later texts. These are all different means of "letting language itself speak," which corresponds to Heidegger's understanding of the primordial meaning of *Dasein*'s phenomenology: "Let the means of disclosing's self-disclosing be seen from itself

(*Das was sich zeigt, so wie es sich von ihm selbst her zeigt, von ihm selbst her sehen lassen*)."[23] This is definitely not a typical case of "paying excessive attention to wording," but is in fact like what he called "the circular dance of self-appropriation (*der Reigen des Ereignens*)."[24] Through this kind of mutual projection, the hard outer crust of language is "bitten and chewed" open, and pulled, stretched, and appropriated as a completely interlinked region. This is just what Heidegger speaks of in a poem he wrote as "the glory of the simple (*Die Pracht des Schlichten*)."[25]

The key point here is that neither man nor language themselves are metaphysically substantive, but rather are the "there (*Da*)" itself. Therefore, the revelation or repetition of this "there" is never meaningless, because it does not have a substance that it could preserve by being closed up within itself. Like the repetition of music and poetry, its own openness and closeness must constitute or continue the original, preconceptual meaning of existence (*Existenz*). Therefore, Heidegger also says: "Language itself is poetry (*Dichtung*) in the essential sense. . . . The essence of poetry is the establishment (*Stiftung*) of truth. . . . Establishment is overflowing and gift-giving. . . . This genuine poetic projection (*Entwurf*) is the opening up of that in which *Dasein* as historical (being) is already thrown."[26] That *Dasein* can understand that which language speaks, rather than merely being spoken of by language, is because it fundamentally has the nature of *Da*, and thus belongs to this realm of appropriation. We can speak language because, first of all, we can hear language's speaking,[27] and more importantly because we and language both belong to the realm of—or stand in the midst of—self-appropriation.[28]

According to this train of thought, language itself is not just an empty means of communication, nor is it just the rules of a game which only gains meaning in use; it is rather an ontological region that carries primordial "news" and meaning. It holds together, nurtures, and preserves our existential world. It is with this meaning in mind that Heidegger said "language is the house of being (*das Haus des Seins*)."[29] The same thought lies behind his statement: "The hermeneutic method does not primarily discuss meaningful explanation (*das Auslegen*), but only brings news (*das Bringen von Botschaft und Kunde*). . . . Because language determines the hermeneutic relation."[30] Chapter 21 of the *Laozi* speaks of a region of "way" that contains preconceptual news: "In his every movement a man of great virtue / follows the way and the way only. / As a thing the way is / shadowy, indistinct. / Indistinct and shadowy, / yet within it is an image; / shadowy and indistinct, / yet within it is a substance. / Dim and dark, / yet within it is an essence. / This essence is very genuine / and within it there is something reliable. / From the present back to antiquity / its name has never deserted it. / It serves as a means for inspecting the origin of the multitude. / How do I know the disposition of the origin of the multitude? / By means of this." The essence of the way is the "shadowy and indistinct" region of appropriation. This "shadowy indistinctness" is not completely chaotic, nor is it purely empty; it contains "an image," "a substance," "an essence," "something reliable." This is just to say that it carries on the primordial news and "great image." In this way, the movements of a man with great virtue (that is, emptiness charged with the highest virtue) must necessarily "follow the way and the way along," and follow this shadowy and indistinct great way and "know the disposition of the origin of the multitude" (that is, the primordial situation of beings).

THE WAY'S SPEAKING

The above brief comparison, as well as all of the comparative research between Heidegger's thought and the Chinese way, point out and demand an understanding of the linguistic dimension of the way. However, down to the present day, the work required to arrive at such an understanding seems not yet even to have begun. There are two main reasons that this research has been obstructed and people tied up in the vague formula "the way fundamentally does not speak." The first is relatively technical, namely, that many scholars deny or do not know that in pre-Qin Lao-Zhuang thought, "*dao*" already carried the meaning of "speak."[31] The second reason is interpretive: the belief that both Lao and Zhuang completely deny a genuine relationship between the way and language. This kind of viewpoint has not only been transmitted very widely, but from a chronological perspective, can actually be traced back to Wang Bi of the Wei-Jin period. The following discussion will make clear that these two views are mistaken or, in the case of the latter, merely superficial; we can call them "two dogmas of the way" which use slogans in place of evidence. On top of this, and more important, the essay will strive to explain that disclosing the meaning of the ontologically constituted, nonrepresentational "way language" is, from the perspective of the operation of thought itself, appropriate. It is "appropriate" because this kind of new interpretation is not without justification; it is also of use in understanding the profound mystery of the way's "being and nonbeing producing each other"; and it also does no harm to the way's fundamental meaning. Let me emphasize that this interpretation does not claim that "*dao*" can only be understood as "speak." It only stresses that the ontological meaning of "*dao*-language" should be one among the plentiful meanings of "*dao*," and in addition, it is more appropriate and more interesting than interpretations which conceptualize *dao*—like viewing it as "the supreme principle from which all things originate" or "the most universal principle (the substance of matter and its laws).[32] Simply put, "way language" is an interpretation of "*dao*" which derives both from the needs of thought itself (that is, it has hermeneutical significance), and from linguistic justifications. Below, I will begin with the meaning of the word "*dao*."

The earliest meaning of "*dao*" was "road." In the *Shuowen Jiezi* we find: "*Dao*: the *dao* on which one walks."[33] In the *Book of Poetry* "The Zhou *dao* was like a whetstone, its straightness like an arrow" [*Xiaoya, Dadong*], where "*dao*" indicates a flat and straight road. Several other meanings developed from this primordial meaning. Several of the important ones are "unobstructed (or open up)," "guide (teach, direct)," "standard," and "speak (or speech)." Below I will give examples of each, the most important point naturally being the meaning of "speak" or "speech."

For "*dao*" to mean "(make something) unobstructed" seems like a natural extension of "road." The "Yugong" chapter of the *Book of History* says: "The nine rivers were *dao*," it means that the rivers were dredged and rendered clear for passage. The *Zuo Commentary*, 33rd year of Duke Xiang, says: "That was not as good as making it *dao*;" it also uses *dao* in this sense.

Dao also has the meanings of "guide," "lead," or "direct." For instance, here is *Analects*, 1:5: "The master said, in guiding (*dao*) a state of a thousand chariots, approach your duties with reverence and be trustworthy in what you say; avoid excesses in expenditure and love your fellow men; employ the labor of the common people only in the right seasons."

Dao solidified into a noun, and thus came to mean "standard," "method," "moral norm," "morality," and "origin." Two examples are *Analects*, 1:11:"If for three years he makes no changes to his father's ways (*dao*), he can be called filial," and *Analects*, 5:13: "One cannot get to hear the master's views on human nature and the way (*dao*) of heaven." [my fn: Lau, pp. 61 and 78]

Finally, and most important for our purposes, in the pre-Qin period, no later than the time of the language in which the *Laozi* and *Zhuangzi* were written, *dao* already had the meaning of "speak." The text of the "Announcement to the Prince of Kang" in the "Book of Zhou" chapter of the *Classic of History* contains the sentence: "If [the offenders] confess (*dao*) unreservedly their guilt, you may not put them to death." [34] The *dao* in this sentence can only be interpreted as "speak out" or "confess." Cai Shen annotates this sentence as follows: "Since he confesses (*dao*) on his own and tells all the facts without daring to conceal [anything], even though his guilt is great, he should not be killed."[35] At another point in this same book of the *Classic of History*, we find: "Our great lord, leaning on the gem-adorned bench, declared (*dao*) his last charge, and commanded you to continue the observance of the lessons. . . . " This *dao* can also only be read as "said."

It should be pointed out that those who study ancient texts unanimously feel that the twenty-eight chapters of the *Classic of History*, which exist in both the "new text" and "old text" redactions are genuine, and among these the "Book of Zhou" section "is [made up of] original documents that have been preserved."[36] Therefore, these two pieces of evidence make clear that in the early years of the Zhou dynasty (1000 B.C.E.), *dao* already had the meaning "speak."

Besides this, the *Analects*, which was composed at roughly the same time as the *Laozi* (some believe even earlier than the *Laozi*), has passages like this: "The master said: 'There are three things that make up the way (*dao*) of the gentleman, none of which I have succeeded in following: 'a man of benevolence never worries,' 'a man of wisdom is never of two minds,' and 'a man of courage is never afraid.' Zigong said, 'What the master has just said (*dao*) is a description of himself.'" The second of these "*dao*" has been interpreted by commentators as the expression of language. For example, Zhu Xi annotated this as: "*Dao* is saying. [When] one says [something] of oneself, one is self-deprecatory."[37]

In the *Mencius*, which was produced in the same era as the *Zhuangzi*, there are at least two places in which *dao* is used in the sense of "saying." The first is in chapter 1A: "Mencius answered, 'None of the followers of Confucius spoke (*dao*) of the history of Duke Huan and Duke Wen. It is for this reason that no one in subsequent ages passed on accounts.'" Zhu Xi annotates as follows: "*Dao* means spoke." The second instance is in chapter 6B: "Here is a man. If a man from Yue bends his bow and takes a shot at him, one can recount (*dao*) the incident in a light-hearted manner. The reason is simply that one feels no concern for the man from Yue. If it had been one's own older brother who did this, then one would be in tears while recounting (*dao*) the incident. The reason for the difference is simply that one feels concern for one's brother." Zhu Xi annotates this as: "*Dao* means to speak." Anyone who carefully reads the contexts of these two statements can see that other than the likes of "say" or "speak," no other interpretations of *dao* are possible here.

In line one of the first chapter of the *Laozi*, namely, "The way (*dao*) that can be spoken (*dao*) is not the constant way (*dao*)," the second "*dao*" has from ancient times to the present been broadly interpreted as "say" or "speak." If this is the case, how can the first and third *dao* have absolutely no relationship with speaking? The most common interpretation is that this line precisely is absolutely denying a relation between the inexpressible "essence of the way" and the "*dao*-language." But if one reads through the whole chapter, one can see that this widespread and popular view is not reasonable. The whole passage runs as follows: "The way that can be spoken is not the constant way; / the name that can be named is not the constant name. / Non-being names the origin of heaven and earth; / being names the mother of the myriad things.[38] Therefore, let there always be nonbeing so that we may see their subtlety, and let there always be being so that we may see their outcome. The two are the same, but after they are produced, they have different names. They both may be called deep and profound. Profound and more profound, this is the gate of all subtleties." Here *dao* and *ming* (name) are juxtaposed in parallel fashion; it cannot be, as many commentators think, that the two are completely opposed to one another, deprecating "name" and promoting "way." The second line—"the name that can be named is not the constant name"—has the same structure as the first line, namely, "X that can be Xed is not the constant X." Therefore, the first "name" and the third "(constant) name" have the same status as the so-called essence of the way. However, who can deny that "constant name" is a kind of being that is related to "name" or language? Of course it is different from the second, conceptualized and standardized, "name," but it is nonetheless still a "constituent name." Laozi and Zhuangzi regularly in this way use the "small" (expressible, conceptual, logical) to disclose the "great" (pure disclosing, preconceptual, superlogical). The "constant way" spoken of here is the "great way" or the "(boundless) great name"; where is the complete opposition between the essence of way and the essence of name? What we have is just a kind of (productive) opposition between "great way" and "small way," between "great name" and "small name." Therefore, the following lines immediately say: "The two [being and nonbeing, or named and nameless] are the same, but after they are produced, they have different names. They both may be called deep and profound. Profound and more profound, this is the gate of all subtleties." Those who want to separate "way" from "name," "nonbeing (or nameless)" from "being (or named)," have no way to interpret these lines. In addition, this precisely expresses the essence and subtlety of Laozi's thought.

There are many examples in the *Zhuangzi* of *dao* being used in the sense of "*dao*-language." For instance, in the chapter "The Sorting which Evens Things Out," we find: "The greatest *dao* does not commend, / the greatest discrimination is unspoken, / the greatest benevolence is non-benevolent, / . . . Who knows an unspoken discrimination, an untold *dao*? It is this, if any is able to know it, which is called the Treasury of Heaven." This is a method often used in ancient Chinese texts, and particularly in the *Laozi* and *Zhuangzi*, to express subtle meanings: give a series of parallel sentences, each one containing the structure "great X not *x*" or something very like it. The X refers to the meaning which transcends dualisms and cannot be expressed using conceptual language; the *x* refers to the meaning that is still trapped in dualistic, conceptual language. "X" and "*x*" are sometimes the same word, as in "great benevolence is non-benevolent" and "highest virtue is not virtuous"; other times different but similar words are used, like "discrimination" and "speak" or "*dao*" and "commend." Therefore, saying, "The greatest *dao* does not commend" makes clear that in Zhuangzi's mind, "*dao*" and "commend" are close in meaning, and have connotations of "say" or "speak." Relying on this meaning, Zhuangzi uses "the greatest *dao* does not commend" or "the greatest *dao* does not *dao*" to deny that the great *dao* can be expressed as an object of conceptual language (commend, small way, small name), and to disclose the primordial and spoken nature of *dao* itself. Put in Heidegger's terms, this becomes: "speech (*dao*) speaks (*dao*)," and cannot be "spoken (*dao*)"; the "*dao* that can be *dao*-ed" is not "*dao* itself" because "*dao* daos" is precisely the premise of "can be spoken (*dao*-ed)," just as "great discrimination" is the premise for "speaking." Who can deny the connection between "unspoken discrimination" and "un *dao*-ed *dao*," on the one hand, and the activity of nonconceptual language, on the other? Otherwise, why does Zhuangzi say "discriminate" and "*dao*" instead of "quietude," "pattern," "nature," or "essence?"

In chapter 33 of the *Zhuangzi*, "Below in the Empire," there is a passage which gives further philological evidence. It reads: "The *Book of Poetry* serves as *dao* to the intent, the *Book of History* to *dao* the work, the *Book of Rites* to *dao* conduct, the *Book of Music* to *dao* harmony, the *Book of Changes* to *dao* the *Yin* and *Yang,* and the *Spring and Autumn Annals* to *dao* names and portions. After this was variously spread through the empire and established in the central states, the scholars of the hundred schools sometimes commended (*cheng*) and expounded (*dao*) it." A few commentators interpret the first six *dao* as "reach" or "guide," but all read the seventh *dao* as "(commandingly) speak."[39] This is because the use of *dao* and *cheng* side by side serves to remove all other interpretive possibilities. In addition, the sixth *dao* is also not completely devoid of the connotation of "speaking." In "The *Book of Poetry* serves as *dao* to the intent," and "the *Book of History* to *dao* the work," at the very least, these uses of *dao* can be understood as related to speaking. Of course, glossing them here as "understand" or "reach" is also correct. From this we can perfectly well see that the development of the meaning of *dao*—from "road" to "open," "guide," (make something) reach, "method," "principle," "teaching," and ultimately "speaking"— is so natural. Therefore, Heidegger's opinion in his essay "The ontological nature of language" that the original meaning of *dao* was "road," and also that it was the locus of the "complete secret of the reflective speaking (*Sagen*),"[40] are well-founded interpretations. For humans, the most important means of "reaching out" is "saying" or "speaking." According to Laozi and Zhuangzi, only saying (*daochu*) itself (*dao*-speak, great *dao*), rather than its retrograde form (human speech, the *dao* that can be spoken) is the most fundamental reaching out and source.

From the foregoing discussion and analysis, we can see that not only did the word *dao* have the meaning of "saying" by the Western Zhou period at the very latest, but this meaning also had closely related manifestations in the *Laozi* and the *Zhuangzi*. Why did both Laozi and Zhuangzi want to discuss the relation between *dao* and language? This is precisely because the actual relationship between language and ultimate foundations had already entered into their fields of vision and become a question of the first importance. In addition, as we have already seen, although they deny that language which submits to conceptual thinking can reach *dao*, they absolutely do not deny the *dao*-saying of *dao* itself, nor that the shadowy and indistinct, image-creating nature of the way (*dao*) is to speak (*dao*). Otherwise, there would be no possibility of: "They both may be called deep and profound. Profound and more profound, this is the gate of all subtleties." This is just to say that Laozi and Zhuangzi use the method of "the way that can be spoken is not the constant way" and "the great way does not commend" to indicate a nonrepresentational, unconceptualizable view of language that is embodied in the great *dao* and the great language (*dayan*). *Zhuangzi* more directly expresses the inseparable relationship between this view of language and its understanding of the *dao* itself. In the chapter "The Sorting which Evens Things Out," in addition to the passage already quoted above, there is also language like "Great wit is effortless, / petty wit picks holes. / Great speech is flavorless, / petty speech strings words." This manifestly distinguishes between the superconceptual expression of "great speech" and petty speech that expresses concepts and objects. In fact, all of the *Zhuangzi* is constituted from this kind of great speech. Another passage from "The Sorting which Evens Things Out" describes the method of this kind of great speech:

> It makes no difference whether the voices in their transformation have each other to depend on or not. Smooth them out on the whetstone of heaven, use them to go by and let the stream find its own channels; this is the way to live out your years. What is meant by Smooth them out on the whetstone of heaven? Treat as right even what is not, treat as so even what is not. If the right is really right, there is no longer a difference for disputation from what is not; if the so is really so, there is no longer a difference for disputation from what is not so. Forget the years, forget duty, be shaken into motion by the limitless, and so find for things lodging places in the limitless.[41]

Those who understand Heidegger's view of language and Wittgenstein's theory of "language games," can draw many conclusions from this passage. "Voices in their transformation" means transforming in accord with context, rather than being subject to fixed ideas and objects. *Dao*-speech which "depends" on this realm in fact is all the more "non-dependent" and non-subject to expressive objects. The phrases "treat as 'right' even what is not, treat as 'so' even what is not" can be understood in terms of the expressive technique discussed above for "great benevolence is non-benevolent" and "great *dao* does not commend," together with "do non-doing," "taste the tasteless," and "formless form": it uses "not right" to dissolve the conceptual language of the "small right" and publicize the "right itself" and the "so itself." Precisely because this "right (itself) is the disclosure of *dao*-speaking itself, so "there is no longer a difference for disputation [between what is right] and what is not." In this way, both "right" and "not right" ultimately end up "finding lodging places in the limitless," which is just to say in the region of the great way's appropriation.[42]

In the *Zhuangzi* chapters "Imputed Words" and "Below in the Empire," Zhuangzi also uses "saying from a lodging place," "weighty saying," and "spillover saying" to express his "speech that does not speak" view of *dao*-speech. He views them as ways of following the *dao* akin to "alone with the quintessential-and-*daemonic* in heaven and earth going to and for" or "assenting to transformation and being released from things." It is difficult to say whether "weighty saying" can be interpreted as "*dao dao*-ing," "birth birthing is called change," or "love loving is great." From the "Below in the Empire" chapter, we can see that Zhuangzi himself, or the interpretation of his thought shared by his followers, has an extremely prominent view of language:

> Zhuang Zhou got wind [of the ancient tradition of the way] and delighted in it. With his outrageous opinions, reckless words, extravagant formulations, he was sometimes too free but was not partisan, he did not show things from one particular point of view. He thought that the empire was sinking in the mud, and

could not be talked with in too solemn language. He thought that "spillover" sayings lets the stream find its own channels, that "weighty" saying is the most genuine, that saying "from a lodging place" widens the range. Alone with the quintessential-and-daemonic in heaven and earth he went to and fro, but was not arrogant toward the myriad things. He did not make demands with a "That's right, that's not," and so he got along with conventional people. (*Zhuagzi* chapter 33)

Although his writings are extraordinary there is no harm in their oddities. Although his formulations are irregular, their enigmas deserve consideration. What is solid in them we cannot do without. Above, he roamed with the maker of things; below, he made friends with those for whom life and death are externals and there is neither end nor beginning. As for the root, he opened it up in all its comprehensiveness, ran riot in the vastness of its depths; as for the ancestor, it may be said that by being in tune he withdrew all the way back to it. Nevertheless, he assented to transformation and was released from things, and set forth principles that can never be shuffled off. Veiled and arcane, he is one who has never been completely comprehended.

Could all this "extraordinary and odd" and "irregular and enigmatic" talk of "spillover saying," "weighty saying," "saying from a lodging place," and "outrageous opinions" really just be a kind of individual expressive style possessing only literary value? Obviously not. *Dao*-saying with this kind of nonconceptual appearance is exactly the way (*dao*) to reach the original, ontological realm that Zhuangzi describes as "What is solid in them we cannot do without. Above, he roamed with the maker of things; below, he made friends with those for whom life and death are externals and there is neither end nor beginning." Only this kind of great *dao* and great speaking can indicate and disclose the origin that small *dao*s and small speech have no way of approaching. Therefore, "As for the root, he opened it up in all its comprehensiveness, ran riot in the vastness of its depths; as for the ancestor, it may be said that by being in tune he withdrew all the way back to it." Of course, this disclosure is neither linear nor fixed conceptually, but topological or situational. Therefore, "when one he assents to transformation and is released from things, [one can] set forth principles that can never be shuffled off. Veiled and arcane, [one will be] one who has never been completely comprehended."

THE MUTUAL EVOCATION OF *DAO* AND SAYING

The introduction and discussion of the first two sections suggests the following conclusion: for Heidegger and for Laozi and Zhuangzi, language or "speaking" has two kinds of meaning, one of which is the means or symbol system used to convey information, the other of which is the primordial, purely disclosing ontological region or realm of occurrence. The first is only for ready-to-hand (*vorhanden*) beings to make contact with one another and express or convey the ideas, thoughts, or concepts in their minds. The truthfulness of this kind of linguistic activity only lies in the correspondence between external "actual states of affairs" and "statements" or "formal propositions." In this sense, we can say that this kind of linguistic activity is confined to conceptual or ideal modes of thought, and so is a kind of concept-presenting language, or in other words, a "small language." It presupposes and reinforces the dualistic ontological and epistemological division between subject and object. Conversely, the second view of language holds that primordial speaking or *dao* (saying) is prior to any dualistic ontology or epistemology. "In the beginning was the word (*dao, logos*)": this *dao* and the most fundamental substance (being itself or perfect *dao*) form a one-into-two-and-two-into-one relation of mutual, constitutive evocation. Heidegger called this "*Ereignis*" (self-appropriation). In Daoism it is shown through the various ways that "return is the movement of the *dao.*" In the places in their works that Laozi and Zhuangzi speak of "wordless" or "nameless," in fact both are denying that concept-expressing small language, or human language, can reach the perfect *dao*, though this is not to completely deny a relationship between language and *dao*: to the contrary, this kind of expression precisely aims at using "return" or "losing" small language in order to attain the great language of the *dao*. Otherwise, the "irregular formulations" of Laozi and Zhuangzi, like "eternal name," "its name does not depart," "great saying," and "roam with the maker of things" will have no justification.

Many self-contradictions in traditional interpretations of Daoism result from confusing these two meanings of "*dao* (saying)." In the eyes of those interpreters who follow Wang Bi, speech and names can only indicate concepts, and so can only make contact with "being" or "physical things." With respect to the metaphysical "essence of the *Dao*," one can only be "wordless." However, the *Laozi* and the *Zhuangzi* themselves, as well as all later interpretations, were created with words. At this point, these interpreters can only say: the essence of the *dao* cannot speak, but we cannot help but speak about it, and so we provisionally, reluctantly have no choice but to speak about it, in order to try, though our words, to reach the realm of the wordless *dao*. This is what is meant by the sentence, "Attain the meaning and forget the words, catch the fish and forget the fishtrap." This seemingly profound statement contains an extreme and insurmountable defect, however: if *dao* in fact cannot speak, then how are you going to use language to speak about it and attain its meaning? Isn't this just to deepen the grip that "nothing" has on you and leave the "great source" further behind? There is only one way to undo this knot entangling language and *dao*: admit that in the midst of language itself there is something that mutually "harmonizes, suits, and satisfies" with *dao*, a preconceptual dimension of language, and through this, or in its very midst, *dao* tells (*dao*) us that which it says (*dao*). As the preceding two sections have made clear, for both Heidegger and for Laozi and Zhuangzi, this dimension of language does indeed exist and it is of the first importance.

When dealing with language and ultimate reality, philosophers can adopt one or the other of two different attitudes. They can hold that the essence of language is concept-representing or else non-concept-representing. Similarly, they can hold that ultimate reality is a conceptual entity or a non-conceptual entity. There are thus several different possibilities. Philosophers who believe that the essence of both language and reality are conceptual, like traditional metaphysicians, will pay absolutely no attention to the ontology of language. Those who hold that language is concept-representing but believe reality to be a non-conceptual entity, or those who hold the reverse, namely, that language is non-representational but ultimate reality is a conceptual entity—both of these must pay attention to the problem of "*dao* language" or "expressing reality through language." They typically deny the *dao*-ness of language and furthermore adopt skepticism, relativism, intuitionism, or mysticism. The first two of these attitudes are actually protests against traditional metaphysics and scholasticism, but the latter two cannot avoid falling into the knot of language and *dao*. This is just to say that on the one hand, intuitionism and mysticism strive to pursue nonlinguistic ways of realizing the *dao* or enlightenment, like yoga, *qigong*, meditation, ascetic practices, divination, rituals, or icons; but on the other hand, they discover that they cannot pursue understanding or transmitting the *dao* without using language (broadly construed). They have no choice but to resort to the "language-fishtrap" slogan discussed above, which just leaves them tied up in an inextricable knot.

With regard to the question of language and reality, the attitude of the fourth possible combination mentioned above is to hold that both are non-conceptual and constituted. There are thus no ontological differences between primordial language and primordial reality. They appropriate and constitute one another, and form a coherent whole. Heidegger and Laozi and Zhuangzi all have this kind of insight.

Those committed to the "language-fishtrap" theory, or the theory that language is a tool, typically believe that Laozi "looks on non-being as the original [substance]," and so at the most crucial points in their interpretations of *dao*, their "language is trapped and their road cut off" and they leap into obscurity and mystery. As we have seen from the previous section, though, Laozi's and Zhuangzi's most fundamental view of *dao* is instead that "being and non-being originate in one another," "they both may be called deep and profound," and "assent to transformation and [be] released from things." However, the text of *Laozi* does in fact contain language like chapter 40: "The myriad things of the world originate in being, / and being originates in nonbeing." When reading this kind of sentence, though, one must connect it to the context in order to see its deep meaning. For instance, the whole of the passage in which this sentence appears runs like this: "Reversal is the movement of the *dao*; / weakness if the function of the *dao*. / The myriad things of the world originate in being, / and being originates in non-being." Speaking of "being originat[ing] in nonbeing" is one of the methods by which the *dao* can return; its goal is to remove people's ever-so-common commitments to "small being" and reveal the profound realm of "being and non-being originating in one another" (chap. 2) which is "shadowy, indistinct" (chap. 21). In no way is this passage asserting that nonbeing is a metaphysical substance which, like a black hole, completely sucks in being without ever spitting it back out. The whole text of the *Laozi* is filled with this kind of mutual, life-giving reversals which are the "movements of the *dao*." Where "nameless" is discussed, we also find "named" (chaps. 1, 32); where "non-action" appears, we also find "act without acting" (chaps. 3, 37, 63). This life-blood of the *dao* is even more developed and glorious in the *Zhuangzi*, where it appears in a myriad of guises. The result of indicating that being and nonbeing originate in one another, that "that" and "this" are mutually constituted, and that affirming and denying cause one another, is to make people reach the self-illumination of the "affirmation which goes by circumstance (*yinshi*)" (*Zhuangzi*, chap. 2), which is just to say "reach the essence of affairs" or "the essence of *dao*," and make *dao* speak itself, rather than being cut off through representation and conceptualization (the small name and small language).

Therefore, when a thinker says that "nonbeing" is more primordial than "small being," he is not necessarily asserting that nonbeing is conceptual and substantial. In *Being and Time* and "What is Metaphysics," Heidegger speaks of the ontological priority of nonbeing to beings, but he absolutely does not do this in the course of viewing nonbeing as a substance, contrary to the interpretations of some Asian scholars. It is through his discussion of the nonbeing of *Dasein* that [we see how] being itself is disclosed, and thus beings can be where they are and affirm that which they affirm.[43] To put it a little more simply, he reaches "great being" or "being itself" through "nonbeing." Therefore, this nonbeing is just the "there (*Da*)" of *Dasein*. We can see that for this extremely thorough thinker, speaking of nonbeing does not obstruct genuine being, and speaking of being does not obstruct genuine nonbeing.

Theorists prone to conceptualize thought (like Wang Bi), however, can rarely reach the regionalized appropriation of being and nonbeing originating in one another. Though such a person can, from a conceptual perspective, talk of the dialectical relationship between being and nonbeing, but it will be completely lacking in the profundity and mystery of mutual evocation. An important expression of the dull and shriveled nature of this kind of view is its denial of the mutual evocation of *dao*-saying and *dao* itself. Such thinkers believe themselves to be denying *Dao* any aspect of being or conceptual graspability, little imagining that they were viewing *dao* itself as a most abstract kind of concept; at the same time that they got rid of the small being of *dao*, they lost its great being. Almost all schools of thought have some subsequent, authoritative interpreters who use this kind of method to cut off their own connection to the *dao*. Hinayana Buddhists toward Sakyamuni; Song dynasty Confucians toward Confucius; mechanical, follow the [recorded] conversation-style Chan monks toward Hui Neng—all are like this.

After the pre-Qin period, Daoist philosophical thought entered a period of continuous decline, the most important reason for which was its loss of its constitutive insight that being and nonbeing originate in one another, leading it to be trapped in theories of "*dao* is fundamentally nonbeing" or "*dao* fundamentally does not speak." These are forms of mysticism or intellectual laziness forced on Daoism by a conceptual mode of thinking (The substance of a metaphysical *dao* can only be nonbeing, and language and the phenomenal world can only be being). If *dao* and linguistic thinking lack any kind of fundamental connection, what options does someone seeking the *dao* have but to become a *qigong* master, an alchemist, or a prophet? Using Heidegger's technical terminology, at this point Daoism willingly withdrew from the realm of "pure being" or "pure thought" which constituted humanity's historical authenticity, and fell into the loose world to which ready-to-hand beings belong. The constitutive insight of the Daoism ancestors ended up relying on later Buddhists (Huayan, Tiantai, and Chan) to expound and propagate.

When Heidegger and Laozi and Zhuangzi speak of "nonbeing," it typically has a connotation of "function" or "nonfunctional great function." This connotation is connected to the attitude they hold toward language or *dao*-saying. To put it simply, they all use "nonbeing" or "nonfunction (of ready-to-hand, small being)" to "lose" (*Laozi*, 48) conceptual, representative small names and small language, and thus to manifest an original, pure region of language or *dao*-language, and make people dissolve into it and attain the great functioning of the true *dao*. Heidegger describes this pure realm of language with terms like "hermeneutical position," "region of self-appropriation," "opening," "game space," and so on. Laozi typically describes it as the "gateway of the mysterious female" (chap. 6) which is "shadowy, indistinct, dim, and dark" (chap. 21), "concentrating one's energies to be supple" (chap. 10), "empty without being exhausted: / the more it works, the more comes out" (chap. 5), "acting with extreme emptiness" (chap. 16), and "revolving without pause" (chap. 25). This confusedly formed realm of *dao* contains "images," "essences," "things," and "reliability" (chap. 21); it can be called "dimly visible; it seems as if it were there, / yet use will never drain it" (chap. 6). What has the inflexible "essence of nonbeing" to do with all this? And for Zhuangzi, this realm of *dao*-language which is prior to concepts, names, and ideas is all the more boundless and unrestrained.

It cannot be denied that the ways in which Heidegger, on the one hand, and Laozi and Zhuangzi, on the other, express their views on language are different. Heidegger's experience studying theology in university awoke his concern for hermeneutics, and this had a great influence on his views of phenomenological ontology and the nature of language. Because of this, the question of the ontological significance of language occupies a particularly prominent position in his thought. After the 1930s, the group of questions represented by "language" was the central topic of his writings. Although the relation between language and reality was an extremely important question for Laozi, he always used the idea that "true saying is paradoxical" to express himself, and thus through denying the *dao*-nature of concepts and names, indicated the great *dao*, great image, and great language. In the *Zhuangzi*, the *dao*-nature of language itself received more direct discussion. Heidegger certainly has a more definite and direct discussion of the ontological dimension of language than do the Daoists. Nonetheless, the preceding discussion has shown that not only are the views of Heidegger and Laozi and Zhuangzi on this subject not contradictory, but also in fact they communicate deeply with one another. Therefore, even though Heidegger knew that the original meaning of the Chinese word *dao* was "road," he still believed that "the word '*dao*' has hidden in it the complete mystery of saying."[44] The analysis and argumentation in the second and third sections of this essay have made clear that this opinion is justified both by philological evidence and by intellectual stimulation. In one sense, it helps us to see the plentiful meanings of *dao*, and especially the ways in which these meanings mutually relate to and shed light on one another.

For Heidegger, Laozi, and Zhuangzi, the key to pursuing truth lies in dispelling small names and small beings, and allowing the most fundamental constitutive region, represented by the great *dao* and by being itself, to be revealed. The more purely and completely revealed this primordial region, the more it affinitively unfolds it constitutive nature, and "says" or *dao*s the non-conceptual "news" it contains in itself. In these circumstances, no matter whether it is from the wordless outdoors, the disclosure of poetry or music, the inspiration of innate goodness or innate ability, or indicated through linguistic investigation, we will all be able to hear the surging call of this region itself.

NOTES

1. Martin Heidegger, *Identity and Difference* (Shanghai: Sanlian Shudian, 1996), pp. 28–30; *On the Way to Language*, p. 198. Translated from Chinese.

2. Heidegger, *Identity and Difference*.

3. Su Shiyi, "Our encounters in the wood market," in *Remebering Martin Heidegger* (Beijing: Sanlian Shudian, 1997), pp. 119–129.

4. Heidegger, *On the Way*, p. 96. Translated from Chinese.

5. Ibid., pp. 95, 121.

6. Heidegger, *Being and Time*, p. 37. Translated from Chinese. (Beijing: Sanlian Shudian, 1987).

7. Heidegger, *On the Way*, pp. 98–9.

8. Ibid., p. 252.

9. Ibid., p. 254.

10. Ibid., p. 124.

11. Martin Heidegger, "What are poets for?" p. 124. Translated from Chinese. (Shanghai: Sanlian Shudian, 1996).

12. Heidegger, *On the Way*, p. 261.

13. Heidegger, *Identity and Difference*, p. 30.

14. Ibid., pp. 254–5; and *On the Way*, p. 12.

15. "Things," in *Collected Speeches and Essays*, p. 166. Translated from Chinese. (Shanghai: Sanlian Shudian, 1996).

16. Heidegger, *Being and Time*, p. 328.

17. Ibid., p. 331.

18. Heidegger, *On the Way*, p. 197.

19. Heidegger, *Being and Time*, p. 133.

20. Heidegger, *On the Way*, p. 247.

21. Ibid., p. 247.

22. Ibid., p. 187.

23. Heidegger, *Being and Time*, p. 34.

24. Heidegger, "Things," p. 173.

25. Martin Heidegger, *From a life of thought*, (1947), p. 13. Translated from Chinese. (Shanghai: Sanlian Shudian, 1996).

26. *Holzwege*, pp. 61–2. Translated from Chinese. (Shanghai: Yiwen Press, 1997).

27. Heidegger, *On the Way*, p. 254.

28. Ibid., p. 260.

29. Ibid., pp. 111, 166, 267.

30. Ibid., p. 122.

31. For example, see: Alan Watts and A. C. Huang, *Tao: The Watercourse Way* (New York: Pantheon Books, 1975), pp. 38–9. Here Watts says that in the third century B.C.E. (the period in which he believes *Laozi* was written), "*dao*" did not have the meaning of "say."

32. See Feng Youlan, *Zhongguo zhexue shi* [*History of Chinese philosophy*] (Beijing: Zhonghua Shuju, 1961), 1:218; and Ren Jiyu, ed., *Zhongguo zhexue shi* [*History of Chinese philosophy*] (Beijing: People's Press, 1966), 1:44.

33. Xu Shen, *Shuowen jiezi* (1963), p. 42.

34. *Sishu wujing*, vol. 1 (Beijing: Zhongguo shudian, 1958), p. 88.

35. *Sishu wujing,* p. 126.

36. Liu Qi, *"Shang shu,"* in *Shujing qiantan* (Beijing: Zhonghua shuju, 1984), p. 20.

37. *Lunyu jishi* (Beijing: Zhonghua shuju, 1990), 3:1011.

38. These two lines can also be punctuated as follows: "The nameless is the beginning of heaven and earth; / the named, the mother of the myriad things." "Without desire (*wu yu*)" and "having desire (*you yu*)," below, can also be punctuated in this alternative fashion. These differences do not influence the point under discussion.

39. See Guo Qingfan, ed., *Zhuangzi jishi* (Tainan: Weiyi Book Center, 1975), p. 1069.

40. Heidegger, *On the Way,* p. 198.

41. See Wang Xianqian, ed., *Zhuangzi jishi* (Beijing: Zhonghua shuju, 1954), p. 17.

42. Although I know that Heidegger's—and Western philosophy's more generally—notion of "being (*eon, sein*)" is different in many ways from what Zhuangzi here means by "*shi* (treat as right)," I cannot avoid reminding us of the relations and comparability between the two.

43. Heidegger, "What is Metaphysics?" in *Basic Writings* edited by D. S. Krell (New York: Harper and Row, 1977), p. 110.

44. Heidegger, *On the Way,* p. 198.

Speech from Beyond
the Reach of Language

A Response to Zhang Xianglong

Merold Westphal

It is with the deepest appreciation that I recall the days of dialogue between Chinese and American philosophers in which I was privileged to participate in Beijing in 1998. The Chinese scholars came from Peking University and from other universities throughout China, just as we Americans came from a variety of institutions. So I consider it an honor to have been invited to respond to the paper by Zhang Xianglong, all the more so since it seeks to elicit a dialogue between Heidegger and Lao-Zhuang, philosophers I find to be more than worth the effort it takes to try to understand them.

I turn to this task having just finished giving my undergraduate course on Chinese philosophy. In reading the Confucian classics, I invited my students to juxtapose these ideas to contemporary American culture, to identify points of affinity and divergence, and above all to read the texts as we might well read Plato, namely, as a challenge addressed to us across great expanses of time and space. I have to confess that I did not have the courage to do this as seriously when it came to Lao-Zhuang, but relied, for comparative purposes, primarily on possible relations between these texts and the various schools of Chinese Buddhism we studied. Implicit in this procedure, I suppose, was a sense that Daoism and Buddhism represent a concentrated and deliberate assault on "common sense" in a way that Confucianism does not. For example, whereas the latter places great emphasis on the rectification of names (an interesting critique of "spin" and "hype" in American culture), Daoism and Buddhism try to show the impotence of names, the ultimate inadequacy of language to mirror the world.[1]

It is not surprising that when Zhang chooses a Western dialogue partner for Lao-Zhuang, he turns to Martin Heidegger, whose philosophy of language represents a departure from those Western philosophical traditions about the *logos* that have most deeply shaped the "common sense" view of the world in the West and its "Confucian" view of language.

Zhang begins his illuminating paper with a section entitled "Heidegger's View of Language." He characterizes this view by calling it a "nonrepresentational and constitutive view of language." This suggests that Heidegger is a certain kind of Kantian, a hermeneutical Kantian perhaps. To say that language is nonrepresentational is not to say that it does not refer to anything outside itself, but rather that it is not its task to mirror the world, nor does it fall within its power to do so.[2] To say that language is constitutive is to say that neither its chore nor its competency is to copy the world or correspond to it but to create it. This does not mean, of course, that language creates the world *ex nihilo* or that it operates under no constraints. It is rather to say that the world, the meaningful *Umwelt* that is the wherein of our concernful dealings with entities of various sorts, is not simply given to our cognition, a set of prefabricated facts to be duplicated in our propositions. It is rather the product (in the mathematical sense) of *(a)* what is given to us by nature and tradition, and *(b)* our construal or interpretation of it. Knowledge is interpretation, and interpretation is translation. Just as no translation is simply a copy of the original text but a creative construal of it, so language in general is not a mirror image of the world as passively "out there" but joins in the very constitution of the world as the meaningful horizon of all experience and knowledge.

This view of the matter is nicely expressed by two thinkers we might describe as Heideggerian Kantians. Hans-Georg Gadamer tells us that "understanding is not merely reproductive but always productive activity as well."[3] In a similar way, Jacques Derrida tells us that while deconstruction "is always deeply concerned with the 'other' of language" and indeed is "above all else the search for the 'other' and the 'other of language,'" it is also true that "*There is nothing outside of the text.*"[4] John D. Caputo has nicely expressed the dialectical, even paradoxical nature of the situation: "For while there is nothing which, for Derrida, would escape the constraints of textuality [read: language], it is no less true that everything that Derrida has written has been directed toward the other of language, toward the alterity by which language is claimed."[5]

There is no doubt that the "nonrepresentational and constitutive view of language" we have been discussing is to be found in *Being and Time*. But how? Against interpretations that make a sharp distinction between the "early" and the "late" Heidegger, William J. Richardson's Heidegger I and Heidegger II,[6] Zhang argues that at least on the question of language there is only one Heidegger. He argues that in the hermeneutical context of the analytic of *Dasein*, language is existentially significant, that language is about disclosure more than about communication, that there is a realm of disclosure and thus of language prior to spoken language, that this priority is that of the horizon that enables language to play its constitutive role, and that Heidegger is already beyond traditional notions of the subject. These claims are beyond dispute.[7] But are they sufficient to support the following claim about his view of language in *Being and Time*: "Corresponding to his view of *Dasein*, he does not believe that primordial language is in any sense a ready-to-hand thing . . ."

I do not think so. In the first place, the case is not made textually. The exposition of Heidegger's view of language is taken overwhelmingly from later texts. The texts cited in this section from *Being and Time* are not specifically about language and neither individually nor collectively do they support the above claim.

This is not surprising, for, in the second place, the analytic of *Dasein*, in its polemic against the priority of the present-at-hand (*vorhanden, Vorhandenheit*) insists that proximally and for the most part (*zunächst und zumeist*) *Dasein* operates within the horizon of the ready-to-hand (*zuhanden, Zuhandenheit*). Heidegger is not a crude pragmatist, but in his analysis of beings as equipment, and in the famous example of the hammer, he suggests that everyday *Dasein* is a fairly crude pragmatist. Absent clear evidence to the contrary, we have every right to suppose that this applies to *Dasein*'s attitude toward language.[8]

However, and thirdly, instead of clear evidence to the contrary, when Heidegger turns specifically to language (*Sprache*), he presents us with *Dasein* in its everyday inauthenticity, as falling in idle talk, curiosity, and ambiguity. Far from making a clean break with the pragmatism of *Zuhandenheit*, we find *Dasein* here, as elsewhere, proximally and for the most part immersed there. Perhaps there is a theory of "primordial language" that is "not in any sense a ready-to-hand thing" to be found explicitly or implicitly in *Being and Time*, but Zhang has not shown us where or how to find it.

The case for a discontinuity between early and later Heidegger is, if anything, even stronger when we take note of two other features of Heidegger's view of language as presented by Zhang. One of these is the idea that "language is more powerful than we are," a notion nicely expressed in the phrase, "*die Sprache spricht*."[9] The other is that it is the "horizon for understanding being," indeed the very "house of being." But in *Being and Time*, *Dasein* is more powerful than language, and Heidegger does not say "*die Sprache spricht*" because in idle talk, curiosity, and ambiguity, it is *Dasein* who speaks. And precisely because the horizon for *Dasein*'s understanding is framed by its own projection in everyday inauthenticity, it is a horizon for understanding beings and not being. Language is not the house of being for *Dasein* because in its absolute preoccupation with beings, whether as *zuhanden* or as *vorhanden*, its horizon is for misunderstanding being. Heidegger had hoped to use *Dasein* as the key to the meaning of being, but, as he himself recognized, he never got beyond *Dasein* as too busy with beings to worry about being, or to listen to language as the house of being. Like the "we" in Hegel's *Phenomenology of Spirit*, which hopes to see past the finitude and unhappiness of natural consciousness, the "we" of *Being and Time*, if "we" are sympathetic readers, hopes to get past the everydayness of *Dasein* to something more genuinely primordial than what *Dasein* is proximally and for the most part. But whereas Hegel's text purports to reach its lofty goal, Heidegger's does not. So we should not expect to find the essentials of Heidegger II's philosophy of language in Heidegger I.[10]

Even if this conclusion is right, I do not think it is very important. For even if it is not to be found in the early Heidegger, there surely is a philosophy of language in the later Heidegger that (1) is beyond the instrumentalism of the world of the ready-to-hand, (2) portrays language as stronger than we are, and (3) portrays language in its primacy as the house of being, the horizon for understanding being. And the project of bringing this philosophy of language into dialogue with Lao-Zhuang is an exciting one indeed.

There is, of course, a major obstacle to such a project. Heidegger may well have a philosophy of language that takes us beyond both the ordinary uses of language and the ordinary understanding of what language is. According to this view, language is the house of being, indeed the very voice of being. When *die Sprache spricht*, silencing *Dasein*, or at least revealing to attentive listeners the trivial nature of ordinary language, we might well say that *Sein selbst spricht*. But doesn't the *Laozi* famously open with the line: "The way that can be spoken is not the constant way?" Does this not mean that "the way fundamentally does not speak?" Do not "both Lao and Zhuang completely deny a genuine relationship between the way and language?" Are not way (*dao*) and name (*ming*) "completely opposed to one another?"

In a word, no, replies Zhang, and it is to defend this resounding negative that his second section, entitled "The Way's Speaking" is devoted. There is a link between the way and language because, among its other meanings, "*dao*" means "saying." Already in the Zhou dynasty (1000 B.C.E.), in the *Classic of History*, there are two passages where "*dao*' can . . . only be read as 'said'." Other passages in the *Analects* and the *Mencius,* which are more or less contemporary with Lao-Zhuang, respectively, confirm this linguistic usage, reinforced by the annotations of Zhu Xi on the latter text. Finally, there are ample indications of such usage in the *Laozi* and the *Zhuangzi* themselves.

The argument is at once linguistic and textual. I am in no position to question the linguistic portion of this argument. In any case, I am not in the least inclined to do so since the textual argument is persuasive and the linguistic argument helps to explain it. It is important to be clear, however, that Zhang is not challenging the entire traditional reading (and translation) of the opening line of the *Laozi*. The way is indeed beyond names, not because it has no relation to language, but because it cannot be captured and adequately mirrored by names (or propositions) in the way in which ordinary language is ordinarily thought to capture and correspond to the world. Zhang elegantly formulates the ways in which the way both is and is not beyond language: " . . . although [the

Laozi and the *Zhuangzi*] deny that language which submits to conceptual thinking can reach *dao* itself, they absolutely do not deny the *dao*-saying of *dao* itself,
nor that the shadowy and indistinct, image-creating nature of the way (*dao*) is
to speak (*dao*)." They hold to a "nonrepresentational, unconceptualizable view
of language that is embodied in the great *dao* and the great language (*dayan*)."

We have already seen that a nonrepresentational view of language signifies a
view that does not revolve around such notions as copying, mirroring, corresponding, and adequation. But how shall we understand "unconceptualizable?"
Since Zhang is trying, with help from Heidegger and Lao-Zhuang to articulate
a distinctive view of language, it is presumably not the view of language that is
unconceptualizable, but language itself, in its most primordial mode, that is
unconceptual in something like the way in which it is nonrepresentational. This
can hardly mean that the language in question does not use concepts, for, to take
only the most conspicuous example staring us in the face, the opening line of
the *Laozi*, presumably the bearer or locus of *dao*-speech, uses such concepts as
'way,' 'name,' and 'constant'. We would do better to take the claim to mean that
the language in question, when it does use concepts, does not use them in the
commonly understood way, noetically (in the private commerce between the mind
and the world) to mirror the essences in things by duplicating them in the mind
(the immaterial reception of the forms), and then pragmatically for purposes of
communicating these meanings to others. Rather, this kind of speech, here
attributed to the *dao*, has a "shadowy and indistinct, image-creating nature . . ."
Adumbration, we might say, not adequation. Here language seeks to say what
cannot be said, at least not in conceptual-representational ways. But this is a
mode of speaking, a way we might describe as poetic, both because of the poetic
nature of the texts of Lao-Zhuang and because of the way Heidegger explicitly
thematizes the poetic nature of primordial language.

This account of the way in which the *dao* speaks to us surely invites comparison with Heidegger's account of the language of being (subjective genitive)
which occurs when *die Sprache spricht*, and language becomes the very voice of
being. Heidegger writes: "The soundless gathering call, by which Saying moves
the world-relation on its way, we call the ringing of stillness [*das Geläut der
Stille*]. It is: the language of being."[11]

In his third section, "The Mutual Evocation of *Dao* and Saying," Zhang
begins this comparison by developing two themes. First, he argues that both
Heidegger and Lao-Zhuang have a dual (not dualistic) view of language. On the
one hand, there is ordinary language or "small" language. It is characterized by
a conceptual-representational self-understanding; its pragmatic horizon is communication among human speakers; its epistemic norm is correspondence between proposition and fact;[12] and it is incapable of reaching the *dao*, or of
getting beyond beings to being itself. It is useful but ontologically impoverished.
On the other hand, there is *dao*-speak or *Ereignis*, primordial language which is
beyond the dualisms of subject and object, proposition and fact. But this is

language, not intuitionism or mysticism. It is of central importance to Zhang to deny the claim that while we can speak about the *dao*, it cannot itself speak to us. This would lead to an intuitionism or a mysticism which would "strive to pursue nonlinguistic ways of realizing the *dao* or enlightenment. It is primarily in these terms that Zhang seeks to distinguish Daoism from Buddhism.

Those who deny *dao*-speak might also turn to skepticism and relativism, and Zhang wants to distinguish Daoism just as sharply from this alternative. It would seem that Zhang agrees with Robert Allinson's argument against interpreting Zhuangzi as a relativist.[13] In the Buddhist traditions, skepticism and relativism are often the prolegomena for what is here called "intuitionism or mysticism." But they could equally well play a penultimate role in Zhang's Daoism. For the argument that the *dao* speaks is fully compatible with a skeptical relativism toward "small" language: not only does it not reach the *dao*, but it does not give us finitude in anything but radically perspective modes.[14] It is hard not to find this kind of skeptical relativism in Lao-Zhuang. But the skeptical relativism Zhang has primarily in mind is not a prolegomenon to transcendence but a final philosophical resting place for those complacently assured that they are called by no Truth.

Beyond the skeptical relativism which uses language to establish its own superiority to the language that it judges to be inadequate, and on this side of the intuitionism and mysticism which give up on language without giving up on the Ultimate, the *dao* speaks. In spite of the relativism and the mysticism which, in giving up on human language, render the Ultimate mute,[15] the *dao* speaks. That is the central point, which Zhang seeks to reinforce with his second theme. Both Heidegger and Lao-Zhuang give a prominence to nonbeing in their thinking that is atypical of the contexts in which they have emerged. But they do not, Zhang insists, give priority to nonbeing; they are not ontological nihilists. Their view is better described as the "mutual evocation" of being and nonbeing. Like Hegel, they find being and nonbeing unthinkable apart from each other.[16] To be sure, their talk of nonbeing is a challenge, even a threat, to the ultimacy of ordinary discourse.[17] But it does not signify a first principle, nor is nonbeing some kind of substance. Rather, they use the language of nonbeing, in its reciprocity with the language of being, for two purposes: first, to undermine conceptual-representational thought, which takes being to be a first principle and, in some form or other, a substance; and second, in this way to clear the way for something better, "to manifest an original, pure region of language or *dao*-language" so that "we will be able to hear the surging call of this region itself."

We are addressed. The point of Daoism is to render us open (vulnerable, available, receptive, welcoming) to this "surging call" which comes to us from beyond the reach of our own, merely human language. In the above citation from Heidegger about *das Geläut der Stille*, a phrase we might render as "the language beyond language," emphasis is on the fact that the voice is the voice of being. Now we can also notice that what sounds through the stillness is a call:

"The soundless gathering *call* . . . we *call* the ringing of stillness" (emphasis added). We are called, and not only this. Our own calling, in this case a naming, is a response to a prior call. Heidegger has been careful to prepare us for this discovery, emphasizing in the preceding paragraphs first, that the initial language is "not a mere human faculty," and second, that "as Saying of the world's four-fold, language concerns us . . . who can speak only as we respond to language."[18]

Here Heidegger only repeats what he said in an earlier essay on language:

> *Language speaks as the peal of stillness* [*das Geläut der Stille*]. . . . The peal of stillness is not anything human. But on the contrary, the human is indeed in its nature given to speech—it is linguistic. The word "linguistic" as it is here used means: having taken place out of the speaking of language. What has thus taken place, human being, has been brought into its own by language, so that it remains given over or appropriated to the nature of language, the peal of stillness. . . . Only as men belong within the peal of stillness are mortals able to speak in *their own* way in sounds. . . . Poetry proper is never merely a higher mode (*melos*) of everyday language. It is rather the reverse: everyday language is a forgotten and therefore used-up poem, from which there hardly resounds a *call* any longer. . . . But human speech, as the speech of mortals, is not self-subsistent. The speech of mortals rests in its relation to the speaking of language. . . . Mortal speech must first of all have listened to the *command*, in the form of which the stillness of the difference *calls* world and things into the rift of its one fold simplicity. . . . Mortals speak insofar as they listen . . . by receiving what it says from the *command* of the difference, mortal speech has already, in its own way, followed the *call*. Response, as receptive listening, is at the same time a recognition that makes due acknowledgment.[19] (emphasis added).

Beyond all the obvious and not so obvious differences between Lao-Zhuang and Heidegger, there is a profound affinity: we are called by a language which comes to us from beyond the reach of our own language. In response to Zhang's eloquent presentation of this significant meeting of East and West, I want to mention another place in the Western tradition where a strikingly similar move occurs and the claim is made that we are addressed by that which exceeds the reach of our language, at least in its conceptual-representational mode.

I have in mind Augustine. He is very clear about the fact that God is an ineffable mystery, one who exceeds our conceptual grasp. This is not to say that he is bashful about describing God, about attributing properties and actions to God in a classically theistic way. But he is aware that our words are arrows that, however appropriate, do not reach their target but fall short of the glory of God. So, early in the *Confessions*, in the midst of an eloquent and exuberant explica-tion of the divine being, he describes God not just as "most present among us" but also as "most hidden from us . . . ever enduring and yet we cannot compre-hend you." He concludes, "Can any man say enough when he speaks of you? Yet woe betide those who are silent about you! For even those who are most gifted with speech cannot find words to describe you."[20]

Similarly, in *De Doctrina Christiana*, he writes, with reference to the Trinity of Father, Son, and Holy Spirit,

> It is not easy after all, to find any name that will really fit such transcendent majesty. . . . Have I said anything, solemnly uttered anything that is worthy of God? On the contrary, all I feel I have done is to wish to say something; but if I have said anything, it is not what I wished to say. How do I know this? I know it because God is inexpressible. . . . And from this it follows that God is not to be called inexpressible, because when even this is said about him, something is being expressed. And we are involved in heaven knows what kind of battle of words. . . . And yet, while nothing really worthy of God can be said about him, he has accepted the homage of human voices, and has wished us to rejoice in praising him with our words. That in fact is what is meant by calling him God. Not, of course, that with the sound made by this one syllable any knowledge of him is achieved.[21]

God is the Ultimate Mystery, not because there are things we do not know about God (while the things we do know are perfectly in order); rather it is because none of our language about God is adequate to the divine being,[22] none of our propositions represent divine facts by mirroring them in our minds. In this sense, the God of Augustine is beyond language.[23]

But this is not to say that God has no relation to language. After all, as Creator, a role Augustine constantly recalls, God is the source of our ability to speak. But far more importantly, God speaks. In biblical language, Creation itself is a speech act: "Then God said, 'Let there be light'; and there was light" (Gen. 1:3).[24] It is as a speaker that God is the First Cause, a fact that decisively separates Augustine's God from Aristotle's Prime Mover and from Plotinus' One. God has called human language into being out of nothing, along with everything else finite. But the ultimate miracle of divine speech for Augustine is not that God speaks us into being and in doing so give us the power of speech; it is that God speaks to us. His God is First Cause, to be sure; but far more profoundly, God is First Interlocutor. As immersed as Augustine is in the vision metaphor inherited from Platonism, he regularly performs an *Aufhebung*, a teleological suspension of vision in speech. God is an essence we long to behold; but even more deeply (and immediately) God is a voice to which we must listen. The deepest reason Augustine says "You" to God, and not he, she, or it, is because he is always reminding himself and us, "You called me."

Thus, when remembering in the *Confessions* how he panted for "Truth! Truth!" when he read Cicero's *Hortensius* and how what the Manichees offered him left a taste in his mouth that "was not the taste of truth," he confesses to God, "you are Truth itself. . . .Yet the things [the Manichees] gave me to eat were not in the least like you, as now I know since you have spoken to me" (*Confessions* III: 6). One medium of this speech was the Incarnation. "Our Life himself came down into this world and took away our death. He slew it with his own abounding life, and with thunder in his voice he called us from this world to return to him in heaven. . . . He did not linger on his way but ran, calling us to return to him, calling us by his words and deeds . . ." (*Confessions* IV: 12). Even, or should we say especially, in his most mystical moments, God is the one who addresses Augustine. He describes one moment of rapture when "I entered into the depths of my soul . . . and with the eye of my soul, such as it was, I saw the Light that never changes casting its rays over the same eye of my soul, over my mind. . . . It was above me because it was itself the Light that made me. . . . I gazed on you with eyes too weak to resist the dazzle of your splendor. Your light shone upon me in its brilliance, and I thrilled with love and dread alike." The Platonic cast of this discourse in conspicuous, but so is its interruption as Augustine continues, "I realized that I was far away from you. It was as though I were in a land where all is different from your own and I heard your voice calling from on high. . . . And far off, I heard your voice saying, *I am the God who IS.* I heard your voice, as we hear voices that speak to our hearts, and at once I had no cause to doubt" (*Confessions* VII: 10).

Finally, there is the famous experience of mystical ecstasy that Augustine experiences with his mother, shortly before her death. Realizing that they had had a foretaste of glory divine, they speculate about what turns out to be not just the beatific vision but the beatific listening as well:

> Suppose, we said, that after giving us this message and bidding us listen to him who made them all, [created beings] fell silent and he alone should speak to us, not through them but in his own voice, so that we should hear him speaking, not by any tongue of the flesh or by an angel's voice, not in the sound of thunder or in some veiled parable, but in his own voice, the voice of the one whom we love in all these created things; suppose that we heard him himself, with none of these things between ourselves and him . . . suppose that this state were to continue . . . would not this be what we are to understand by the words, *Come and share the joy of your Lord?* (*Confessions* IX: 10)

I spoke above of Augustine's thought as "strikingly similar" to that of Heidegger and Lao-Zhuang. Here, once again, we find ourselves addressed in a speech that comes from beyond the reach of our own language. But Augustine's thought is also strikingly dissimilar, more different from Heidegger and Lao-Zhuang, I believe, than they are from each other. In all three cases we are addressed by a call. But only in Augustine's case does the call come from a caller. Augustine's God is a personal being capable of performing conscious, intentional acts, among which speech acts can be numbered. This is not to say that the categories used in the previous sentence are adequate to the divine reality any more than any other categories. But it is to claim, with all the genuinely theistic traditions of the East and the West, that they are more appropriate, more nearly adequate to the divine reality than impersonal categories. Even before one particular human being, Jesus of Nazareth, is said by Augustine and the Christian tradition to which he belongs, to be the best indication of who God is, human persons generically are said to be created in the image of God, among all the created beings with whom we are most immediately in contact, the ones who provide us with the best clue of who God is. Human speech is not merely a response to a call; it is a participation, an imitation of divine speech acts without which God would not be God. In this sense, the claim that God speaks is a literal claim and not a metaphor.[25] There is a call because there is a caller.

This does not seem to be the case with Heidegger and Lao-Zhuang. They seem rather to affirm a call without a caller. At least I do not find them affirming the eminently personal character of being or the *dao*. In *Being and Time,* the call emerges most clearly as the call of conscience. Two features distinguish this call from the call to which Augustine refers. First, the call says nothing: "*Conscience discourses solely and constantly in the mode of keeping silent.*" Second, although the calls comes both "*from* me" and "*from beyond me,*" the caller is *Dasein* itself and the "beyond me" only signifies that it is *Dasein* in its uncanniness, not its everydayness, that is the caller. Immanuel Kant would be proud of the way Heidegger holds uncompromisingly to the Enlightenment (modern) ideal of autonomy. There is a caller, but it is *Dasein* itself, and here we encounter once again the primacy of *Dasein* which Heidegger must overcome to get to a philosophy of language that can be compared with that of Lao-Zhuang.

In the later writings, the call "speaks" once again in the mode of silence (*das Geläut der Stille*). In this case, however, the call comes more decisively "from beyond me." And yet, this beyond is not a personal being who performs speech acts of promise, direction, command, forgiveness, and so forth, but language itself (*die Sprache spricht*) or being (which is not a being and a fortiori not a personal being). As already suggested, it is to the later Heidegger that Lao-Zhuang are most closely related. *Dao*-speak is only metaphorically vocative and it's not interpreted in terms of promise, command, forgiveness, and so forth, precisely because it is not viewed as emerging from a personal being capable of such speech acts.

By contrast, the call to which Augustine refers emerges from just such a personal being. For just this reason it is not a voice of silence but has what is sometimes called "a propositional content." We should not understand this to mean that divine speech acts are primarily declarative. They are as likely to be promises or invitations or commands as to be assertions. But they have a specific content. Thus, in one dramatic instance, Augustine heard through the voice of a child a command from God to take up the Bible and read it.[26] The specificity of this speech act betrays the radically personal character of its source.

More generally, Augustine also refers us to "your commandments, the three which proclaim our duty to you and the seven which proclaim our duty to men" (*Confessions* III: 8). This reference to the Ten Commandments follows Jesus' summary of the law as the commands first to love God with all our hearts, and second to love our neighbor as we love ourselves (Matt. 22:34–40). For Augustine, of course, God's commands are never separated from divine promises. So he is also able to translate the language of duty into the corresponding language of happiness: "Blessed are those who love you, O God, and love their friends in you and their enemies for your sake" (*Confessions* IV: 9).

This linkage of neighbor love with love of God is typical for Augustine. Thus, he emphatically affirms the teaching of 1 John 4:20, "*Whoever does not love the brother whom he sees cannot love God whom he does not see.*[27] One important gloss on this linkage comes in the following passage: "But when the mind loves God . . . it can rightly be commanded to love its neighbor as itself. For now it loves itself with a straight, not a twisted love, now that it loves God."[28] This notion of straight as distinct from twisted self-love is further glossed as follows: "Whoever therefore loves men should love them either because they are just or in order that they might be just. This is how he ought to love himself . . . in this way he can love *his neighbor as himself* (Mark 12:33) without any danger. Anyone who loves himself any other way loves himself unjustly. . ."[29]

This is not the place to develop in detail Augustine's understanding of the linkage between the command to love God and the command to love the neighbor. The point is to notice here a second distinctive of Augustine's notion of the call. Beyond the fact that the call comes from a caller, it is a twofold call. It calls us away from the world of finitude to the Infinite, from the world of time to Eternity, from everything relative to the Absolute. But having done so, it sends us back to the finite, temporal, relative world in which we live cheek by jowl with our neighbors—our families, our friends, our acquaintances, our enemies, and the strangers in our midst— and it commands us to love them as we love ourselves.

On this point, it seems to me once again that Augustine's understanding of the call differs significantly from that of Heidegger and Lao-Zhuang. There has been much debate over whether there is an ethics in Heidegger. I think there is undeniably a normative element in his thought, an ethos to which he thinks we are called. But in *Being and Time,* it is an *ethos* of authentic self-relation, while in the later writings it is an openness to being, to language, even to beings. But of an obligation to care for those around us, even if they are not our friends, I find nothing in Heidegger. And I cannot help but wonder if this absence contributed to his blindness to the real significance of National Socialism in the 1930s.[30]

To the best of my knowledge, there has been no similar flirtation between Daoism and evil. But I wonder if it has a sufficiently robust ethics of worldly life, of human interaction. To be sure, its notion of *wuwei*, along with the use of such symbols as water, the female, the infant, and the valley, represent a serious and sustained skepticism about the value of the self-asserting, aggressive ego. The self at the center of self-interest is decentered in relation to the *dao*. But I do not find in Lao-Zhuang a corresponding positive imperative to caring, compassion, and charity toward the neighbor in general, or the widow, the orphan, and the stranger in particular.[31]

When the term "mysticism" is applied to Daoism with pejorative connotations, it might be that people have overlooked what Zhang has so effectively pointed out, the linguistic nature of the *dao* itself. But it might be for another reason, namely, that we are called beyond the finite, the temporal, and the relative to the Infinite, the Eternal, and the Absolute without ever being sent back into Plato's cave on missions of mercy. The focus is so heavily on the relation of the individual to the Ultimate that the relation between the individual and the little people within the reach of "small" language suffers unnecessary neglect.

We are indebted to Zhang for pointing out so clearly the fundamental point of contact between Heidegger and Lao-Zhuang: they hear the call that comes to us from beyond the language games that make up the world in which we live proximally and for the most part. My question is whether they have properly identified the voice that calls. Is it possible that it is the voice of God who is so eminently personal that we can speak literally and not metaphorically about divine speech acts?[32] And is it possible that such a personal God is love itself and for that reason commands us to love each other in ways that Heidegger and Lao-Zhuang have not clearly heard?

NOTES

1. See Richard Rorty, *Philosophy and the Mirror of Nature* (Princeton: Princeton University Press, 1979); *Contingency, Irony, and Solidarity* (New York: Cambridge University Press, 1989); and *Essays on Heidegger and Others* (New York: Cambridge University Press, 1991. The latter volume actually contains an essay entitled "Wittgenstein, Heidegger, and the Rectification of Names." I use the term "inadequacy" deliberately to remind us of the classical Western medieval definition of truth as *adaequatio intellectus et res.* This equality of the intellect and the thing is perhaps best understood in terms of Aristotle's theory of knowledge as the immaterial reception of the forms. The form in the intellect is exactly the same as the form in the thing. Only the matter, itself ultimately unintelligible, has been omitted. I use the term "mirror" deliberately to remind us that an important metaphor for this relation has been that of mind as a mirror of nature, providing an exact copy. Richard Rorty's critique of these notions draws significantly upon Heidegger.

2. See previous note.

3. Hans-Georg Gadamer, *Truth and Method,* trans. Joel Weinsheimer and Donald G. Marshall, 2d ed. (New York: Crossroad, 1991), p. 296. By concluding with the words "as well," Gadamer makes it clear that constitution is not creation *ex nihilo,* but includes a receptive or reproductive dimension.

4. The first quotation is from Jacques Derrida, *Dialogues with Contemporary Continental Thinkers: The Phenomenological Heritage,* ed. Richard Kearney (Manchester: University of Manchester Press, 1984), p. 123. The second is from Jacques Derrida, *Of Grammatology,* trans. Gayatri Chakravorty Spivak (Baltimore: Johns Hopkins University

Press, 1976), p. 158. In the paragraph before saying this, Derrida notes that while interpretation cannot be reduced to reproduction or what he calls "doubling commentary," this moment has its legitimate place as a "legitimate guardrail." It would seem that he and Gadamer are in basic agreement on this point. See previous note.

5. John D. Caputo, *The Prayers and Tears of Jacques Derrida: Religion without Religion* (Bloomington, IN: Indiana University Press, 1997), p. 16.

6. William J. Richardson, S. J., *Heidegger: Through Phenomenology to Thought*, 2d ed. (The Hague: Martinus Nijhoff, 1967).

7. We would do well to remember that the concept of hermeneutics and interpretation are broader than the concept of language in *Being and Time*. Accordingly, in paragraph 33 assertion (*die Aussage*) is a derivative mode of interpretation. I have discussed the problem of pre-predicative interpretation in "Hermeneutics as Epistemology," in *The Blackwell Guide to Epistemology*, ed. John Greco and Ernest Sosa (Oxford: Blackwell, 1999).

8. These themes in Heidegger link him to Wittgenstein, who assimilates words to tools and reminds us that "we do the most various things with our sentences." See Wittgenstein, *Philosophical Investigations*, trans. G. E. M. Anscombe (Oxford: Blackwell, 1958), pp. 6–13. For more detailed comparison, see Stephen Mulhall, *On Being in the World: Wittgenstein and Heidegger on Seeing Aspects* (New York: Routledge and Kegan Paul, 1990).

9. See, for example, Heidegger, *On the Way to Language*, trans. Peter D. Hertz (New York: Harper and Row, 1971), p. 124, and *Poetry, Language, Thought*, trans. Albert Hofstadter (New York: Harper and Row, 1971), p. 197. Zhang cites passages from *Being and Time* in which Heidegger speaks this way about time, for example, *"Zeitlichkeit zeitigt"* (5), but not about language.

10. This is compatible with the terms on which Heidegger is willing to accept Richardson's distinction, which is "justified only on the condition that this is kept constantly in mind: only by way of what Heidegger I has thought does not gain access to what is to-be-thought by Heidegger II. But [the thought of] Heidegger I becomes possible only if it is contained in Heidegger II." But this is not to say that Heidegger II is contained in Heidegger I. See William Richardson *Heidegger: Through Phenomenology to Thought*, p. xxii.

11. Heidegger, *On the Way to Language*, p. 107. That this is a subjective and not an objective genitive is clear from the preceding page, where Heidegger makes it clear that the language of which he speaks is "not a mere human faculty."

12. There is an irony here. Correspondence theories and pragmatic theories of truth are usually treated as opposed to one another. But here pragmatism is the horizon and home for correspondence.

13. See Robert Allinson, *Chuang-Tzu: For Spiritual Transformation* (Albany: State University of New York Press, 1989).

14. It could well be argued that this relativism of "small" language is present in the hermeneutical circle as presented by Heidegger in *Being and Time*. See "Hermeneutics as

Epistemology." From this viewpoint the "turn" from Heidegger I to Heidegger II is made necessary precisely because *Being and Time* never gets beyond hermeneutical relativism, in spite of its desire to do so.

15. Of course, when we render the *dao* mute, we render ourselves immune to its call, a position not unwelcome to our individual and collective egos. The bodhisattva ideal in Mahayana Buddhism, already embodied in Siddhartha Gautama, is a resistance to this temptation. It is a response to a call for compassion in relation to those around us.

16. Thus, in the Wing-Tsit Chan translation of *The Daodejing*, we read:

> Therefore let there always be non-being . . .
> And let there always be being . . .
> The two are the same . . .
> But after they are produced, they have different names . . .
> Being and non-being produce each other . . . (stanzas 1 and 2).

But in the light of the Ivanhoe translation, English speakers must be careful here, for the same text reads:

> Always eliminate desires . . .
> Always have desires . . .
> These two come forth in unity but diverge in name . . .
> To have and to lack generate each other . . .

For Chan, see *A Source Book in Chinese Philosophy*, trans. Wing-Tsit Chan (Princeton: Princeton University Press, 1963), or *The Way of Lao Tzu* (text and commentary), trans. Wing-Tsit Chan (Indianapolis, IN: Bobbs-Merrill, 1963). For Ivanhoe, see *Readings in Classical Chinese Philosophy*, ed. Philip. J. Ivanhoe and Bryan W. Van Norden (New York: Seven Bridges Press, 2001).

17. See, for example, Heidegger, *What is Metaphysics,"* in *Pathmarks*, ed. William McNeill (New York: Cambridge University Press, 1998).

18. Heidegger, *On the Way to Language*, pp. 107–108.

19. Heidegger, *Poetry, Language, Thought*, pp. 207–209. While the use of the term "dif-ference" here invites a dialogue with Derrida, but we should not overlook its relation to the ontological difference as well.

20. Augustine, *Confessions*, trans. R. S. Pine-Coffin (Baltimore: Penguin Books, 1961), I: 4.

21. Augustine, *Teaching Christianity*, trans. Edmund Hill. O.P. (Hyde Park, NY: New City Press, 1996), I: 5–6.

22. Let us not forget the full force of this claim: in terms of the classical definition of truth as *adaequatio*, nothing that we say about God is, *strictly speaking*, true, which is not to say that some predications are appropriate and in some qualified sense "true" as distinct from others which are inappropriate and in an equally qualified sense "false."

23. Jean-Luc Marion shows how typical of Christian teaching Augustine is on this point. See Jean-Luc Marion "In the Name: How to Avoid Speaking of 'Negative Theology,' " in *God, the Gift, and Postmodernism*, ed. John D. Caputo and Michael J. Scanlon (Bloomington, IN: Indiana University Press, 1999).

24. Thus, speaking of the world, the Psalmist says, "God spoke, and it came to be; he commanded, and it stood firm" (Ps. 33.9). The *Revised English Bible* juxtaposes this concept of creation with the artisan model.

My hand founded the earth,

my right hand spread the expanse of the heavens;

when I summoned them,

they came at once into being. (Isa. 48:13)

25. For a wide ranging discussion of God as a performer of speech acts, see Nicholas Wolterstorff, *Divine Discourse: Philosophical Reflections on the Claim that God Speaks* (New York: Cambridge University Press, 1995). In relation to his claim that God literally performs speech acts, I have discussed the need to combine this claim with the claim that we do not speak univocally when we speak of human and divine speech acts. See Merold Westphal, "On Reading God the Author," *Religious Studies*, Vol. 37, No. 1 (September 2001), 271–91, with a response from Wolterstorff.

26. Augustine, *Confessions*, VIII: 12. Wolterstorff (see previous note) has an illuminating analysis of the double discourse involved here, one which does not reduce the divine speech act to the human speech act.

27. See Augustine, *The Trinity*, trans. Edmund Hill, O.P. (Brooklyn, NY: New City Press, 1991), VIII: 12.

28. Augustine, *Trinity*, XIV: 18.

29. Augustine, *Trinity*, VIII: 9.

30. On this question I find John D. Caputo's *Demythologizing Heidegger* to be especially helpful. (Bloomington, IN: Indiana University Press, 1993).

31. Against the background of the Jewish Bible, these are the specific forms of the Other focused on by Levinas in *Totality and Infinity*, trans. Alphonso Lingis (Pittsburgh, PA: Duquesne University Press, 1969) and elsewhere.

32. See note 25 above.

CONTRIBUTORS

STEPHEN C. ANGLE received his B.A. from Yale in East Asian studies and his Ph.D. in philosophy from the University of Michigan. He specializes in Chinese philosophy, particularly in the relations between modern (nineteenth- and twentieth-century) Chinese thought and the Confucian tradition. He also has research interests in contemporary Western metaethics and philosophy of language. He is the author of *Human Rights in Comparative Perspective: The Challenge of China* and the coeditor of the *Chinese Human Rights Reader*.

MIRANDA D. BROWN is an assistant professor of early Chinese culture at the University of Michigan. Under the direction of Professors David Keightley and Michael Nylan, she completed her dissertation, "Men in Mourning: Ritual, Politics, and Human Nature in Warring States and Han China 206 BC-AD 220" in May 2002. She has traveled throughout the People's Republic of China and during fall 2000, she was a visiting fellow at the Chinese Academy of Social Sciences in Beijing. There, she conducted dissertation research and studied paleography under the direction of Professors Xie Guahua and Hou Xudong. In addition to mourning ritual, her research interests include early Chinese science, philosophy, and culture.

CHEN LAI is professor in the Department of Philosophy, Peking University. He is one of the last graduate students of Professor Feng Youlai (Fung Yu-lan, 1895–1990), the most outstanding philosopher in Chinese modern time. Professor Chen is the author of *Ancient Religion and Ethics: The Origin of Confucian Thought,* (Beijing: Life, Reading and New Knowledge Publishing House, 1996), *Philosophy and Tradition: Modern Confucian Philosophy and Modern Chinese Culture,* (Taipei: Yun Chen Publishing Company, 1994), *Song Ming Neo-Confucianism,* (Liao Ning: Education Publishing House, 1992), *The Realm of You and Wu: The Spirit of Wang Yang-ming's Philosophy,* (Beijing: People's Press, 1991), *A Chronological Study of Zhu Xi's Letters,* (Shanghai: Shanghai People Press, 1989), *Research in Zhu Xi's Philosophy,* (Beijing: China Social Science Publishing House, 1988).

KELLY JAMES CLARK is Professor of Philosophy at Calvin College. He earned his doctorate at the University of Notre Dame. His dissertation director and mountain climbing partner was Alvin Plantinga. He has published over thirty articles and seven books including *Return to Reason,* (Grand Rapids, MI: Eerdmans Publishing Company, 1990), *When Faith is Not Enough,* (Grand Rapids, MI: Eerdmans Publishing Company, 1997), *Philosophers Who Believe* (Downer' Grove: InterVarsity Press 1993) and *The Story of Ethics: Human Nature & Human Fulfillment.* (New Jersey, Prentice-Hall, 2003).

STEPHEN T. DAVIS is Professor of Philosophy and Religious Studies at Claremont McKenna College. He is the author of some seventy articles and eleven books (including *Encountering Evil: Live Options in Theodicy* (Atlanta: J. Knox Press, 1981), *Risen Indeed: Making Sense of the Resurrection* (Grand Rapids: Eerdmans Publishing, 1993) and *God, Reason and Theistic Proofs* (Grand Rapids: Eerdmans Publishing, 1993). He has written on various topics in the philosophy of religion, as well as on topics in Christian theology, ancient philosophy, and higher education.

ROBERT W. FOSTER received his doctorate in Chinese history from Harvard University's Department of East Asian Languages and Civilizations in 1997. His dissertation, entitled *"Differentiating Rightness from Profit: The Life and Thought of Lu Jiuyuan (1139–1193),"* couches the philosophy of Lu Jiuyuan within the historical context of the Southern Song, including Lu's debates with Zhu Xi. Foster is currently Associate Professor of History and Coordinator of Asian Studies at Berea College in Kentucky.

ERIC L. HUTTON holds a B.A. in Classics and Asian Languages from Stanford University and an M.A. in East Asian languages and civilizations from Harvard University. He also obtained his Ph.D. in philosophy from Stanford University, where he wrote his dissertation on Xunzi. His main research interests are pre-Qin Chinese philosophy, Greek philosophy, and contemporary moral philosophy. He is currently assistant professor of philosophy at the University of Utah in Salt Lake City.

LIU ZONGKUN, received his Ph.D. from the Department of Philosophy at Peking University in 1999. He was Extraordinary Fellow in the Center for Philosophy of Religion at the University of Notre Dame, 1999–2000. His area of research includes comparative philosophy, social ethics, legal and political theory. He is the author of *Waiting For God or Waiting for Godot?* (Beijing: Chinese Social Press, 1996) and *Max Weber* (Baoding: Hebei University Press, 1999).

ALASDAIR MACINTYRE is a research professor of philosophy at the University of Notre Dame. He is the author of *A Short History of Ethics* (New York: Macmillan, 1966), *After Virtue* (IN: University of Notre Dame, 1981) and most recently *Dependent Rational Animals—Why Human Beings Need the Virtues* (Chicago: Open Court Publishing, 1999).

ALVIN PLANTINGA received his B.A. from Calvin College in 1954 and Ph.D. from Yale in 1958. He has taught at Wayne State University, Calvin College, and the University of Notre Dame, and is at present the John A. O'Brien professor of philosophy at Notre Dame. His most recent books are *Warrant: the Current Debate* (New York: Oxford University Press, 1993), *Warrant and Proper Function* (New York: Oxford University Press, 1993) and *Warranted Christian Belief* (New York: Oxford University Press, 2000). He is presently working on issues involving the relation of religion and science.

KWONG-LOI SHUN received his B.A from Oxford University and Ph.D. from Stanford University in addition to earning degrees from the University of Hong Kong and University of London, all in philosophy. He is a professor of philosophy at the University of California at Berkeley and has taught at the university since 1986. Dr. Shun is author of *Mencius and Early Chinese Thought*, the first volume of a three volume work on Confucian thought, and is currently writing the second volume, *The Development of Confucian-Mencian Thought: Zhu Xi, Wang Yangming and Dai Zhen*. He has written numerous articles on Confucius, Mencius, and various other topics in Chinese Philosophy.

EDWARD SLINGERLAND, assistant professor at the University of Southern California, holds a joint appointment with the Departments of Religion and East Asian Languages & Cultures. His specialties and teaching interests include Warring States Chinese thought, cognitive linguistics, evolutionary psychology, and methodologies for comparative religion and philosophy. His *Effortless Action: Wu-wei as Conceptual Metaphor and Spiritual Ideal in Early China*, was published by Oxford University Press in March 2003, and a full critical translation of the *Analects* of Confucius—complete with traditional commentary—Hackett Publishing Company September 2003. Professor Slingerland has also published various articles and reviews in *Philosophy East & West, Journal of the American Academy of Religion, and the Journal of Religious Ethics*.

BRYAN W. VAN NORDEN is an associate professor in the philosophy department and in the Asian studies program at Vassar College. He edited and contributed to *Confucius and the Analects: New Essays* (New York: Oxford University Press, 2002), and is a coeditor (with Philip J. Ivanhoe) and contributor to *Readings in Classical Chinese Philosophy* (Indianapolis: Hackett Publishing, 2003).

WAN JUNREN is the professor of ethics and west philosophy, and chair of Department of Philosophy at Tsinghua University, China. He is the author of *A History of Contemporary West Ethics* 2 vols. (Beijing: Peking University Press, 1990–1992), *A New Approach to Ethics: Toward Modern Ethics* (Beijing: China Youth Press, 1994), *In the Depth of Nothingness: Reading of J-P. Sartre* (Chengdu: Sichuan Press, 1995), *We All Live Near By Our God* (Shenyang: Liaoning Press, 1997), *Contrasting and Perspectives: A Comparative Modern Horizon of Chinese Ethics vs. Western Ethics* (Guangzhou: Guangdong Press, 1998), *In Search for A Universal*

Ethics (Beijing: Commercial Book House, 2001). He has published more than 150 articles both at home and abroad, and translated 16 books from English into Chinese, including Professor Alasdair MacIntyre's *Whose Justice? Which Rationality?* and John Rawl's *Political Liberalism.*

ROBIN R. WANG is Director of Asian and Pacific Studies and an assistant professor in philosophy at Loyola Marymount University. Her teaching and researching interests include ethics, contemporary moral problems, Chinese philosophy, women and gender in philosophy of East and West. Since the 1990s, she has actively engaged in the academic exchanges between China and the United States. Her publications include: *Reason and Insight Western and Eastern Perspective on the Pursuit Moral Wisdom,* co-author with Timothy Shanahan, 2nd ed. (Belmont, CA: Wadsworth, 2002) and *Images of Women in Chinese Thought and Culture: Writings from Pre-Qin to Song Dynasty* (Indianapolis, IN: Hackett Publishing, 2003). She is a vice-president of the Association of Chinese Philosophers in America.

MEROLD WESTPHAL received his B.A. from Wheaton College (in Illinois) and his Ph.D from Yale. He is Distinguished Professor of Philosophy at Fordham University. He is the author of two books on Hegel, two on Kierkegaard, and two in the phenomenology of religion. His current work involves exploring the religious significance of postmodern philosophies and trying to bring Levinas and Kierkegaard into dialogue.

ZHAO DUNHUA is professor and chair of Department of Philosophy, Peking University. He received his Ph.D. in philosophy from Louvain University, Belgium, 1988. His specialties are history of philosophy, philosophy of religion, comparative philosophy and applied philosophy. He is the author (all in Chinese) of *Plotinus* (Taiwan: San Min Books Publisher, 1998); *The Essence of Contemporary Anglo-Saxon Philosophy* (Beijing: Modern China Press, 1997); *A General History of Western Philosophy,* vol. I (Ancient and Medieval Period) (China: Peking University Press, 1996); *A Thousand and Five Hundred Years' Christian Philosophy* (Beijing: People's Press, 1994); *Karl Popper* (Taiwan: Joint Publisher Hong Kong and Yuanliu Press, 1992); *A Commentary of Rawls' A Theory of Justice* (Taiwan: Joint Publisher Hong Kong and Yuanliu Press, 1988); *Wittgenstein* (Taiwan: Joint Publisher Hong Kong and Yuanliu Press, 1988). Professor Zhao has also published more than fifty articles in different Chinese academic journals. He is vice president of the Chinese Association of Religious Studies, Executive Commissary of Beijing's Philosophical Society and Member of Degree Commission in Beijing Area. He has been a visiting scholar in Australia, Canada, Hong Kong, Taiwan, and the United States.

ZHANG DAINIAN is professor in the Department of Philosophy at Peking University and the oldest Chinese philosophy scholar alive today. (He is ninety-three years old and is a brother-in-law of Feng Youlai (Fung Yu-lan). He has published extensively since 1931. His book: *An Outline of Chinese Philosophy* (1943; reprint, Beijing: *Zhongguo Zhexiu Dagang*, 1958 second edition, and 1982 third edition) has been a must read textbook for every philosophy major student in China. All of his important books, articles, and lectures are included in the *Collections of Zhang Dainian*, (Shijiazhuang: Hebei People's Press 1997) (8 volumes and over 5200 pages). He was the president of the Chinese National Association of the history of Chinese philosophy, 1979–1989 and the honorary president since 1989. His influence and contribution to Chinese philosophy has been carried in the history of Chinese philosophy.

ZHANG XIANGLONG received his B.A. in philosophy at Peking University 1981 and his Ph.D. in the Department of Philosophy at State University of New York, Buffalo in 1992. Now he is a professor and the director of Institute of Foreigner Philosophy at Peking University. He has specialized in comparative philosophy, phenomenology, and the history of Western philosophy. He is the author of *Heidegger's Thought and Chinese Dao of Heaven* (Beijing: Shanlian, 1996), *A Biography of Heidegger* (Shijiazhuang: Hebei People's Press, 1998), and *From Phenomenology to Confucius* (Beijing: Shangwu Press, 2000), which has been the best seller in China.

INDEX